THE COMPLETE BASEBALL PLAY BOOK

JIM TRAINOR

THE COMPLETE BASEBALL PLAY BOOK

Photographs by George T. Kagawa

DOUBLEDAY & COMPANY, INC.
Garden City, New York   1972

LIBRARY OF CONGRESS CATALOG CARD NUMBER 77-165387
COPYRIGHT © 1972 BY JAMES FRANCIS TRAINOR
ALL RIGHTS RESERVED
PRINTED IN THE UNITED STATES OF AMERICA
FIRST EDITION

To a mom and dad who saw to it that I had every chance to play the game as a kid, and to my wife, Rocky, who responds to everything I pursue now with unwavering support.

CONTENTS

PREFACE

Just what do we hope to accomplish with this book? The reader deserves an answer before we ask him to start poring over the pages that follow.

Unlike much of the material that has been published on baseball, this book is intended for players as well as coaches. Although several chapters are directed specifically to the player, and several others to the coach, the book as a whole should be of interest and value from both points of view.

We also hope that the information presented here is applicable to all levels of competition. We have attempted to describe the fundamentals in such a manner that even the individual who has had very little experience with the game can understand what we are talking about. On the other hand, we have included many of the finer points of baseball, some of which would be appropriate only for advanced players and their coaches.

We have tried to be as thorough as possible in describing the various fundamentals and coaching techniques. We wanted to give the reader a complete and detailed analysis of every movement so that the book can actually be used as an instruction manual. Because of this devotion to detail, we have found it necessary, in most instances, to focus on a single approach to teaching and learning the game. In other words, this book does not represent an exhaustive study of all the different ways in which baseball can be played. We are offering you a step-by-step analysis of one method which we favor and which we know from experience and observation is sound, practical and "professional."

There are other ways to approach the game; perhaps there are better ways, but we could not recommend them here because we have not used them. We have tried to avoid recommending something to you with which we have not had some personal experience. You will not be reading about methods that "sound" as if they should work; you will be reading about methods that have proven to be successful in practice on the field.

We have also made an effort to concentrate on those fundamentals that we feel are the most effectively taught. For example, the reader will notice that we do not discuss hitting quite as extensively as we do some of the other fundamentals. There is good reason for this. Learning to hit a baseball requires considerable hard work on the part of the young player, but hitting is also a highly *individual* skill. That is, a batting technique that would be appropriate for one athlete might not be for another. Our text includes suggestions on hitting that we feel are *basic*. They are relatively few in number but vitally important. Beyond these basic fundamentals there is much room for individuality. No two big league hitters look the same at the plate, but they are *all* good hitters by our standards. On the other hand, we have gone into great detail in presenting our views on other fundamentals, particularly with regard to defense. Not because we think the defensive game is more important, but simply because this phase of baseball is more coachable and more readily learned from a book.

We have gone to great lengths to emphasize the educational aspects of the game. The author is convinced that there can be a much deeper meaning to competitive sport than most coaches and players realize. Coaches, in particular, tend to justify their athletic programs on the basis of what it is doing for the "character" of young boys. Yet, as a rule, few coaches really put much thought into this important responsibility. We become so engrossed in the technical side of the game, that we leave everything else to chance. Therefore, more than anything else, we want the reader to see baseball as something more than merely good exercise, recreation and competition. This is a book on how to play the game, but it is also, and more importantly, a book about how baseball can help participants gain a better understanding of themselves and each other.

Some comment should be made about the sources of the information that appears in the succeeding pages. Although all of these techniques have been used by the author in his playing and coaching experiences, almost none of them originated there. This book represents years of conscientious "brain picking." We have borrowed from fellow coaches, players, professional scouts and even fans. The only credit we can claim for ourselves is the manner in which the material has been arranged.

How can the book best be used? This will depend on the needs of the individual. Coaches may want to read it in its entirety and select the material within each chapter that is appropriate at their level of competition. The beginning coach will find that he has a great deal to learn about the game, particularly regarding those positions at which he has not had playing experience. The more experienced coach will want to pick and choose. Perhaps he will find something helpful in our explanation of bunting or sliding techniques. Maybe he can use our system for organizing a practice session or preparing for a ball game. We would imagine that almost every coach will find something here that could make him a more effective teacher.

The player who takes time to plow through these pages already has proven that he has something of what it takes to be successful at the game. I have not written this book with the idea of making it entertaining. Probably only the most dedicated of athletes will want to read every word to improve his performance. Others will be selective, according to their needs and positions. My objective is to provide the young athlete who has sufficient desire with enough detail to learn any and all aspects of the game. Above all, this book is not only meant to be read; it is meant to be *used*. What I would like to see would be a tattered copy of it in the hip pocket of every boy as he walks to the park for a workout.

Jim Trainor

THE COMPLETE BASEBALL PLAY BOOK

1

An Introduction to the Game

As a Spectator Sport

Baseball appeals to people in different ways. Some of us enjoy the relative stability of the game. With everything around us undergoing revolutionary change, the playing rules of baseball remain basically the same as they were back in the days of Ty Cobb and Honus Wagner.

Some argue that baseball just happens to be *the* perfect sport. The game which Alexander Cartwright formulated back in the late nineteenth century provides the fan with a rare combination of individual competition and teamwork. The ingenious geometry of the diamond is such that close plays and decisions occur with astonishing regularity. Even the bat and ball are objects of finely sculptured beauty and near perfect functional design.

The less aesthetic among us are more impressed by the incredible difficulty of playing baseball well. We see the game as one that requires most players to possess a multitude of basic athletic abilities as opposed to those sports that require but a few—such as great speed or extreme height. The major league performer must have them all. Speed, quickness, strength, co-ordination and a tremendous ability to concentrate under pressure. Courage? Can you imagine the "guts" it takes to stand up at the plate and think about hitting while a guy fires balls under your chin at speeds exceeding ninety miles per hour?

Many feel that baseball has to be among the greatest of pressure sports. Whether it's a ball or a strike, a hit or an error, one individual either succeeds or fails on every play. And as the athlete makes a play he *knows* he may be failing his teammates as well as himself. In fact, the winner of a close game is usually determined in the end by the ability of a single player to deliver in the "clutch" while another is failing miserably.

Baseball appears to be as easy to follow for the spectator as it is difficult for the athlete to play. Perhaps this is why literally millions of women have become almost fanatical baseball fans. The game is so popular with housewives that most baseball broadcasts are sponsored, at least in part, by makers of household goods.

Although baseball is looked upon as a "blue collar" or working-man's sport, it is also quite popular among intellectuals. Could it be that these "brains" are attracted to baseball for the same reasons they are to the game of chess? Both games move along at a rather slow and leisurely pace, with each participant trying to anticipate his opponent's next move.

Of course, the vast majority of us are baseball fans today simply because we spent a good part of our youth on a ball diamond. In a sense, baseball games give us an opportunity to relive that youth. Most of us don't just watch a game; we *experience* it, as if we were right out there on the field ourselves. Whether Willie Mays takes a called third strike or hits one out of the park, we know exactly how he feels. No wonder some of us get a little carried away in our appreciation for the game.

As a Learning Experience for the Player

Most of us started playing baseball as young boys simply because we found it enjoyable. As we grew older the game lost its luster for some but not for others. For those of us who retained an interest beyond the Little League stage, baseball became more than just another sport. It became a dream. We began to think in terms of a professional career and perhaps one day wearing the uniform of our favorite major league team. We really could not imagine being paid to play baseball, but we dared to hope and somehow no price was too much.

Of course, we soon realized that the dream becomes a reality for only a very few. Instead of enjoying big league fame and fortune, we went on to become rather obscure citizens. But what about all that time we spent on a baseball diamond? Certainly the experience must have provided something for those of us who never received a dime for our efforts.

Baseball did provide us with something. Something far more valuable than exercise and good, clean fun. The game was a learning experience for all of us, whether we made it to the big time or not.

Through baseball, many of us have gained a better understanding of ourselves. The pressures of competition tend to bring out the worst as well as the best in an individual. The game becomes so important to us that we allow our immaturity to interfere with our performance. In an effort to improve as athletes, each of us finds it necessary to take a closer look at himself as a person.

Baseball also gives many of us our first indication of what it takes to be successful at something. Not too long ago one of my athletes came to the unpleasant conclusion that he was never going to become much of a hitter until he learned how to hit a curveball. From that moment on the boy insisted that he be thrown only curveballs in batting practice. Before long, his efforts began to pay off. He became a better-than-average curveball-hitter and finished the season batting well over .300. This boy was rewarded for his hard work by being named to the all-league team. But the fact that he experienced success through dedication may prove to be more valuable to him than any awards he wins as he faces future challenges, on and off the field.

Perhaps more than any other sport, baseball teaches self-discipline. The outfielder who has not had to make a play in the field all day must be just as alert as the catcher or pitcher. We won a ball game recently because our rightfielder had learned that nothing is ever taken for granted in a baseball game. When our usually reliable shortstop overthrew first base the rightfielder was there backing up the play, thus preventing the runner from advancing to second base. If it had not been for this individual's ability to keep his "head in the game," the next hitter's single would undoubtedly have scored the tying run.

Baseball has helped many of us become better "competitors." I don't think I will ever forget a picture showing a dejected but resolute Jackie Robinson checking to see that Bobby Thomson touched every base after hitting the home run that won the pennant for the Giants in 1951. Thomson's home run was a catastrophe for the Dodgers, but Robinson was a competitor and he wasn't about to concede defeat until the game was completely over.

The game is so difficult to play that even the best of players fail quite regularly. An error in a crucial situation. A strike-out with the bases loaded. In almost every game someone ends up being the "goat." And yet, the nature of the game is such that the player must learn to pick himself up and get ready for the next play or game right away. Isn't that what life is all about too?

Baseball can develop a boy's appreciation for sportsmanship. The young athlete learns early in his career that the rules of the game are essential if teams are to compete on an equal basis. He also learns that baseball has a code of ethics that extends beyond the rule book. An infielder, for example, does not fake a tag to lure a baserunner into making an unnecessary slide. It is not that such a maneuver would be against the rules, it is simply a matter of showing some concern for another athlete's safety.

More important than anything else, baseball has given us an opportunity to work closely with others. It has provided us with valuable lessons in teamwork because boys on the same team have to depend upon each other in their efforts to arrive at a common goal. They get to know each other well. Social barriers such as race and economic level tend to diminish in importance as individuals are judged solely on their ability to play the game. It is no wonder that many lifetime friendships began on a baseball field.

The Basic Requirements

The degree to which a boy is able to realize the full educational value of his baseball experience may be determined in part by factors beyond his control. Not every youngster possesses the physical qualifications to play the game on a highly competitive basis. Even if he does, his community may or may not provide him with sufficient opportunities to develop those talents. Supportive parents also make it easier, and good coaching represents another important ingredient.

But even if these factors are helpful, they are certainly not essential. Boys with fairly limited ability have found many satisfactions in the game, and there are players in the big leagues who have practically taught themselves how to play. Willie Mays developed his great natural talents playing "stickball" in the streets of New York. He learned the game without the benefit of top-quality equipment and well-groomed ball diamonds, items that some modern "Little Leaguers" almost take for granted.

Clearly, the basic requirements must be provided by the player himself. It's the same old story: An athlete is going to find himself taking from the game no more than he is able to put into it. Baseball will afford him a truly valuable learning experience but only to the extent to which he is capable of approaching it with the following attitudes:

1. *A sincere desire to play the game.* The boy who turns out for the squad in order to please his frustrated athlete of a father or because he likes the looks of the team's major league style uniform rarely finds much satisfaction on the diamond. An athlete should be aware of some of the well-meaning but misleading pressures that are used to lure boys into some of our youth league baseball programs. When appraising the true nature of his interest in the game, a genuine desire to play must be foremost.

2. *A desire to be the best possible performer.* It is not enough just to want to play the game. At least it is not for the individual who is looking for more than mere recreation and good exercise. The true athlete competes because he wants to prove something for himself, and he enjoys the experience only when he is performing to the limit of his natural ability. Playing for fun is fine, but that is not what we are talking about here.

3. *An overwhelming desire to win for the team.* There are athletes who enjoy the game and play hard, but only because they derive a certain amount of satisfaction from their own performance. Let's face it, baseball is a *team* sport, and a player simply cannot be competing to the limits of his ability unless he is thinking in terms of team success first.

Becoming a Winner

Of course, most youth athletes do not perform up to their physical capabilities. If the average boy is accused of not giving his best, he will deny it. He will deny it simply because he probably believes that he *is* giving his best. Athletes are rarely aware of their own potential because they really do not completely understand what goes into a total effort.

What do we mean when we say we want an athlete to give his best? Perhaps it is time we dispensed with the vague generalities and began describing some specific forms of behavior. Baseball players often refer to the guy who has a solid approach to the game as a "winner." On the other hand, they often use the term "busher" to identify the player whose attitude leaves much to be desired. But even the best of big leaguers are not "winners" in every respect, and certainly no athlete good enough to play at any level should ever be labeled a "busher." For the purpose of illustration, however, let's assume the super player, or "winner," and the totally inept player, or "busher," do exist and see how each of them might respond on the field under similar circumstances.

THE WINNER DEMONSTRATES:

WHILE THE BUSHER:

1. *Courage* by showing his willingness to get in front of hard-hit ground balls, "hanging in there" on tag plays and sliding *hard* into second base to break up a double play.

Turns his head away and tries to backhand hard-hit balls; tries to watch the runner and ball at the same time on tag plays—usually missing both—and slides only when there is no other alternative.

2. *Daring* by taking chances on the bases and trying for the "shoestring" catch when the percentages are not in his favor.

Is content to stay put on the bases, advancing only when it is a sure thing, and usually gives up on balls hit in front of him, regardless of the percentages.

3. *Fortitude* by insisting on playing despite an injury that may be bothersome but not dangerous. Of course there are players who seem to have a higher pain threshold than others. The great Yankee star Mickey Mantle played most of his career with both legs taped from the calf to the thigh. Mantle possessed great natural abilities, but those who played alongside him will probably remember him more for his tremendous courage and fortitude.

Uses almost any excuse to stay out of competition and often points to a minor injury as an explanation for a poor performance.

THE WINNER DEMONSTRATES:

WHILE THE BUSHER:

4. *Dedication* by performing every assignment given him as if the game depended upon it, even if that job amounted to no more than warming up a relief pitcher or coaching first base.

Feels that certain tasks are beneath him and approaches non-playing assignments with cool indifference.

5. *Concentration* by his ability to exclude everything from his consciousness but the task at hand. As a hitter, he stands up at the plate against a hard-throwing pitcher and thinks about one thing—getting a base hit.

Is easily distracted—often bothered by the opposition's bench jockies, irregularities in the field, weather, etc. As a batter, he is usually more concerned with not being hit than with getting a hit.

6. *Pride* in the way he wears his uniform. He *looks* like a ballplayer from the time he steps on the field until he re-enters the locker room.

Usually looks as though he is in the "process" of getting dressed. Shirttail out, no belt, pant legs bloused incorrectly and cap askew. He may also wear different colored sleeves, stretch the stirrup in his stockings or use white laces in his shoes just to set himself apart from the other players.

THE WINNER DEMONSTRATES:	WHILE THE BUSHER:

7. *Poise* by the manner in which he conducts himself on the field. He is content to let his performance speak for him and usually refrains from shows of temper, disgust or amazement when he makes a mistake or has a call go against him.

Plays to the crowd by displaying his feelings for all to see. If he boots a ball or strikes out, he lets everyone know how disgusted he is by kicking the dirt, throwing his bat or helmet, etc.

8. *Confidence* by approaching every game situation with the feeling that he will succeed. For example, the pitcher who has confidence in his ability does not hesitate to throw his curveball when he is behind in the count. He *knows* he can get it over.

Approaches crucial situations *hoping* things will break his way. He would not think of throwing his curve when behind in the count because deep inside he doubts his ability to throw it for a strike.

9. *Tenacity* by his willingness to listen to a coach's suggestion once and then go out and practice the skill a thousand times to perfect it.

Usually has to be told something a thousand times before he will practice it once.

10. *Respect* by the manner in which he treats umpires. He may disagree with a call and occasionally lose his temper, but he never questions the integrity of an official. His extensive knowledge of the rules allows him to dispute "interpretation" calls intelligently.

Considers all umpires as adversaries and treats them accordingly. He argues often and loudly. When he is on his home field he is particularly demonstrative because he knows most of the spectators will side with him. He finds it easy to blame an umpire for a loss.

11. *Loyalty* in his relationship with his coach and his teammates. He recognizes his coach as a teacher of the game, not infallible but certainly as interested in winning as any player.

Often accuses the coach (not to his face) of selecting his line-up on the basis of personality rather than ability. He also tends to read something "personal" into the coach's criticisms of his

THE WINNER DEMONSTRATES:

WHILE THE BUSHER:

He is quick to excuse another player for a mistake. A sincere interest in team morale prevents him from breaking training rules.

play. His relationships with teammates are superficial at best. Training rules are of no great importance to him because he considers them unnecessary restrictions rather than a mutual sacrifice that helps to bind team members together.

12. *Consideration* by the manner in which he treats his opponents. He does everything within the rules to defeat rivals on the field but never makes the game a personal matter. He observes the basic "courtesies" of the diamond such as retrieving the catcher's mask and telling baserunners not to slide if there is no play. He gives his best regardless of the score. After the game he extends himself to thank his opponents for their efforts. As a loser he is gracious but offers no excuses. As a winner, he is humble but not phony.

Likes to belittle an opponent as well as defeat him. He is usually an accomplished bench jockey and his jibes are often of a personal nature. If his team happens to be winning the game easily, he tends to ridicule his opponent by displaying an indifferent attitude for the remainder of the contest. If his team happens to end up on the short end of the score, he finds it extremely difficult to give his opponents credit for being the better team on that day. His comments usually include "they got all the breaks" or "they were lucky."

2

The Fundamentals of Hitting

There are few baseball players at any level who do not like to hit. Even pitchers tend to brag about their successes at the plate before they do their victories on the mound. However, the enjoyment a player gets out of hitting and his ability to hit may be different matters entirely.

Hitting is probably the most difficult skill in the game. Some people claim that good hitters are born and not made. Perhaps this is true in the sense that the ability to hit a baseball with consistency and power requires quick reflexes, strength and coordination. But given these natural talents in some quantity, an athlete's success or failure with the bat will be determined largely by his willingness to work at it, not only conscientiously but also intelligently.

There are several important concepts that we feel are basic to an understanding of this particular skill:

A boy must *want* to hit if ever he hopes to become a good hitter. Ted Williams was blessed with great physical skills, but he became a great hitter primarily because he was willing to spend hour after hour swinging at baseballs. He would hit before school, after school and all day on weekends. No one forced him to do this. He simply loved to hit, and he wanted to make the most of his God-given talents. The player who has to be talked into taking extra batting practice stands little chance of improving his hitting ability. If great hitters are born, it is their desire to excel that sets them apart from the others as much as their inherent physical ability.

We also believe that hitting is an *individual* skill. The variety of batting techniques (stances, etc.) used by successful major league hitters illustrates this fact quite clearly. How can we claim that one approach is better than another when individual players are constantly finding success with unorthodox methods? Few coaches would ever recommend a closed stance to a player, yet Stan Musial used such a stance to break almost every batting record in the National League. Roberto Clemente "steps in the bucket" and goes after bad pitches, but he has won three consecutive batting titles. Even Ted Williams' somewhat classical stance and swing might be inappropriate for many young players. Therefore, it seems obvious that there really isn't any *one* way to hit a baseball.

Another one of our basic beliefs is that a young player will be better off in the long run if he learns to *hit to all fields*. Matty Alou's success with the Pirates represents an excellent illustration of why learning to hit to all fields is particularly good advice for the smaller player. Matty was an inconsistent hitter at best in his early years with the Giants. As a lefthanded hitter he seemed to be trying to pull everything to rightfield because of the strong wind usually blowing in that direction at Candlestick Park. He was traded to Pittsburgh and immediately became a high average hitter. With the Pirates, Matty gave up thinking about hitting for distance and began to concentrate on spraying the ball to all fields. There were no strong winds at Forbes Field and even the big boys found it difficult to reach the distant fences. The good pitchers have always said that they much prefer pitching to the pull-hitter because they know *where* to pitch to him: "Keep the ball away from him and you've got him."

Young players will also be more effective hitters if they *emphasize bat control over power*. The harder a batter swings, the less he is able to control the bat and the more often he will strike out. Since even a feeble ground ball to the pitcher can be booted or take a bad hop, striking out represents the ultimate in failure for a batter. On the other hand, a long fly ball is usually less effective with younger players because they often play on open fields and even 400-foot drives can be caught. Rough playing fields and relatively inconsistent defenses give a batter a chance as long as he makes contact with the ball.

Because we have seen boys hit successfully with almost every possible kind of stance and style, we have to believe that *hitting is at least 50 per cent mental.* In the following paragraphs we have made an effort to describe some of the psychological factors that appear to be essential to batting success:

1. *Determination*—The good hitter looks upon each trip to the plate as a private duel between himself and the pitcher. He literally dares the pitcher to throw the ball by him.

2. *Concentration*—The good hitter has that rare ability to eliminate every unnecessary stimulus from his consciousness. He's not bothered by fan noise, irregularities in the playing field or razzing from the opposing team. He rarely concerns himself with the possibility that he may be hit by a pitched ball. Even against pitchers who throw extremely hard and are somewhat wild, he has the courage to concentrate on hitting rather than being hit.

3. *Intelligence*—The good hitter learns something every time he goes up to the plate. He learns when he can afford to guess and when he must protect the plate. He studies each pitcher he faces and usually learns to think along with him.

4. *Confidence*—The good hitter *knows* he can hit a pitcher. As a former pitcher, the author can verify the fact that the "look" in the hitter's eyes as he faces you can make a difference. I will never forget facing a particularly "cocky" hitter in a relief situation. The pitcher preceding me had been hit hard and bases were loaded as I entered the game. No one was going to "dig in" on me, so I let go with my best fastball, high and tight. The ball hit the visor of the batter's cap and turned it around, but he never moved his head! He then proceeded to hit the next pitch—a good curveball on the outside corner—to right center for a bases-clearing double. That hitter *knew* he was going to get a base hit! He did not go up to the plate hoping he could hit the ball or trying to secure a base on balls. The only thought in a hitter's mind should be taking a good cut at the first pitch that comes into the strike zone.

The Selection of a Bat

There are no definite guidelines for selecting a certain kind of bat, and in most instances the player will choose a bat simply on the basis of how it "feels" to him. However, a hitter should make an effort to select a bat that will be most likely to support his particular style of hitting. For example, long-ball hitters usually prefer long, narrow-handled bats because they allow for a maximum amount of whip action. On the other hand, the punch-hitter will probably choose a bat with a fairly thick handle to give him more hitting surface.

Of course, most hitters do not fall into either of these categories entirely. The majority of players want some whip action, but they want a bat that has sufficient hitting surface too. And probably more important than anything else, they want a bat which has good balance.

The balance of a bat is affected by its length, weight and shape.

Most high school and college players swing a bat which is between 33 and 35 inches in length. Boys at this age level can usually handle a bat at least 33 inches long, and as a general rule a player should swing the longest bat he can control with his wrists alone. On the other hand, a bat over 35 inches long is generally too difficult to control by all but the strongest of young players.

The weight of the bats used by amateur players usually corresponds with their length. That is, a 34-inch bat normally weighs 34 ounces. The professional player can afford to be a little more selective. Most professional players sign a contract with a manufacturer to have their bats built according to their own particular needs. Therefore, the player at this level may choose to have a bat made for him that is 34 inches long but weighs 36 ounces.

The shape of a bat largely determines the distribution of its weight. Because of this, the shape of the bat is probably more important in terms of balance than overall weight. For example, a 34-ounce bat that has most of its weight in the barrel because of an extremely narrow handle, will probably be difficult to control. On the other hand, a 34-ounce bat that has a moderately thick handle will be much easier to control because the weight is more evenly distributed.

As we mentioned previously, whip action and hitting surface are also used as criteria for the selection of one bat over another.

The narrow-handled bat provides a maximum amount of whip action. That is, the bat actually bends somewhat upon impact and serves to catapult the ball. Many experts feel that it is the wider use of the narrow-handled bat that is responsible for the ever-increasing number of home runs that are being hit in the major leagues and not a livelier ball. There seems to be a good deal of justification for this theory. The old-timers used bats that were almost "bottle" shaped and the home run was a rarity. Their bats had very little whip action but they did provide for a maximum amount of hitting surface.

The durability of a bat should also be a primary consideration. Obviously, an extremely narrow-handled bat will be more likely to break if the ball is hit on the handle than will the moderate-to thick-handled bat. A player should also avoid using a large bat that appears to be extremely light in weight. These bats may feel good but they'll probably break on the first pitch that is not hit solidly.

There is one additional factor the hitter must consider in his selection of a bat. I am referring to the location on the handle at which the player holds the bat. Needless to say, the balance of the bat, and therefore the hitter's ability to control that bat, will be affected by the nearness of the hands to the fulcrum (the balance point). In other words, if a player wants to use an extremely long bat, he should "choke up" on the handle somewhat to compensate for the extra length. If the player chooses a relatively short bat, he can probably hold it down at the end without sacrificing control.

The Grip

As a general rule, the middle knuckles of the top hand should be lined up somewhere between the first and second knuckles of the bottom hand. This grip will aid the hitter in breaking his wrists on the follow-through.

The bat should be gripped primarily with the fingers rather than deep in the palm of the hand against the thumb.

The location of the hands on the bat was mentioned in the previous section. Again, the closer the hands are to the fulcrum of the bat the easier it will be to control. Most hitters use a modified "choke" grip by placing the hands from 1 to 2 inches

up the handle from the end of the bat. Some hitters prefer a full-choke grip and move the hands up as far as 3 to 5 inches from the end.

Ty Cobb used a split grip, which he claimed gave him even greater control. He allowed a 2- to 3-inch spread between the top hand and the bottom hand. Some hitters use this grip today, but the split is usually less than an inch wide.

The hands should be relaxed on the bat until the start of the forward swing. Any tenseness before the swing is likely to interfere with the hitter's concentration.

Position in the Box

Opinions differ considerably when it comes to deciding where the hitter should stand in the batter's box.

Many hitters allow the pitcher on the mound to determine their position for them. They stand in the rear of the box against hard throwers and they move up and stand in the front of the box against the curveball-pitcher. The theory is that they will have more time to swing against the hard thrower and that they can hit the curveballer's pitch before it breaks.

Most hitters also will adjust their position in the box slightly if they see that a pitcher shows a tendency to throw to a certain area of the strike zone. Ted Williams and Ty Cobb, two of the greatest hitters the game has seen, both advocate moving around in the batter's box, *if* there is a logical reason for doing so. For example, some righthanders, particularly those who throw sidearm, throw a fastball that breaks in on the righthanded hitter. The smart hitter will recognize this after a time or two at bat and move away from the plate so he can hit the ball with the barrel of the bat rather than the handle. On the other hand, against a pitcher who is consistently hitting the outside corner, the hitter would be wise to move in closer to the plate so he is in a better position to reach that pitch.

Some hitters prefer to occupy the same position in the box regardless of the talents of the pitcher on the mound. Their theory is that all pitchers throw several different pitches and that it is unrealistic to assume that a hitter can adjust his position in the box from one pitch to the next with any degree of effectiveness. These hitters feel that there is more value in seeing every pitch from the same position in relation to the strike zone than there is moving around in an effort to anticipate a particular pitch.

Some hitters also vary their position in the box to improve their effectiveness as bunters. In most cases, the player will move up to the front of the box so that the ball will be a little less likely to fall in foul territory.

The Stance

The stance of the hitter just prior to the swing will vary considerably from one individual to the next. However, there are a few features that are almost universally accepted by the better hitters:

1. The *feet* are usually shoulder-width apart or slightly more. If the feet are close together, a longer stride is necessary. A long stride is *not* advisable as the hitter must commit himself to swing at the pitch too early.

2. The *front foot* may be slightly behind, parallel with or slightly in front of the rear foot. A closed stance, for example, would have the front foot much closer to the plate than the rear. An open stance would mean that the rear foot is much closer to the plate. Actually, the position of the feet in relation to the plate before the swing is not

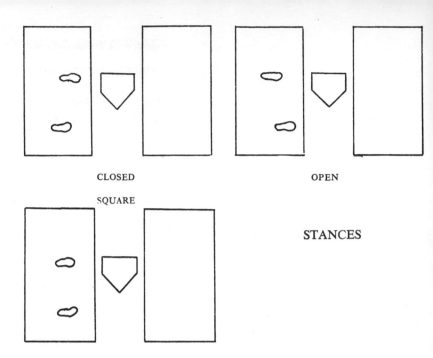

CLOSED   OPEN

SQUARE

STANCES

that important. What is important is the direction of the stride during the swing.

3. The *knees* are slightly bent and the *hips* are slumped inward toward the plate. This places the weight of the body on the balls of the feet and not on the heels.

4. The *back* is usually bent slightly toward the plate.

5. The *front shoulder* is angled in toward the plate and remains slightly lower than the rear shoulder.

6. The *hands* hold the bat approximately 6 to 8 inches out in front of the rear shoulder and even with or slightly to the rear of the back leg.

7. The *head* remains absolutely motionless with the *chin* close to the front shoulder.

8. The *eyes* concentrate on the ball.

The Swing

1. *Cocking.* Many hitters feel they add momentum to their swing by using a cocking action just prior to bringing the bat forward. They rotate the front shoulder, knee and hip forward, then backward, and then forward again into the pitch.

2. *The stride.* As the pitch is released, the weight is shifted so that it is predominantly on the back foot. The front leg strides forward with the foot close to the ground and the hands, hips and weight held in reserve. The stride should be in the general direction of the pitcher. Some good hitters stride away from the plate but they keep their weight moving into the pitch. Ken Boyer, a former Most Valuable Player Award winner for the Cardinals, emphasizes that the stride foot should also land softly, "like stepping on a baby."

3. *Meeting the ball.* The rear hip pushes the front hip out of the way as the hitter makes his decision to swing. The front foot is planted no more than 6 to 8 inches in front of its original position. The hands follow the hips and swing the bat down, through the ball. The bat meets the ball at the instant the hitter's weight coming off the back foot returns to both feet.

4. *The follow-through.* The rigid front knee acts as a barrier against the thrust of the hitter's weight and provides the necessary leverage.

The top hand rolls over the bottom hand immediately after contact is made with the ball and the bat is allowed to come all the way around on the follow-through.

Watching the Ball

The most important single fundamental in hitting is to watch the ball. The hitter must learn to concentrate on the ball from the time he steps into the batter's box until it hits his bat. He should literally try to "see" the ball hit the bat. One of my former players carried this theory a step further. He not only watched the ball until it hit his bat, he also followed the ball with his eyes into the catcher's glove when he did not swing.

Know the Strike Zone

The strike zone is defined by the rule book as the space over home plate that is between the batter's shoulders and his knees when he assumes his natural batting stance. Obviously, the hitter who offers at pitches that are outside of this area will be giving the pitcher an unnecessary advantage. However, a hitter should not become so conscious of swinging at a bad pitch that he becomes more of an umpire than a hitter.

Good hitters visualize the strike zone as being slightly larger when

they are behind in the count. With two strikes on them, they realize the limitations of their own judgment, and the umpire's for that matter, and swing at any pitch that could be called a strike. With no strikes on him, the batter can afford to be more selective and offer at a pitch only if it is "right in there."

Hitting the Ball Where It Is Pitched

As we have said before, we advocate trying to hit the ball where it is pitched. For example, we do not feel that a young player has the strength to "pull" an outside pitch and still hit with any degree of authority.

On a *high* pitch the batter should chop down on the ball with a "tomahawking" motion.

On a *letter-high* pitch the hitter should bring the bat down into the ball from its higher position before the swing. The batter will feel as though he is swinging down, but in actuality the bat will be traveling on an almost level plane.

On a *low* pitch the hitter brings the bat down into the ball and

attempts to "pick it up." This is done by bending the rear leg and hitting the ball out in front of the plate.

On an *inside* pitch the batter brings the barrel of the bat around quickly and meets the pitch out in front of the plate. The hands remain behind the end of the bat as the ball is pulled into leftfield by the righthanded batter.

On a pitch *down the middle* of the plate the hands are almost even with the barrel of the bat as the ball is driven toward centerfield.

The hitter hits the *outside* pitch by concentrating on keeping his weight back. He catches the inside of the ball after it has passed his hands and tries to hit the ball to the opposite field. That is, a righthanded batter who would pull an inside pitch to leftfield should hit an outside pitch to rightfield.

Of course, since every pitch will be coming to him on two planes, vertical and horizontal, the batter will have to learn how to combine these techniques.

Hitting Different Kinds of Pitches

As a general rule, a batter should look for a fastball on every pitch. Then if a slower pitch is delivered he will have time to adjust his swing accordingly.

The *slider* is delivered with the same motion and is thrown almost as hard as a fastball. It breaks much less than a curveball but in the same direction. To hit a slider, the batter must keep his weight back on the rear foot and the hips slumped in toward the plate as most pitchers will try to keep this pitch low and away. He should also cut down on his swing slightly for better bat control. As with the curveball, he should try to hit this pitch in the direction in which it is breaking.

To hit a *curveball,* the batter should look for a pitch that is released off the side of the index finger rather than off the tips of the fingers as on the fastball and slider. The curveball is an intimidating pitch. That is, the righthanded pitcher will throw his curve *at* the righthanded batter to make it break over the outside half of the plate. Therefore, the batter must have the courage to stay in there, keeping his weight on the rear foot and the hips slumped in toward the plate. At the last split second he strides into the pitch with the elbows well away from the body for good leverage. As a rule, he will have better results in hitting the curveball if he tries to hit it in the direction in which it is breaking. The curve is delivered much slower than the fastball and by trying to push it to the opposite field, the hitter will be less likely to get around on it too quickly. Of course, anytime the hitter gets a curve that "hangs" up and inside, he should try to pull it. A friend of mine, a former minor league ballplayer, came out to work with my players on hitting the curveball. He was having some difficulty getting one boy to keep his weight back and wait on the pitch. My friend decided to demonstrate what he was talking about. Picking up a bat, he stepped into the batter's box and directed the pitcher to throw him a curveball. The pitch "hung" and he hit it onto the roof of a house about fifty feet beyond the rightfield fence. The boy didn't learn much about waiting on the pitch, but he sure received a vivid demonstration of what to do with a hanging curveball.

The batter should hit a *change-up* in pretty much the same manner as he does a curveball. He should look for a pitch that is delivered with the same motion as the fastball but only about half as fast. Again, the secret is to keep the weight back on the rear foot and not to try to pull the ball. Unless he has two strikes on him, he should not offer at a change-up that has him off-balance, even if it is a strike. Some pitchers will use a slow curve for a change-up. This pitch should be attacked in the same way.

On occasions, a batter will find himself up against a pitcher who relies on some sort of *trick* pitch for his effectiveness. Trick pitches are delivered in varying speeds. Some, like the forkball or knuckleball, tend to "flutter" due to a lack of spin. Others, like the screwball or sinker, tend to break down and in the opposite direction of the curveball. The batter should generally try to hit these pitches in the same manner he does any other off-speed pitches. He should keep his weight back to prevent starting the swing too soon. He should cut down on his swing for better bat control and attempt to hit the ball where it is pitched.

Getting Out of the Way

Every hitter should know how to get out of the way of a pitch that may hit him.

On pitches at the head, the hitter should throw his legs out from under his body and fall on the seat of his pants.

If a pitch is directed below the head, the batter should turn his

head away from the pitch, drop his back shoulder, and turn his back to the ball. These pitches, particularly curveballs that fail to break, should be taken in the back or hip.

Also, any time a hitter has to get out of the way of a wild pitch, he should drop his bat in an effort to keep the ball from hitting it and having to take an unnecessary strike.

Common Batting Faults

Although a positive approach to hitting is essential, there are a number of bad habits which almost all batters develop at one time or another in their careers.

1. *Pulling the head:*

a. This fault is becoming increasingly common as more and more hitters attempt to hit the long ball. When the hitter turns his head with the swing of the bat in his eagerness to hit with power, he is not going to see the ball in that last split second when it converges on the plate.

b. A hitter who pulls his head is particularly weak on pitches on the outside half of the plate, particularly curveballs and other change-of-speed pitches.

c. To correct this habit the batter must discipline himself to keep his head still and his eyes on the ball. In fact, as one old-timer put it, a batter ought to be able to hold a glass of water on his head and take his stride without spilling a drop.

2. *Stepping in the bucket:*

a. In most cases, this fault is developed by the batter because he is afraid of being hit by a pitched ball or is trying to pull everything. The "foot-in-the-bucket" hitter strides away from the pitch rather than into it.

b. Foot-in-the-bucket hitters usually have trouble with any kind of a pitch on the outside half of the plate.

c. To correct this fault the batter must first conquer his fear of being hit. He can usually do this as long as he is willing to face up to it. From a mechanical standpoint, the batter can help to eliminate this habit if he will keep his weight off of his heels. Merely striding away from the plate is not, in itself, a bad fault. (Willie Mays is a notorious "bucket" hitter, but he's swatted many an outside pitch over the rightfield fence.) As long as the batter has his weight moving into the pitch upon contact, his stride foot can land almost anywhere.

3. *Uppercutting:*

a. The uppercutter swings the bat in an upward arc at the pitch, regardless of where it is pitched.

b. The hitter who swings up on the ball is particularly weak against high pitches. Even if he hits a high pitch, it usually results in a high pop fly at best.

c. This fault can be virtually eliminated once the batter is convinced that he really is uppercutting. Most hitters will deny that they are swinging up on the ball because to them it feels as though they are swinging level. The uppercutter must learn to swing "down" at the ball. (Former Cleveland and Yankee great Joe Gordon suggests that all hitters should swing down on the ball to compensate for an almost natural tendency to uppercut.) He can learn to do this by watching himself in a mirror and by concentrating on keeping his front shoulder down. For some hitters, holding the bat a little higher prior to the swing may also help.

4. *Overstriding:*

a. Few hitters can afford to stride more than 6 to 8 inches. The reason for this is that the longer the stride, the more difficult it is to time the pitch. It only stands to reason that the hitter who uses an extremely long stride will have to commit himself earlier and will be more likely to lunge at the ball.

b. The overstrider has a great deal of difficulty hitting any pitch that approaches the plate at a slower speed. Many young players develop this habit because they are accustomed to hitting against pitchers who have not yet learned how to mix up the speeds of their pitches. To get more power, the hitter rears back and takes a long stride into the pitch because he can anticipate its speed.

c. Many hitters who overstride use a stance that has their feet fairly close together. By spreading the feet so they are at least shoulder-width apart, the hitter will be less likely to take a long stride. Another technique that has been used effectively is to place a small object or draw a line at the point in the batter's box where the batter thinks he should be striding. He can then check to see where his stride foot is landing and adjust accordingly.

5. *Sweeping:*

a. This fault may be the result of improper coaching. In telling young hitters to keep their hands away from the body, a coach can lead the player into thinking that his arms should be fully extended throughout the swing. In other words, he "sweeps" at the ball as if his arms were an extension of the bat.

b. The batter who has this fault will have trouble hitting any pitch with authority, and he will probably find himself breaking a lot of bats on inside pitches.

c. Correcting this habit is usually a simple matter once the fault is discovered. The batter merely reminds himself to keep the bat closer to his body and to extend the arms only when the fall is being met by the bat out in front of the plate.

6. *Hitching:*

a. This habit is common with almost all hitters, but for some it becomes a problem because it produces a swing that is slow and unsmooth in its execution. Hitching merely refers to the movement of the bat in the hands just prior to the beginning of the swing forward. The timing of the pitch becomes difficult when this preliminary movement causes the batter to begin the swing with the bat in different positions from one pitch to the next.

b. The batter who has this problem will have difficulty getting his bat around against a pitcher who has a good fastball. He will also have that much more difficulty timing change-of-speed pitches.

c. The hitter must learn to time his "hitch" so that it does not interfere with the swing. He should use a cocking action but do it early so that the bat is back in position in time for the swing. The alternative would be to not use any preliminary movement and keep the bat in contact with the rear shoulder. Of course, this should be done in practice only and just as a means of correcting a hitching problem by getting the hitter to hold the bat still.

7. *Dragging the bat:*

a. This fault is exemplified by the hitter who has difficulty bringing the bat around fast enough to hit the ball with any authority. He usually hits the ball to the off field and has very little power.

b. This type of hitter will always have more trouble with fastballs than with slower pitches.

c. The fault may be due to a lack of strength. If this is the case, the player should develop the strength of his wrists and forearms by performing the exercises presented in Chapter 23. This kind of batter may be helped if he tries to "throw" the bat at the ball so that the hitting end of the bat does not lag on its forward swing. If the hitter will visualize himself swinging a rope with a heavy weight on the end, he may better understand this important concept. He should also practice tightening the wrists more quickly and vigorously on the forward swing.

3

The Fundamentals of Bunting

Bunting, while closely associated with hitting, is an art in itself. Many mediocre hitters are excellent bunters, and many fine hitters are barely adequate bunters.

Bunting is one of those baseball skills at which almost any player, regardless of his natural ability, can become quite proficient if he has the determination to master the fundamentals. Good bunters are usually excellent team players. They tend to be unselfish athletes in that they spend a good deal of time perfecting a skill that will bring them very little personal glory. A few seasons back I was privileged to have a boy on my squad who was an excellent bunter but could do little else. In fact, if it were not for his bunting ability, he would not have made the team. On more than one occasion, we had him pinch-hit for one of our better hitters if the situation called for a bunt. This boy had very limited physical ability, but he made the most of what he had by perfecting a skill that was within his capability.

The Sacrifice Bunt

There are a number of ways in which the sacrifice bunt can be executed effectively. The oldest and still one of the best methods has the batter bringing his entire body around so that it is facing the pitcher prior to laying the ball down.

We prefer a technique that calls for the batter to "square around" but leave his feet in place. We feel that this method enables the

batter to visualize the strike zone from essentially the same position as he would be if he were hitting away. Also, the batter does not have to commit himself quite as early using this technique.

To execute the sacrifice bunt from his regular batting stance, the batter:

1. Pivots his body around on the balls of both feet as the pitcher brings the ball back to throw. Younger players should square around a little earlier than this until they can assume a good bunting position almost automatically.

2. The top hand slides up the handle of the bat to the trade-mark, gripping it with the thumb and forefinger. The bottom hand remains near the end of the bat.

3. The knees are slightly bent and the weight is supported on the balls of both feet.

4. The rear foot may be allowed to fall forward toward the plate for better balance.

5. The bat is held well away from the body, close to the top of the strike zone. The barrel of the bat should be slightly higher than the handle.

6. The ball is literally caught with the bat. The batter allows the bat to recoil slightly upon impact. He does not push at the ball. Nor does he pull it back.

7. The batter offers at strikes only!

8. Since he is holding the bat at the top of the strike zone, he always works down on the ball, never up. This is done essentially by bending the knees rather than by extending the bat down with the arms.

9. The bat is angled in the direction the ball is to be bunted.

10. The batter must dispel all thoughts from his mind about getting to first base until after the ball has been bunted.

As a general rule, a sacrifice bunt is most effective when it is directed down the first or third baseline. However, the younger player will find it easier if he bunts the ball where it is pitched. For example, the righthanded batter would push the outside pitch down the first baseline.

We will have more to say about specific bunting situations in Chapter 17.

The Short Bunt

This technique is used by both left- and righthanded batters to get on base. The lefthanded batter tries to dump the ball down the third baseline. The righthanded batter can lay it down either baseline.

The short bunt is performed in the same manner as the sacrifice bunt, except that it is executed quicker and with more deception:

1. The batter doesn't commit himself until the pitcher is about to release the ball.

2. At that point he squares around into the bunting position and attempts to drop the ball down either baseline.

3. As the ball hits the bat the weight is almost entirely on the front foot and the rear foot is beginning to come around for the first step toward first base.

The Push Bunt

The push bunt is performed in the same manner as the sacrifice and short bunts, except that the batter attempts to push the ball by the pitcher rather than down the baseline. With a righthanded pitcher on the mound, who has a tendency to finish his delivery on the first-base side, the batter would try to direct the ball at the shortstop. With a lefthanded pitcher on the mound, who has a tendency to finish on the third-base side, the batter would push the ball at the second baseman. Of course, the objective is to bunt the ball hard enough that it goes by the pitcher but not so hard that an infielder can make a play on it.

This bunt is particularly effective on hard, fast infields. The bunter need not be a speed-burner either. If the ball is placed accurately, almost any player should be able to beat it out. The captain of our

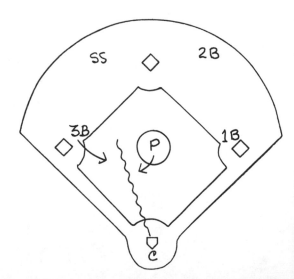

team of a couple of seasons ago was an excellent bunter, but he simply did not have the speed to beat out a bunt for a base hit. Time and time again, he would place the ball perfectly down the baseline only to be thrown out at first base. Then he decided to try pushing the ball by the pitcher instead of dumping it in front of the first or third baseman. Because he was already a good bunter, he found almost immediate success. In fact, we moved him from seventh to second in the batting order because he became a much greater threat at getting on base.

The Drag Bunt (see photos, top of pages 34 and 35)

Many people refer to almost any effort to get on base by bunting as a drag bunt. Actually, the drag bunt is executed only by the left-handed batter when he attempts to place the ball down the first baseline.

To execute a drag bunt the batter assumes his normal stance in the batter's box. Then as the pitcher is about to release the ball he:

1. Slides the top hand up to the trade-mark and brings the bat around to a position parallel with the ground. At almost the same time, the left foot (rear foot) is brought forward toward the pitcher.

2. A second step is then taken with the right foot in the same direction but angled slightly toward first base. On this step the body is leaning toward the baseline, but the hands and bat stay back to make contact with the ball.

The Slash Bunt

This technique is used by both left- and righthanded batters. It is most effective when the defense is expecting a bunt and the first and/or third basemen will be charging in to cover. Actually, "slash bunt" is just a streamlined name for the "fake bunt and hit," a technique that is almost as old as baseball itself.

1. From the normal batting stance the batter pivots around to a position facing the pitcher just as he would if he were bunting. The top hand comes up to the trade-mark and the bat is extended over the plate. This bunting position is assumed a bit earlier than usual so the defense has enough time to react.

2. As the ball is released, the bat is brought back to a position over the shoulder and the bottom hand slides up the handle near the top hand.

3. The batter then takes an easy, downward swing at the ball, stepping into the pitch with a low, short stride and, hopefully, hits it by the charging infielders.

4

The Fundamentals of Baserunning

Four factors determine a player's value to his team when he is on the base paths: (1) his natural speed and quickness, (2) his awareness of and ability to size up the game situation, (3) his mastery of baserunning fundamentals, and (4) his aggressiveness and ability to hustle.

Of the four, a player's concept of the word "hustle" is probably the most important. Nothing can be taken for granted in baseball, particularly on the bases. The batter who has just singled to the outfield should be thinking in terms of taking two bases. The runner rounding second base has to be looking for a chance to go to third. The baserunner who anticipates the error or bad hop will be ready to take all he can get. The runner who lacks this aggressiveness and hustle will not be in a position to take advantage of the unexpected when it happens. Ty Cobb was not the fastest man in baseball during his playing days and neither was Maury Wills in his prime. Yet these two players are generally regarded as the two best baserunners in the game's history. To them, baserunning was an art and they worked hard to perfect the fundamentals. They developed an instinct which told them when to go for that extra base and when not to. Above all, they were both extremely aggressive on the bases and were never satisfied until they crossed home plate.

Running Form

Many young players could improve their effectiveness on the bases by simply improving upon their running form:

1. The athlete should run on the balls of his feet and use high knee action.

2. He should check to see that as he strides each foot is landing directly in front of his nose.

3. The elbows should swing straight ahead and in the opposite direction of the corresponding feet. The arms should not swing across the body in front of the chest.

4. Whenever possible, the eyes should be focused on the base or destination.

Baserunning from Home Plate

1. As the ball hits the bat the hitter transfers his weight to the front foot and takes the first step toward first base with the rear foot.

2. The runner should not look for the ball but should focus his eyes on first base.

3. As he approaches the bag he looks to the first-base coach for one of three hand signals:

    a. Palms down—which means to slide to avoid a possible tag by the first baseman. (Ty Cobb would often slide on close plays at first base, even when the throw was on target and he was not trying to avoid a tag by the first baseman. Cobb felt that sliding into first base might not get him to the bag faster, but it might tend to prejudice the umpire's decision in his favor.)

    b. Circling left arm—which means to run on past the bag.

    c. Circling left arm, right hand pointing toward second base—which means to take a hard turn and look for the ball.

4. The runner attempting to beat a throw to first base should not leap for the bag. He should run through the bag full speed, slow down quickly and turn in toward the diamond without making an indication that he is going to second.

5. Before rounding first base the runner should veer outside the baseline so that he can cross the bag heading toward second base. The bag should be touched on the inside corner without breaking stride and with the body leaning toward the infield.

6. First base should be rounded with the intention of going on to second base, and the runner should not return to the bag until the

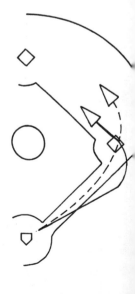

ball is actually fielded by an outfielder. The runner rounding first base is on his own on balls hit to left- and centerfields. Only on balls hit behind him to rightfield will the base coach yell "back" if trying for second base is a poor risk.

7. There are two generally accepted ways a baserunner may return to the bag after taking his turn (if a slide is not necessary):

a. He can reach for the far corner of the bag with his left foot, turn clockwise toward the infield and look for an opportunity to advance.

b. Or, he can reach for the far corner of the bag with the right foot. This method places the runner with his back to the infield, but it will enable him to see a ball that goes by the first baseman a little sooner.

From First Base

1. Immediately following each pitch or play the baserunner looks to the bench for a possible signal. He should always take the sign with one foot on the bag and should never leave the bag until he actually sees the ball in the pitcher's hand.

2. He takes his lead off the bag using one cross-over step (the left over the right) followed by several slide steps. This should be done deliberately and carefully. If he does it too quickly the pitcher may catch him leaning the wrong way and pick him off.

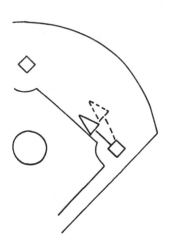

3. The amount of lead a runner takes at first base will depend on the player's speed and the game situation. Many coaches feel that a runner has an adequate lead only if he has to dive back into the bag on a pickoff attempt. Others feel that a more secure lead is best, even for the fastest of baserunners.

4. The runner must also be careful to take his lead *in the baseline* and not behind it. Many players get into the habit of leading off the bag in the direction of centerfield rather than second base. This just gives them that much farther to run, whether it is back to first or on to second base.

5. Once he has taken his lead, the runner should assume a balanced position with the weight on the balls of the feet. Normally, he should be moving toward second base when the pitch reaches the batter. However, he may cause the pitcher to hurry his delivery by taking a few quick strides toward second on the pitch, and then quickly returning to the bag. A baserunner will not bother most pitchers by merely bouncing around, yelling and throwing dirt in the air.

The mechanics of stealing second base will be described in Chapter 7.

Rounding Second Base

1. The runner should look for the ball as he approaches the bag and, unless the ball is behind him in rightfield, he should decide for himself whether to go on to third.

2. If the ball is in rightfield the runner should be watching the third-base coach for one of two signals as he rounds the bag (see Chapter 8).

   a. Circling left arm and pointing to third base with the right— means keep coming to third.

   b. Both hands up, palms facing the runner—means hold up and return to the bag.

From Second Base

1. The runner on second base should also look for a signal before he leaves the bag. He listens for additional instructions from the third-base coach and takes his lead only after the pitcher is ready to pitch.

2. The runner watches the pitcher, and the third-base coach watches the infielders for a possible pickoff play.

3. The runner on second base should look for an opportunity to relay the catcher's signals into the batter.

4. The lead at second base should be longer than at first as the catcher has a greater distance to throw for the pickoff.

5. The runner should take a few quick steps toward third as the ball is delivered, being careful to watch the catcher for a possible pickoff throw if the ball is not hit.

Approaching Third Base

1. As the runner approaches third base he should look to the base coach for one of three signals (see Chapter 8):

    a. Palms down—which means to slide (to the side indicated).

    b. Circling left arm—which means to round the bag.

    c. Circling left arm, right hand pointing toward home—which means to keep going and try to score.

From Third Base

1. The runner takes the sign, finds the ball and assumes his lead *outside* of the baseline. He stands in foul territory to eliminate the possibility of being hit by a batted ball (in which case he would be out).

2. He will normally use a walking lead. That is, he simply starts walking toward home as the pitcher takes his windup.

3. In most situations, the runner should take a moderate lead at third; one that will allow him to be moving toward home when the pitch passes the hitter and still return to third safely.

4. Occasionally, a runner can bother the pitcher by breaking almost halfway to the plate before returning to third. The only

thing wrong with this is that the runner has to start back to third before the ball reaches the plate. Therefore, he is in a poor position to advance if the ball is hit by the batter or gets by the catcher.

5. A baserunner should always return to third on the inside of the line so that his body is likely to come between a throw from the catcher to the third baseman.

Approaching Home Plate

1. A runner approaching home plate should look to the on-deck hitter for one of two hand signals (see Chapter 8):

    a. Palms down—which means to slide (on the side indicated).

    b. Palms up and facing the runner—which means to come in standing up.

5

The Fundamentals of Sliding

A player will never become an aggressive, hustling baserunner until he becomes a confident slider as well. If a boy is unsure of his ability to slide at the next base, he will be less likely to want to advance to that base when the opportunity presents itself. Sliding can also be dangerous. In fact, most of the serious injuries in baseball occur while a player is in the process of sliding. Hence the need to learn to slide properly.

Every athlete should be able to execute at least one type of slide before he plays in game competition. We feel that the younger boy will have best results if he concentrates on learning the bent-leg slide. This type of slide can serve many purposes and provides for a maximum of safety. In ten years of coaching, I cannot recall ever having a boy injure himself seriously while sliding. Credit for this lies in the fact that we insist that every boy on the squad learn the bent-leg slide. Once the player has mastered this basic slide, he can then progress to those other types of slides that have their value but are generally more difficult to execute and are somewhat more dangerous.

The Bent-Leg Slide

The basic bent-leg slide is used as an all-purpose slide. It can be used to reach the base quickly, prevent overrunning a base or as a hard slide to jar the ball out of the fielder's hands.

1. The baserunner starts the slide about 10 feet from the bag.

2. He takes off on either the left or the right foot, whichever of the two is the most comfortable for him. The take-off foot becomes the "bent-leg."

3. As soon as the take-off foot leaves the ground that knee is bent at a 90 degree angle. For example, if the right foot is the take-off foot, the right knee is bent after take-off so that the right foot extends underneath and to the far side of the left knee. The shoelaces of the right foot are facing in the direction of the slide.

4. The top leg (or left leg in this case) is about 6 inches off the ground, slightly bent, with the knee cap facing upward.

5. The back bends slightly at the waist and the arms are stretched out to the side for balance with hands well off the ground to avoid being scraped.

6. The slider leans back and lands on the seat of his pants and the upper right leg.

7. Sliding, he touches the bag with the foot of the top leg.

The Pop-Up Slide

The pop-up slide is used to prevent overrunning a base and in situations where the runner might be able to advance after the slide.

The fundamentals of the pop-up slide are identical to those of the bent-leg slide with one exception. The runner is brought to his feet or "pops up" as he reaches the bag. He does this by making contact with the bag with the top foot and pressing *down* with the bottom leg. These actions, along with his momentum forward, lift the slider quickly off the ground into a standing position.

The Take-Out Slide

The take-out slide is another variation of the bent-leg slide. It is used to upset the pivotman on a double-play attempt. The author learned the value of the take-out slide the hard way. I was pressed into service as a second baseman during the last inning of a semipro game. Being a pitcher by trade, I really didn't know what I was doing. However, when a ground ball was hit to our shortstop (there was a runner on first) I did know enough to cover second to take his throw. Just as I was about to relay the ball to first the baserunner crashed into me. The ball ended up in the bleachers behind first base and I landed on my back. Needless to say, that was the last time I ever volunteered to fill in at second base.

1. The baserunner starts his slide a little closer to the bag than usual so that his momentum will be sufficient to upset the pivotman and spoil his throw to first.

2. He directs the slide right at the pivotman, remembering that he cannot slide more than three feet out of the baseline when going after a defensive player.

3. The take-off leg is doubled underneath as normal, but the top leg is held considerably higher.

4. The slider tries to make contact with the fielder's striding foot with his (the slider's) top foot. His objective is to prevent an accurate relay throw by simply knocking the fielder's feet out from under him. Bending the top leg and hitting the fielder with his shin is one way to do it without spiking him.

The Hook Slide

This slide is used to evade a tag, particularly when an infielder has to reach to one side or the other for the ball. It is not a very good slide to beat a throw because the slider does not direct his body straight into the bag.

A player should learn to hook slide to either side. Of course, the

objective is to slide away from the direction in which the ball is coming.

1. The hook slide is executed by taking off on the foot opposite the side of the base the runner hopes to slide to.

2. The baserunner begins to fall away from the baseline as the take-off foot hits the ground.

3. He arches the back and throws the arms out to the side.

4. Both feet are extended toward the base as the body lands on the hip, seat and upper leg.

5. The toe of the inside foot hooks the base, causing that knee to bend.

6. The outside foot continues on past the base and remains off the ground.

7. The slider should be careful to not bend the hooking leg until after it touches the bag. The sooner the slider bends the hooking leg the farther he will have to slide. Many coaches discourage the use of the hook slide for this very reason. The player who has a tendency to bend his leg before making contact with the bag is apt to be traveling more than 90 feet between bases. (Maury Wills refers to this as the "93-foot slide.")

The Back-Door Slide

The back-door slide is used only when the throw to the base has the runner easily beaten. The slider tries to evade an almost certain tag by luring the fielder into thinking he is going to hook the bag with his inside foot.

1. The slider uses a hook slide but directs it farther away from the baseline than usual.

2. Upon reaching the bag, he quickly pulls the hooking leg away from the tag and straightens it.

3. He slides past the bag with both legs extended.

4. He then rolls over toward the bag and grabs for the back corner with his opposite hand.

The Head-First Slide

This slide is probably the best for covering a certain distance in the shortest amount of time. Most players use the head-first slide to get back to the bag on a pickoff attempt. Some players use the head-first slide as their basic slide. (Richie Ashburn of the Phillies

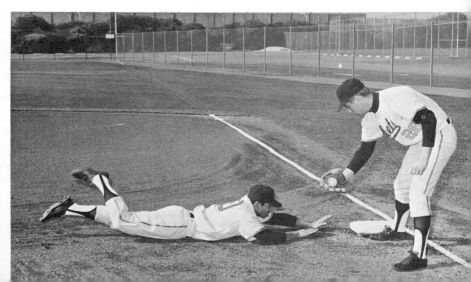

was one, Pepper Martin of the Cards' old "Gas House Gang" was another), and many others use it when they want to protect a leg injury. A young player would be wise to use the head-first slide, if he does not have confidence in his ability to execute one of the feet-first slides. Of course, even the head-first slide can be dangerous if it is not executed correctly.

1. The baserunner bends forward and dives low and directly to the bag. He attempts to do this without breaking stride or losing momentum.

2. The back should be arched, the head up and the arms extended.

3. The impact with the ground is made on the chest and stomach.

4. If the ball beats the runner to the bag, he should delay his reach for the base until after the fielder sweeps down for the tag.

General Tips on Sliding

1. When in doubt, slide!

2. Keep relaxed and stay low to the ground. Do not leap at the bag!

3. Watch the fielder or base coach for an indication of which side of the bag to slide on.

6

Offensive Game Situations

When the team is not attempting a specific play the baserunner or baserunners have some fairly definite rules to guide their decisions on the base paths. Each of the following rules has a purpose. It is not enough that the player merely understand these rules. He must know them so thoroughly that he applies them almost automatically as each situation develops in game competition.

Rules for the Runner on First Base

1. With less than two outs, the runner should:

a. *Hold up* and get caught in a rundown if a ground ball is fielded in the baseline by the second baseman. By doing this the runner can prevent the second baseman from tagging him and throwing to first for an easy double play. This rule really paid off once for the Yankees in a game against the Red Sox. With Roger Maris on first and Hector Lopez on third, a ground ball was hit to the second baseman in the baseline. Maris held up to avoid the tag. The second baseman, a rookie, started to chase Maris back toward first as Lopez edged off third. Maris retreated all the way to first with the second baseman in hot pursuit. At this point, Roger started down the rightfield line, and to everyone's amazement, the rookie infielder continued to chase him! Of course, by the time the second baseman realized his mistake, Lopez had scored.

b. *Slide* into second base on any other ground ball. If the play at second is close, he should slide hard into the pivotman to break up a possible double play. Even if he is an easy out, he should not go in standing up. The pivotman may drop the ball and the runner wants to avoid overrunning the base. He also wants to avoid being hit by the thrown ball. We won one ball game when a player of mine "caught" the relay throw with his forehead because he didn't hit the dirt going into second base. The ball caromed off his head into rightfield and the runner going to third was able to score the winning run. I don't recommend this, for obvious reasons. In this case the player was not hurt, but he did learn that it pays to slide at second base in a double-play situation.

c. *Tag up* on all foul fly balls. He could not advance even if the ball were dropped so there is no purpose in straying off the bag.

d. *Tag up* on any fly ball hit deep enough to advance on after the catch if it appears that the outfielder will be able to make the catch.

e. *Tag up* on a fly ball whenever a lead runner is also tagging up. With a runner on third, break toward second after the catch if the throw goes into the plate.

f. *Get off the bag* as far as possible on any fly ball he could not advance on after the catch.

g. *Get off the bag* as far as possible on any fly ball on which he may be able to score if it is not caught. In this case, the runner could not tag up and advance to second if the ball is caught, but he might be able to score if the ball gets beyond the outfielder.

2. With two outs, the runner should:

a. Run on any ground ball or fly ball.

Rules for the Runner on Second Base

1. With less than two outs, the runner should:

a. If no runner is on first, *hold up* on any ground ball hit in front of him, unless it goes through into the outfield. In this situation the runner does not want to give the defense an easy play on him at third. I lost my temper and benched one of my best ballplayers when he was thrown out trying to advance to third on a ground ball to the shortstop. That was five years ago, and that boy, who is now playing professional ball, says that's the one rule he has never forgotten!

b. *Advance* to third on any ground ball hit past the pitcher to the shortstop's left, or to the rightfield side of the infield.

c. *Tag up* on all foul fly balls.

d. *Tag up* on any fly ball hit deep enough to advance on after the catch.

e. *Tag up* on a fly ball whenever a lead runner on third is tagging.

f. *Get off the bag as far as possible* on balls that he could not tag up and advance on after the catch was made.

g. *Get off the bag* as far as possible on all doubtful catches.

2. With two outs, the runner should:

a. Run on any ground ball or fly ball.

Rules for the Runner on Third Base

1. With no outs, the runner on third should:

a. *Stay close* to the bag and avoid being doubled off on a line drive.

b. *Try to score* on a ground ball only if he can do so without taking a chance on being thrown out.

2. With less than two outs, the runner on third should:

a. *Hold up* on a ground ball hit back to the pitcher or to an infielder who is playing in for a play at the plate.

b. *Try to score* on any ground ball that goes by the pitcher with the infield playing halfway or deep.

c. *Try to score,* regardless of where the infield is playing, if there is also a runner on first. The runner on third must never remain there if a double play possibility exists. If his opponents have him easily at the plate, he should hold up and get caught in a rundown to allow the trailing runners an opportunity to advance.

d. *Tag up* on all foul fly balls. With a runner on first also, the runner on third should bluff toward home after the catch to force the defense to make a throw to the plate and, perhaps, give the runner on first a chance to go to second.

e. *Tag up* on any fly ball hit deep enough to advance on after the catch.

f. *Tag up* on all doubtful catches. If the fielder makes a difficult catch, the runner can still score after the play.

g. *Get off the bag* as far as possible on fly balls he could not advance on after the catch.

3. With two outs, the runner on third should:

a. *Hold up* when attempting to score may provide an infielder with an easier play than the one on the batter. For example, a runner should not try to score on a ball dribbled toward third in such a manner that the third baseman has a fairly easy throw to the plate but an extremely difficult throw to first.

General Principles for All Baserunners

1. A baserunner should use a base coach as an aid but should not rely upon him to make his decisions for him. It stands to reason that if a runner has to wait for instructions from a base coach, he will be just that much slower in getting started. The only exception to this rule occurs when the ball is behind the runner where he cannot see it. In this situation, the base coach is usually in the best position to make the decision.

2. A baserunner should always be thinking of ways to draw throws and force the defense into mistakes. Willie Mays has to be one of the best at this. He seems to know when he can afford to slow up to draw a throw and when he cannot. Just this past season he won a game for the Giants by "loafing" into third base. A rookie rightfielder decided to show off his arm by trying to throw Mays out at third. The throw went past the third baseman and Mays scored the winning run standing up.

3. A baserunner should always be aware of the percentages involved in the chances he takes on the bases. For example, a runner should take a chance on going to third base when there is one out, but he should never take the same chance to reach that base when no one is out or when there are two outs.

4. A trailing runner should always be aware of what the runner ahead of him is doing. Not only does he want to avoid "running

him down," but he also wants to be ready to advance to the next base if a play is made on the lead runner. For example, a batter who has singled to the outfield with a runner on second, should always go on to second base if the throw to the plate is not cut off.

5. A runner who discovers that he is going to be an easy out on a tag play should always hold up and get caught in a rundown if there is another runner behind him. With the defense forced into concentrating longer on the lead runner, the trailing runner(s) may have an opportunity to move up a base. For example, a runner on first may be able to move to second (scoring position) if his teammate going from second to third gets caught in a rundown. Of course, this rule does not apply if there are already two outs.

7

Offensive Plays

A baseball team, like its football counterpart, must have a series of set offensive plays designed to exploit the defense of the opposing team. The extent to which a particular baseball team will make use of these offensive stratagems depends somewhat on the level of competition. By and large, the higher the level of competition, the less a team is likely to rely upon trick plays. Most professional managers play a relatively conservative game in comparison to that at the high school and college levels. The pros go for the long ball and generally play for the big inning. They usually don't take chances on the bases because almost anyone in the offensive line-up is capable of hitting the ball for distance, and defensive arms are strong and quick.

On the other hand, most high school and college teams make good use of a wide variety of set offensive plays. This is true for two general reasons. First of all, younger players often are not strong enough to hit the long ball with any consistency. Secondly, high school and college defenses are not as able to cope with certain offensive techniques as are those in the big leagues. A high school catcher, for example, must throw the same distance to second base as the major league catcher. Naturally, even the best of high school catchers will not be capable of making consistently good throws to second base. Therefore, the steal and double-steal plays become much more effective and are more likely to be attempted by the offensive team.

Regardless of the level of competition, to be effective offensively a baseball team must be able to execute a number of basic plays. Each member of the squad must understand the theory of the play completely in order to be able to execute it properly when he is called upon to do so. The following plays represent most of the basic offensive plays used in baseball. Teams will vary somewhat in the way they execute these plays, but the basic intent is usually the same.

1. Runner on first base, *sacrifice bunt:*

a. Normally used with no outs and in the latter innings of a close game to move a runner into scoring position.

b. The *batter,* being careful to bunt at strikes only, tries to put the ball down the first or third baseline.

c. The *baserunner* takes a good lead but does not leave for second until the ball is on the ground. If the ball is bunted to the third baseman, he looks for a chance to go to third if that base remains uncovered.

2. Runner on second base or first base and second base, *sacrifice bunt:*

a. Used normally with no outs to: (1) move the runner on second to third so he can score on a fly ball or infield hit or error; (2) move both runners into scoring position; and/or (3) avoid a possible double play.

b. The *batter,* being careful again to bunt only strikes, tries to put the ball down the third baseline far enough to force the third baseman to leave the bag and field it.

c. The *runner on second* must get a good lead. Again, he leaves for third only when the ball is on the ground.

d. The runner on first merely advances to second when the ball is bunted.

3. Runner on third base or first base and third, *sacrifice bunt* (safety squeeze):

a. Normally used with less than two outs to score an important run and, in the case of runners on first and third, to avoid a double play.

b. The *batter* bunts only at strikes and tries to put the ball down either baseline.

c. The *runner on third* tries to score once the ball is on the ground if he thinks he can make it. If the ball is not well placed, he waits for the fielder to make his throw to first, then looks for a chance to score on the throw. The *runner on first* simply goes to second once the ball is bunted and looks for a chance to go on to third.

4. Runner on first base, *steal:*

a. Used under almost any circumstances with a fast man on base.

b. The *batter's* responsibilities on this play range from moving to the rear of the batter's box and simply taking the pitch to squaring around and faking a bunt or swinging to miss the pitch. Most teams have the hitter do something to make the catcher's job that much more difficult

c. The *baserunner,* unless he is the first baserunner in the game, should already be aware of what he should watch for in the pitcher's delivery to get a good jump. If a righthander is on the mound, the runner should look for:

1) The pitcher to lift his right heel if he is throwing to first base and to leave it on the rubber if he is throwing home.
2) The pitcher to rotate his shoulders too far in checking the runner. The runner can leave the moment the pitcher starts to rotate them to the right to throw home.
3) The pitcher to stride forward with the left foot to throw home and toward first to throw to first base.
4) The pitcher to develop a consistency in his looks to first base so the baserunner can anticipate when the pitcher will throw home. We won one important ball game when we discovered that an otherwise great high school pitcher always looked to first base only once before throwing to home plate. Every runner who reached first stole second, and it so unnerved him that he completely lost his effectiveness.
5) The pitcher to lean toward home before he actually starts to throw.

If a lefthander is on the mound, the runner should look for:

1) The pitcher always to look home when he is throwing to first and always to look to first when he is throwing home.
2) The pitcher to lean toward home before he actually starts to throw.
3) The pitcher to bring his right foot back behind the left

before throwing home. Once he has done this he cannot throw to first base without balking.

The runner takes a good lead but not so far off the bag that he has to lean back toward first base. Keying the pitcher's delivery, he takes off for second if he gets a good jump.

5. Runner on second or first base and second base, *steal*:

a. Often attempted with one out to get a man on third so he can score on a fly ball or error, and with no outs and runners on first and second when a sacrifice is expected. Generally, third base is an easier base to steal than second because the runner is able to take a much longer lead.

b. The *batter* will usually square around to fake a bunt, hoping to draw the third baseman away from the bag so he cannot take the catcher's throw.

c. The *runner on second* must take a good lead, watching the heel of the pitcher. Left- and righthanded pitchers will lift the heel of the pivot foot if they are going to throw to second. The runner takes off on the pitch and uses a hook slide to the leftfield side of third.

d. The *runner on first* cannot loaf as many catchers will throw to second instead of third.

6. Runner on third, second and third, or the bases loaded, *steal:*

a. Used under almost any circumstances but usually when the opposition is least expecting it. The batter should be righthanded to restrict the view of the catcher, and the pitcher must use his full windup. If the pitcher unexpectedly goes into his stretch delivery, the play is usually called off automatically.

b. The *batter* stands deep in the box to move the catcher farther from the plate. When the pitch is delivered he merely remains in the batter's box and makes the catcher move him out of the way to attempt the tag.

c. The *runner on third* normally uses a walking lead. That is, he merely starts walking toward home as the pitcher readies to pitch, and the instant the pitcher begins his delivery he breaks for the plate. Once a pitcher has started his delivery, he must throw home and he cannot alter his windup to any great extent to get the ball to the plate quicker.

d. *Runners on first or second* simply steal their respective bases and look for a chance to advance in case of a wild pitch.

7. Runner on first base, *delayed steal:*

a. Used under the same circumstances and for the same reasons as the regular steal of second base when the runner notices that neither the shortstop nor the second baseman covers second *after* the pitch.

b. The *batter* merely stands deep in the box to make the throw longer for the catcher.

c. The *runner* takes his normal lead, holds it as the pitcher delivers, then takes off for second as the catcher starts to throw the ball back to the pitcher.

8. Runner on second base, *delayed steal:*

a. Used effectively when a steal may be called for but against a catcher who has a good arm but is careless with his throws.

b. The *batter* merely remains in the box and does not swing.

c. The *runner* takes an unusually long lead off second—to draw the catcher's throw—then breaks for third when the catcher tries to pick him off second.

9. Runner on third base, *delayed steal:*

a. Used against an unalert catcher who does not check the lead of the runner on third before throwing back to the pitcher, or against a catcher who likes to throw to the bases a lot.

b. The *batter* merely remains in the box and does not swing.

c. The *runner* has two alternatives: (1) against a catcher who does not check the runner on third between pitches, he takes a good lead, holds it while the pitch is delivered, then breaks for home just as the catcher releases his throw back to the pitcher; (2) against the catcher who likes to throw, the runner takes an excessive lead to draw the throw, then breaks for home when the catcher throws to third.

10. Runners on first and second, *long lead double steal:*

a. Most effectively used with less than two outs and the offensive team in need of one run. This play should not be attempted unless the opposing first baseman is righthanded and/ or he has a weak or inaccurate throwing arm.

b. The *batter* has no immediate responsibilities on this play. If the ball is delivered to the plate he does not swing.

c. The *runner on first* base takes an exaggerated lead in an effort to draw a pickoff throw from the pitcher or catcher. If the defense does attempt a pickoff play (with the first baseman breaking over to cover or the second baseman coming in behind the runner), the runner immediately takes off for second base.

d. The *runner on second* takes a normal lead and breaks for third as soon as the throw is made to first base. Unless the first baseman (or second baseman) has an exceptionally strong and accurate arm, the runner should be able to get into third before the ball can be relayed back across the diamond. But this play requires excellent timing.

11. Runners on first and third, *early double steal:*

a. Normally used with two outs, in a tight game with an inexperienced pitcher on the mound.

b. The *batter* has no responsibilities other than coaching the runner attempting to score.

c. The *runner on first* takes his lead and breaks for second as the pitcher takes his stretch. If the pitcher does not lose his composure and balk, the runner gets caught in a rundown. His job is to occupy the ball long enough for the runner on third to score. He does not allow himself to be tagged out until he is sure the runner has scored.

d. The *runner on third* takes a good lead and holds it as the runner on first breaks for second. He then breaks for home when his opponents are most occupied with the rundown between first and second base. His best opportunity will come when the ball is farthest from home, and one fielder is just releasing a throw to the other.

12. Runners on first and third, *regular double steal:*

a. Used under the same circumstances as the early double steal with the exception that this variation would be more effective against a weak-throwing catcher, and/or a weak second base-shortstop combination. The requirements for the defense on this play are such that I know of few high school infields that have coped with it successfully with any consistency. However, the Los Angeles Dodgers and the St. Louis Cardinals have used the play with considerable success, despite the sophistication of big league defenses.

b. The *batter* merely remains in the box and does not swing.

c. The *runner on first* breaks for second as he would on a regular steal. However, he holds up, gets caught in a rundown, and does not allow himself to be tagged until the runner on third has scored.

d. The *runner on third* takes his lead in the baseline so the catcher cannot determine the length of his lead at a glance. He holds the lead as the catcher releases his throw to second. Once the ball passes the pitcher's head he breaks for home.

13. Runners on first and third, *long-lead double steal:*

a. Used under the same circumstances as the other variations of the double steal, but with an inexperienced and/or a lefthanded first baseman.

b. The *batter* merely waits in the box and looks for an opportunity to coach the runner trying to score.

c. The *runner on first* takes an exaggerated lead to draw a pickoff throw from the pitcher. He then gets caught in a rundown long enough for the runner on third to score.

d. The *runner on third* holds his lead and breaks for home at the most opportune time. Some teams have the runner on third break for home the instant the pitcher throws to first base.

14. Runner on third, or second base and third base, *suicide squeeze:*

a. This play is used normally with one out and the man on third representing an important run. The batter must be an accomplished bunter, and his chances of getting a good pitch to bunt will be increased if the pitcher is behind in the count.

b. The *batter* sacrifices himself to score the runner on third. He hides his intention to bunt until the pitcher is about to release the pitch. Regardless of where the ball is thrown, the batter must attempt to put it on the ground.

c. The *runner on third* takes a good lead as the pitcher takes his windup. He breaks for home only when the pitcher's stride foot touches the ground. Or he may break when the pitcher's throwing arm is next to his ear on the delivery. In any case, he will tip off the play and give the pitcher time to throw a pitchout if he leaves any earlier.

d. A *runner on second* takes off for third as the pitcher begins his windup. If the ball is bunted to the third baseman, he rounds third and looks for a chance to score on the play on the batter at first base.

15. Runner on first, or first base and third base, *bunt and run:*

a. Used normally with no outs and an extremely fast runner at first base. The theory behind the play being to advance the runner on first to third so he can score on a fly ball or error.

b. The *batter* squares around to sacrifice and tries to bunt the ball down the third baseline. He must offer at any pitch in order to protect the runner.

c. The *runner on first* takes his lead and breaks for second just as he would on a regular steal. If he hears the ball hit the bat, he looks to make sure the ball has not been popped up. If he does not hear the ball hit the bat, he slides into second. If he sees that the ball has been bunted successfully, he goes into second and looks for an opportunity to go on to third on the play at first.

d. The responsibilities of a *runner on third* would be the same as on a safety squeeze. He would score on the bunt or on the throw to first.

16. Runner on first, or first base and third base, *hit and run:*

a. This play is used for a number of reasons but mainly to reduce the possibility of a double play. Normally, it is attempted with one out but may also be used with no outs. The hit and run is most effective when the pitcher is behind in the count and must come in with a good pitch to hit.

b. The *batter's* responsibility is to hit the ball, regardless of where it is pitched. He should shorten up on his swing and attempt to stroke the ball rather than go for power. Some hitters attempt to place the ball in the spot vacated by the man covering second base. For most batters, however, it is enough to just make sure the ball is hit somewhere.

c. The *runner on first* takes off for second as he would on a steal. He must look up when he hears the ball hit the bat to make sure that the ball is not in the air. If the ball is not hit, he slides into second. If the ball goes through into the outfield, he should be able to reach third easily.

d. A *runner on third* simply holds his lead and looks for an opportunity to score on a batted ball or on the throw to second to get the runner.

17. Runner on first, first and second, or first and third, *run and hit:*

a. This play is very much like the hit and run. The only difference lies in the fact that the batter does not swing at the ball unless it is a strike. It is usually attempted with a count of 3 balls and 1 strike or 3 balls and 2 strikes on the batter. With 2 outs and the count 3 and 2, the run and hit is automatic.

b. The *batter* simply hits the ball if it is in the strike zone, or takes it for ball 4 if it is not.

c. The responsibilities of the baserunners are exactly the same as those on the hit and run.

8

Communication on Offense

The baseball team that is unable to operate as a unit on offense will not be a consistent winner, regardless of the talents of its individual players. Situations arise in competition that call for a coordinated effort on the part of the manager or coach, the batter, the baserunners and the base coaches. If any one of these participants becomes confused as to what the others are doing on a particular play, the success of the play is in jeopardy.

Given the basic skills and a thorough understanding of offensive plays and game situations, a team must also be able to communicate with each other. Offensive communication has two important ingredients: a simple but effective system of signals and competent, conscientious base coaches.

Offensive Signals

Baseball teams use a variety of ways to communicate information to hitters and baserunners. The systems employed by major league teams have to be quite complicated. The players and coaches become skilled at stealing the signals of their opponents. Since one team will play another as many as twenty-four times in a single season, it will have ample opportunity to collect information about its opponents. It is no wonder that major league teams go to great lengths to confuse the opposition by changing systems regularly, using "dummy" signals and relaying signals through base coaches.

Most high school and college teams, however, need not concern themselves with a complicated system of offensive signals. The most important factor in selecting a system should be simplicity. The major concern at this level is to make sure that a team thoroughly understands its own signals, not necessarily those of the opposition. (A colleague of mine simply shouts "Now" to the runner on first when he wants him to take off for second on the early steal.)

1. There are several kinds of signals that have proven to be effective with younger players:

a. *Holding Signals*. This kind of signal is probably the best for extremely young players. The manager or coach simply assumes a different stance or position for each signal. For example, standing with the legs apart may represent the "hit away" signal and with the legs together the "take" signal. The arms folded could represent the "steal" and the hands in the pockets the "bunt." This method is effective with young players because the signal is "held" for some time and the batter or baserunner will be less likely to miss it. In fact, many older teams use this type of signal on plays that require several players to pick up the same signal.

b. *Flash Signals*. This kind of signal is probably the most popular at all levels of play. The signal is "flashed" rather than "held." For example, if the "bunt" signal were the cap, the coach or manager would simply touch the cap briefly. The player receiving the signal would have to be looking just as the signal was given in order to catch it. Needless to say, this kind of sign would be much more difficult for the opposition to steal.

c. *Verbal Signals*. This method has been used successfully by a number of teams. Instead of using hand signals, the coach or manager simply relays information by the use of certain "key" words in his normal chatter to his team. For example, reference to a player by his first name might mean to "hit away." Calling the hitter by his last name might mean the "take" is on, and when the coach says "make it be a strike" the hitter knows he is supposed to bunt. A team will rarely use *only* this system. Verbal signals are often used to get information to a batter or runner who is in a poor position to see a visual signal, or on plays that require quick communication.

2. Pre-high-school-age players will be doing well if they are able to learn a few simple holding, flash or verbal signals. High school

varsities and college teams, however, may want to use a slightly more complicated system in order to do a better job of disguising its communications. This can be accomplished in several ways by using either holding signals or flash signals:

a. If a team prefers to use the holding-type signal, it can disguise each signal by setting a preliminary condition. For example, a coach may tell his players that a signal is not "on" unless his (the coach's) feet are apart when he gives the signal. Therefore, if having the arms folded across the chest is the bunt signal, the batter should bunt only if the coach also has his feet apart.

b. If a team prefers to use the "flash" type of signal, it can use any one of several different methods of confusing the opposition:

1) A team can also set a preliminary condition for flash signals. For example, a team may choose to make a given signal "live" (operative) only if it is given with the left hand. If touching the cap is the bunt, then the batter goes ahead and hits away if the coach touches his cap with the right hand.

2) Flash signals can also be disguised by designating a particular signal as a "key" signal. For example, if touching the belt is the key signal, then the signal that the coach gives immediately after he has touched his belt is the one that is on. If the coach touches his cap, then his belt, and then goes to his sleeve, the sleeve is the live signal.

3) Another commonly used method of disguising flash signals is to simply give a series of three signals, but decide beforehand which of the three will be "live."

4) Flash signals can also be disguised by using "colors" to designate certain plays. For example, the coach may touch some part of his uniform which is *red* if he wants the batter to bunt. If the team uniform includes a red cap, red sleeves and red stockings, the coach may touch any of these items to put on the bunt signal.

c. There are methods of giving offensive signals other than those presented here. However, almost any system will work if each player on the squad makes a concerted effort to learn his team's system thoroughly.

3. Regardless of the system used, there are a few basic principles regarding offensive signals that a team should observe to insure good communication:

a. Younger players should take their signals from the team's coach and not from another player coaching the bases. If the coach of the team is not allowed to coach on the bases, he should give the signals from the bench. It only stands to reason that if a signal has to be relayed to a base coach and then to a batter or baserunner, the chances of someone missing the signal are twice as great.

b. Base coaches, however, should give "dummy" signals at the same time the coach is giving live signals to the batter or runner.

c. The best time to give a signal is immediately following the previous play or pitch. This is the time the opposition is least apt to be looking for a signal. If a coach waits until every eye in the park is looking at him, then there is a much greater chance that the signal will be stolen.

d. A batter should not step into the batter's box until he is *sure* what his coach wants him to do. An inexperienced player will often step into the box to hit even if he is confused by the signal. Not being certain of what his responsibility is, he is less able to really concentrate on the pitch. The batter who is unsure of a signal should call time out, step out of the box and look to the coach to repeat the signal.

e. A baserunner should always take the signal with one foot on the bag. If he is confused by the signal, he should call time out and check with the nearest base coach.

f. After receiving a true signal from the coach, the hitter and baserunners should look to the base coaches to acknowledge their dummy signals.

g. Normally, a signal designating a particular play is given only once. It is repeated only if there is an unusually long delay between pitches or either the batter or baserunner requests that it be repeated.

h. A signal is off only if it is "rubbed off" (with a signal used for that purpose) or it is superseded by another signal. For example, a batter coming to the plate is given the bunt signal before he steps into the box. If the first pitch is not a strike, the batter knows that the bunt is still on even though the signal is not repeated.

i. The experienced player knows when to look for a possible signal and when not to. He can recognize the situation in which his coach may want to give him a signal. On the other hand, when his assignment is obvious he does not take a lot of time looking for a signal.

Coaching the Bases

Base coaching represents such an important element in offensive communication at the major league level that former players are hired specifically for that task. In youth league baseball, however, the manager is usually forced to select his base coaches from among those players on the squad who are not in the starting line-up. Therefore, coaching the bases takes on a negative meaning to the young player. He feels that the main reason he is being given the responsibility of coaching a base is that his manager does not consider him a very good baseball player.

These circumstances are unfortunate because a good base coach can be particularly valuable to a team of young, inexperienced players. I have been blessed with few good base coaches in my coaching career. One of the exceptions was a boy who took the job seriously even though we all knew that he would rather be playing. He ran out to the coaching box at the beginning of each inning, and his constant chatter, I am sure, inspired many of our rallies. Certainly, a boy should be disappointed at not being in the line-up, but he should also look upon his selection as a base coach as an indication of his manager's faith in his knowledge of the game and his ability to make quick decisions. The young player should keep in mind the simple fact that if the rules allowed it, the manager or coach of the team would coach one of the bases himself.

A base coach must not only be a good student of the game, he must also know the fundamentals of his assignment thoroughly. Although the responsibilities at first base differ somewhat from those at third, it is vitally important that arm signals and other methods of communication remain as nearly alike as possible. Each member of the team must be able to interpret the directions of both coaches.

General Rules for Base Coaches

1. Both base coaches should *run* to their respective coaching boxes immediately following the last out of the previous inning.

2. A base coach should never appear bored with the game, even when there are no runners on base. Besides offering the batter constant verbal encouragement, he should be looking for ways to pick up the catcher's signals, watching the pitcher for keys to his delivery and checking the position of the infield and outfield.

3. A base coach should avoid unnecessary conversations with umpires, members of the opposing team and fans. His job is an important one, and it will take all the concentration he can give it.

4. Base coaches can even be of help to their team on defense. As he comes off the lines at the end of the inning, the first-base coach should have a practice ball to give to his first baseman for infield warm-up. The third-base coach can make the same provision for the outfielders.

5. As a general rule, the base coach should assume that the baserunner is capable of knowing and doing little if anything without the base coach's help. In fact, a base coach will probably be doing the runner a service if he treats him as if he has never been on base before.

Coaching First Base

1. When the ball is hit to the infield, the first-base coach should move to a position in the box in line with the throw and first base. Then, depending upon the location of the ball and the accuracy of the throw, he will:

a. Signal the runner to run on past the bag by circling the left arm.

b. Signal the runner to slide and avoid the tag with a palms-down signal.

c. Signal the runner to round the bag and look for the ball by circling the left arm and pointing toward second with the right.

2. The first-base coach should remind each runner who stops at his base of the basic rules for a runner at first base:

a. With less than two outs he should tell the runner to:

1) Break up a double play on a ground ball to the infield.

2) Hold up if the ball is fielded by the second baseman in the baseline.

3) Tag up on fly balls that should be caught and are hit deep enough to advance on after the catch.

4) Go as far down the line as possible on doubtful catches and balls he could not advance on if caught.

5) Tag up and bluff toward second on any foul fly hit behind first or second when there is also a runner on third.

b. With two outs he should tell the runner to:

1) Run on a batted ball of any kind.

2) Be running on a 3-2 pitch.

c. Regardless of the number of outs, the first-base coach should always inform the runner of:

1) The number of outs.

2) The position of the outfielders.

3) How the second baseman and shortstop pivot on the double play.

3. The first-base coach must assume the responsibility for the runner's lead at first base:

a. He verbally guides the runner off the bag until he has an appropriate lead.

b. Watching the pitcher, he yells "back" when the pitcher throws to first.

c. When the first baseman plays off the bag and behind the runner, the coach takes a position in front of the box and watches the first baseman for a possible pickoff attempt.

Coaching Third Base

1. The third-base coach is responsible for the runner rounding second base. He should be aware of the percentages involved in taking the extra base prior to the pitch. He then directs the runner by:

a. Circling the left arm if he wants the runner to take his turn at second.

b. Circling the left arm and pointing to third with the right if he wants the runner to come on to third.

c. Holding both arms in the air if he wants the runner to hold up and return to second.

2. The third-base coach should remind each runner who stops at second base of the basic rules for a runner on that base:

a. With less than two outs, he should tell the runner to:

1) Be sure that a ground ball hit in front of him goes through before he advances to third.

2) Tag up on fly balls that should be caught and are hit deep enough to advance on after the catch.

3) Go as far down the line as possible on doubtful catches and on balls he could not advance on if caught.

b. With two outs he should tell the runner to:

1) Advance on any batted ball unless he would be making an easier play for the third baseman or shortstop.

2) Be running on a 3-2 pitch if there is also a runner on first base.

c. Regardless of the number of outs, the third-base coach should always inform the runner on second of:

1) The number of outs.

2) The position of the outfielders.

3. The third-base coach is responsible for the runner's lead off second base:

a. The coach watches the shortstop and second baseman, and the runner watches the pitcher.

b. Cupping his hands over his mouth, the coach guides the runner off the bag by repeating "you're OK, you're OK, you're OK."

c. Once the runner has reached an appropriate lead the coach cautions him to "hold it."

d. If either of the infielders break over and the runner is in danger of being picked off, the coach shouts "back."

4. The third-base coach is responsible for the runner approaching third base. He should be aware of the percentages involved in having the runner try to score before he actually has to make the decision. He directs the runner approaching third by:

a. Holding both hands high in the air if he wants the runner to come in standing up.

b. Giving a palms-down signal to one side or another if he wants the runner to slide (to the side indicated).

c. Moving well down the line toward home plate if he wants the runner to round the bag. (We scored the tying run in a game once because our inexperienced third-base coach didn't move down the line. The baserunner failed to see him trying to hold him up so he continued on toward home plate. Fortunately for us, the throw was wild and the runner scored.) From this position he will:

1) Raise both arms in the air if he wants the runner to hold up and return to third.

2) Circle the left arm and point toward home with the right if he wants the runner to try to score.

5. The third-base coach should remind each runner who stops at third of the basic rules for a runner at that base.

a. With no outs he should tell the runner to:

1) Be careful not to get doubled off on a line drive.

2) Try to score on a ground ball only if he can do so without any danger of being thrown out.

b. With less than two outs he should tell the runner to:

1) Try to score on any ground ball that goes by the pitcher, unless the infield is playing in front of the line for a play at the plate.

2) Hold up and get caught in a rundown if a throw to the plate has him easily beaten and there are trailing runners.

3) Tag up on all fly balls to the outfield and all foul fly balls.

4) Tag up and bluff toward home on a pop fly behind first or third, when there is also a runner on first base.

c. With two outs the coach should tell the runner to:

1) Be running on a 3-2 pitch with the bases loaded.

2) Try to score on any batted ball unless in doing so he will be creating an easier play for the player fielding the ball.

3) Cross the plate as quickly as possible in case a trailing runner is thrown out at another base.

I can recall losing a run in one game because our runner on third did not hustle across the plate on a sacrifice fly. The runner on first tried to advance to second at the same time and was thrown out (for the third out) before the leading runner crossed the plate.

d. Regardless of the number of outs, the third-base coach should always inform the runner on third of:

1) The number of outs.

2) The position of the outfielders and the relative strength of their throwing arms.

6. The third-base coach is responsible for the runner's lead off third:

a. He should caution the runner to take his lead outside of the baseline.

b. He should caution the runner to have his momentum going toward home when the pitch passes the hitter.

c. The third-base coach should take a position in the box that will enable him to watch the third baseman for a possible pickoff attempt.

Coaching at Home Plate

1. The on-deck hitter has the major responsibility for coaching in the area of home plate:

a. He should tell the batter to run on a dropped third strike.

b. He should help the runner approaching home plate by:

1) Removing the bat and catcher's face mask from the area.

2) Holding both hands high in the air if he wants the runner to come in standing up.

3) Signaling the runner with a palms-to-the-ground motion if he wants him to slide.

2. The batter should perform the above tasks when he is in a position to do so. For example, he should indicate to baserunners whether they should advance on a pitch that gets by the catcher.

9

Basic Defensive Skills

There are a few fundamentals that every player should master before he begins to concentrate on the defensive responsibilities of a particular position. A weakness in any of these fundamental skills has to be corrected if the young player is to ever realize his full potential in baseball. Our first baseman of a few seasons back appeared to have everything he needed to make it in professional ball, but he simply could not throw. He had developed some bad habits when he was younger, and when he reached high school age these habits came back to haunt him. Fortunately, this particular boy had the determination to work hard on his throwing, and eventually he was able to improve the skill to the point that he could make the throws required of his position. In fact, he became our league's outstanding player during his senior year and ultimately signed a professional contract with the Pittsburgh Pirates.

The Ready Position

As the pitch is delivered, every infielder and outfielder must have assumed a position that will enable him to react to a batted ball as quickly as possible. This stance is called the "ready position":

1. The feet are comfortably spread, the back is straight, and the hands are on the knees.

2. As the pitch is delivered, the hands are removed from the knees and the weight is shifted forward to the balls of the feet.

3. Many players take a step or two forward on the pitch to get themselves untracked.

4. The fielder watches the ball from the pitcher's hand to the batter's bat in an effort to anticipate the direction in which it might be hit.

Going After a Batted Ball

A fielder's ability to get a good jump on the ball can also be influenced by his initial footwork. A ball hit in front of the fielder should be no problem as he is already moving in that direction. Neither should there be any concern about the footwork used when the ball is hit to one side or the other, provided that the fielder has plenty of time to get in front of the ball.

However, that first step becomes very critical when the fielder has to pursue a ball hit to his *extreme* right or left. Because literally every step counts, the fielder uses a *cross-over* step in starting after the ball. As the ball is hit, he pivots on the foot nearest the ball and crosses over and takes the first step toward the ball with the far foot. For example, if the ball is hit to his right, he would pivot on his right foot and step toward the ball with his left. Why is this important? Simply because the cross-over step enables the fielder to move his body farther with one step than he would by taking the first step with the near foot. Try it and see!

Footwork is also crucial when the ball is hit over the fielder's head. Here again, the fielder takes his first step with the foot farthest from the ball. He pivots on the near foot and "falls" onto the opposite foot as he steps in the direction in which the ball is hit.

Once he is off and running for the ball the fielder must concentrate on getting to it as quickly as possible.

He should cushion his stride by running on the balls of the feet rather than the heels.

He should wait until the last instant before reaching for the ball as the arms serve as valuable aids in running.

If possible, he should try to field the ball in line with the expected throw.

Catching the Ball in the Air

1. Almost all fly balls and many throws and line drives can be caught with the thumbs together so that the fielder can watch the ball all the way into the glove. (Willie Mays would be the first to admit that the younger player should not try to imitate his "basket catch.")

2. Balls that must be received below the waist should be caught with the little fingers together.

3. In either case, the fielder should try to:

a. Shift the weight of the body onto the foot on the throwing side as the catch is made.

b. Catch the ball as near the throwing shoulder as possible.

c. Keep the elbows in close to the body.

d. Receive the ball with relaxed hands, allowing the glove to recoil slightly upon impact.

4. Of course, the ball should be caught with both hands whenever possible.

Catching Throws and Line Drives in the Dirt

1. The body should be positioned in front of the ball with the knees bent, the legs apart and the glove close to the ground.

2. The fielders should try to take the ball on the short hop or long hop, but should try to avoid fielding it on the in-between hop.

3. To catch the ball on the *short hop* the fielder should:

a. Open the glove wide and reach well out in front of the body.

b. Scoop out and up with the glove and cover the ball with the throwing hand.

4. To catch the ball on the *long hop* the fielder should:

a. Straighten the knees slightly and draw the arms back to the waist with the elbows close to the body.

b. Take a short step backward with the foot on the throwing side.

c. Be careful not to turn the fingers of the glove up until the ball bounces higher than the waist.

5. When there is time and on extremely hard-hit balls, the fielder may drop to the knee on the throwing side to block a ball in the dirt.

6. The eyes must watch the ball all the way into the glove. To avoid pulling the head or flinching, the fielder should "explode" the eyes as he attempts to make the catch. That is, he should force the eyes to open as wide as possible to compensate for the natural tendency to close them.

Catching Ground Balls

1. The fielder should charge a ground ball whenever possible.

2. He should position the body directly in front of the ball and assume the basic fielding position:

    a. The feet are slightly more than shoulder-width apart and staggered. That is, the toe on the throwing side is even with the heel of the opposite foot.

    b. The knees are bent and the weight is forward on the balls of the feet.

    c. The glove is open, well out in front of the body and fingertips touching the ground.

3. With the tail low and the eyes on the ball, the fielder receives the ball with "soft" (relaxed) hands and brings it back to throwing position. Our third baseman and captain of the past season did not become a good fielder until he learned to receive the ball with relaxed hands. He had been taught to scoop forward as he caught the ball. This tended to cause all but the hardest hit balls to pop out of his glove.

Throwing (Righthanded)

1. The fielder must learn to grip the ball without looking at it as he takes it out of his glove:

    a. The first two fingers extend across the seams and are spread one-half to three-quarters of an inch apart.

    b. The thumb, slightly bent at the joint nearest the nail, is tucked directly underneath.

2. The thrower shifts all the weight onto the right foot and pivots around so the left shoulder is facing the target. At this point the arm begins its movement to the rear:

    a. The ball is brought out of the glove *wrist* first.

    b. The arm is directed back rather than down.

    c. The elbow is even with or above the shoulder.

    d. The forearm is almost perpendicular with the upper arm.

    e. The top of the wrist and hand are facing *up*.

    f. The striding leg is up and bent at the knee.

3. As the arm starts forward:

    a. The hand, wrist and forearm are rolled over into a *"lay back"* position and the elbow leads them forward.

    b. The hips open and the stride foot is planted softly in line with the target.

    c. The ball is released off the "pads" of the first and second fingers with a snapping action.

4. The arm is allowed to follow through in its arc as the back bends and the pivot foot is brought up alongside the stride foot.

5. Throughout the throwing action the player's eyes remain on his target.

6. The young player should concentrate on perfecting this overhand delivery. Three-quarter and side-arm deliveries can be developed easily once the basic arm action has been mastered.

10

Pitching

Good pitching undoubtedly represents the most important single ingredient of a baseball team. In fact, the team that fields good players at every position but does not have sound pitching will probably finish the season in the second divsion. On the other hand, mediocre teams have won pennants with one or two outstanding pitchers.

Only a few pitchers are gifted with a good enough fastball to throw the ball by the better hitters with any degree of consistency. Pitching becomes an art when the athlete learns to throw a variety of pitches at several different speeds and then learns to use them to best advantage against the hitter.

Qualifications

The boy who wants to become a pitcher must possess a *"live" wrist* even if he cannot throw exceptionally hard early in his career. If his throwing action is fundamentally sound, he will throw harder as he approaches physical maturity. If he throws incorrectly to begin with, his fastball will never be adequate when he reaches higher levels of competition.

A pitcher must be an *exceptional competitor.* Many boys have the physical capacity to become good pitchers but cannot produce in game competition. The boy with limited physical tools will often outduel the pitcher with great "stuff" simply because he has better control of the emotional aspects of pitching. A few seasons back we won a championship behind a boy who really didn't belong on the mound. He was a fine athlete but certainly lacked many of the physical qualities that most good high school pitchers possess. However, this boy, above anything else, was a competitor. He was at his best in a tight situation, and he never beat himself by allowing his temperament to interfere with his performance.

The boy on the mound must *enjoy pitching.* To pitch is to play a position completely unlike any other on the field. It is much more demanding physically than the others, and for the most part, there is much more pressure on the pitcher during the course of a ball game.

Good pitchers are usually *intelligent* athletes. They seem to have an unusual ability to analyze each performance and learn from that experience. They also have the mental capacity to study and remember the characteristics of the hitters they face. When I think of this particular quality I have to recall a boy who pitched for me during my first season in coaching. This boy learned something every time he went out to the mound. At the end of each inning he could tell you exactly how he pitched to each batter, what was hit or wasn't hit, and what he intended to do with that hitter the next time around.

Angles of Delivery

Most pitchers use one of three basic types of delivery:

Overhand—in which the throwing arm travels through a vertical plane perpendicular to the ground.

Three-quarters—in which the throwing arm travels at approximately a forty-five degree angle.

Side-arm—in which the throwing arm travels almost on a horizontal plane parallel with the ground.

The overhand and three-quarter deliveries are the most common simply because they allow the pitcher the type of arm action on the curveball that causes it to break down. The side-arm pitcher has difficulty throwing an effective curve without changing the angle of his delivery. Generally speaking, a pitcher will be more effective if he can throw a variety of pitches from the same angle of delivery.

A young pitcher should determine which angle of delivery is most comfortable for him and then stay with that delivery until

he has mastered it. He should not experiment with a cross-fire pitch for example, unless he can throw all of his pitches for strikes, overhand. Juan Marichal of the Giants is one of the few major league pitchers who has excellent control while throwing from all three angles of delivery. His case is the exception, however, and the young player should remember that it is Juan's control and not his variety of pitches that sets him apart from the average pitcher.

Form

No two pitchers throw exactly alike, or should they. But there are a few basic principles regarding pitching form that almost all successful pitchers follow. These fundamentals will be presented as if they were for a righthanded pitcher who throws with a three-quarter delivery.

    1. The Full Windup:

      a. When it is used:

      1) When there are no runners on base.

      2) When the runners on base are unlikely to steal. With a runner on third only, second and third, or with the bases loaded, the pitcher will normally not use his full windup.

b. Taking the sign and arm swing:

1) The right foot is forward with at least three of the front spikes extending over the rubber. The left foot remains just behind the right. The body faces home plate or is angled slightly in the direction of third base.

2) Prior to the beginning of the delivery the ball should be held out of the view of the hitter. Some pitchers hold the ball behind their back in the throwing hand while others prefer holding it in the glove in front of the stomach.

3) A slow, rhythmical arm swing brings the ball and both arms up to a position just above the forehead. At this point the elbows are apart so as to not hinder the pitcher's view of the target and the ball is grasped with the throwing hand deep in the webbing of the glove.

4) The pitcher's weight should be forward throughout except for an instant at the top of the delivery to allow for the pivot of the right foot.

c. Pivot, leg lift and body lean:

1) The ball and glove are brought down to the crotch simultaneously with a pivot of the entire body toward third base.

2) The left leg is brought up to the level of the hip. Some pitchers allow the lower leg to dangle down; others keep the raised leg extended.

3) The spikes of the pivot foot now straddle the leading edge of the rubber. Or, the entire foot may be placed in front of and parallel with the rubber.

4) At this point the body begins its fall toward home plate with the hips out in front and the right leg extending.

d. Push-off, stride and throw:

1) The right leg literally catapults the pitcher toward his target. (As Lefty Gomez puts it: "A pitcher should get his head so that he's in a position to run head-first across home plate.")

2) The ball is brought out of the glove by the throwing hand and is thrust backward and downward with the wrist leading. When the arm begins its forward movement the elbow leads the forearm and wrist, which are now in a lay-back position. The fingers, hand, wrist and forearm begin to break forward in a rhythmical, co-ordinated action as the stride foot hits the ground.

3) The left arm contributes momentum by being thrust down and to the rear as the throwing arm comes forward.

4) The stride leg should not be rigid upon impact and the foot should land in a direct line with home plate or slightly to the left. The pitcher should be careful not to land on the heel as well since the jarring will impair his control.

5) The rear leg (right) and hip are brought forward with some force. If the rear leg is allowed to "drag" behind, the pitcher will not be able to follow through properly.

e. Follow-through and fielding position:

1) Following the release of the ball the throwing hand is allowed to continue its arc and finishes opposite the left knee, with the back of the hand facing the plate.

2) The back is bent considerably at the waist and the right leg is brought up alongside the left or beyond it.

3) The pitcher should square-off and assume a fielding position *after* he has completed his delivery. He should not restrict his follow-through in order to finish in a good fielding position. I tell my pitchers that if they worry too much about finishing in a good fielding position they will probably inhibit their pitching motion enough to warrant that concern.

2. The Stretch Delivery:

a. The stretch delivery is used whenever a baserunner has an unoccupied base in front of him. With a runner on first base,

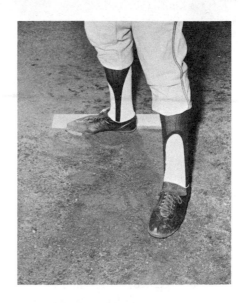

first and second, or first and third, a pitcher must use his stretch delivery to keep the runners from advancing on the pitch. Occasionally, a pitcher will also use his stretch delivery when there is a threat of a squeeze play or steal of home. These plays are a possibility whenever there is a runner on third.

b. The sign is usually taken straddling the rubber or with the right foot against or on the corner of the rubber. The left foot is parallel to the right and about shoulder width from it. The arms hang loosely to the sides and the ball is in the glove or throwing hand.

c. The pitcher comes set by bringing the right foot into contact with the rubber (if he does not take the sign on the rubber) and by bringing the hands together at the belt.

d. With a runner on first base he should:

1) Open his stance in the direction of first base so that he can see the runner by merely tucking the chin close to the left shoulder and turning the head slightly.

2) To throw home, he should take a flat, quick stride and deliver the ball with a minimum of motion.

3) To throw to first base he uses a "jump-shift" type of foot action. That is, he brings both feet off the ground, turns to his left, and makes the throw to first as the feet land facing in that direction.

4) The throw is delivered with a short-arm motion (without reaching all the way back) and at a three-quarter angle of delivery.

e. There are several techniques that will help the righthanded pitcher keep runners close at first base:

1) He should vary the number of times he looks to first so that the runner cannot anticipate when he will be throwing home.

2) He can make his first move to first base slow and awkward to set up his best move.

3) He should look for runners who take a quick lead off the bag. By anticipating when the runner is about to take his lead, the pitcher might catch him leaning the wrong way.

f. With a runner at second base the pitcher can take his stretch with his front foot in line with home plate. His throw to second base is executed with a jump-shift action toward the glove hand.

g. He should hold a runner on third base in the same manner that the lefthanded pitcher holds a runner on first base.

h. Right- and lefthanded pitchers should make sure that they pick up their catcher's target before throwing home.

3. The Stretch Delivery for the Lefthanded Pitcher:

a. The lefthanded pitcher uses the stretch delivery under almost the same conditions as the righthanded pitcher. However, he is less likely to use it with a runner on third because in doing so, he will have his back to the baserunner.

b. The lefthanded pitcher has an advantage over the righthander with a man on first base because he (the lefthander) is facing the runner.

c. However, the lefthander must also be careful not to fall into a pattern that might tip off the runner as to when he is throwing home:

1) For example, he should not get into the habit of throwing home whenever he is looking to first base and throwing to first base whenever he is looking home.

d. The lefthander can afford to use a full leg kick but cannot bring the stride foot behind the pivot leg and still throw to first base.

e. The lefthander's move to first base can be deceptive when it is perfected. He uses the same motion as he does to throw

home. In fact, it is essential that the runner thinks he is going to throw to the plate. At the last instant, the pitcher quickly brings the stride foot to the ground so that it lands on the first base side of a hypothetical line between the rubber and a point on the baseline halfway to home. To step on the home-plate side of this line would be a balk. There are two methods commonly used by lefthanders to keep runners close at first base:

1) The pitcher takes his stretch looking toward first and then turns the head 90 degrees toward home. As the left foot comes off the ground he repeats the same head movement but stops halfway and makes a quick throw to first base.

2) Another technique would be for the lefthander to bring the right leg around, point it at the runner, and then throw home. This delivery will have a tendency to keep the runner close to the bag. If the runner does take too long a lead, the pitcher can make his move to first with a quick overhand throw.

f. The lefthanded pitcher's move to second base is identical to the righthander's. He uses a jump-shift action and turns toward the glove hand.

g. With a runner on third base, he opens his stance somewhat as the righthander would with a runner on first. He watches the runner over the right shoulder and executes his move to third with the same jump-shift action. Whenever possible, the left-hander should use a full windup when there is a runner on third base.

Pitches

Most young pitchers should concern themselves with learning to control a few basic pitches rather than developing a large variety. One boy came to me as a high school junior asking if he could try out for our club as a pitcher. He was a big, strong-looking boy and I asked him why he hadn't played during his sophomore year. He told me he had spent the previous year developing five new pitches to go along with his fastball and curve! We suggested that he ought to concentrate on just a few basic pitches and forget about the "trick" pitches. He did and became one of our more effective pitchers. The boy with a reasonably good fastball and curve will be a winner if he can control those pitches and develop a change-up to go along with them. The slider, screwball, knuckleball and other "trick" pitches are best left alone by young pitchers unless the individual simply does not have the arm to be effective otherwise. Of course, many professional players make good use of these pitches, but only after they have learned to control their fastball, curve and change. Others resort to these pitches later in their careers after they have lost their best stuff.

1. The Fastball:

a. The grip on the fastball can be determined by the angle of delivery the pitcher uses. Generally speaking:

1) A ball delivered overhand will have a greater tendency to rise or "hop" when it is gripped *across* the seams.

2) A ball delivered side-arm will have a greater tendency to sink when it is gripped *with* the seams.

b. By no means should the above factors dictate the kind of grip a pitcher should use. The young pitcher should select a grip that is comfortable for him, and one he can use to throw each of his basic pitches.

c. Once the pitcher has selected a grip he should stick with it until it becomes a natural and automatic part of his delivery.

d. The mature pitcher does not put everything into every fastball he throws. By throwing the majority of his fastballs at about 98 per cent full speed, the pitcher will find that he will be able to control the ball better and he will be able to reach back for the fast one when he needs it. (This fundamental is emphasized by former White Sox and Giant star, Billy Pierce.)

e. Regardless of the angle of delivery a pitcher uses, his fastball is released off the ends of the first and second fingers. The wrist snap should be such that a close observer could actually hear the ball as it is released.

2. The Change-up:

a. There are several methods of changing speeds on the fastball:

1) The pitcher can simply "ease" up on the delivery and not throw the ball as hard. (I asked Stu Miller, formerly of the Giants and Orioles, if he had any special tips on throwing the change. He replied that all he did was ease up on his fastball.)

2) He can reduce the wrist snap and therefore the speed of the pitch by bringing the thumb from underneath the ball to the side.

3) He can use a "choke" grip. That is, grip the ball so that it lies back in the "V" formed by the thumb and forefinger.

4) He can use the "window shade" technique of raising the tips of the first and second fingers from the ball and pulling down on the ball just before it is released.

5) He can simply drag the pivot foot rather than allowing it to come around briskly on the follow-through.

b. Regardless of the technique used, the change off the fastball must be kept low and away from the batter and should be delivered with form as nearly identical to the fastball as possible.

3. The Curveball:

a. The curveball should be gripped as nearly like the fastball as possible. However, many pitchers find it helpful to modify their fastball somewhat to gain better rotation on the curve:

1) The distance between the fingers is reduced slightly.

2) And/or, the middle finger is moved over so that it lies on or next to a seam.

b. The variation in arm action on the curve begins when the ball is adjacent to the ear on its forward motion. Think fastball until the arm gets above the shoulder.

1) At this point, the wrist is rotated inward so that the palm faces the ear.

2) The fingers are on *top* of the ball and not on the outside of the ball.

c. With almost all of the pressure being applied by the middle finger, the ball rolls over the area between the first and second knuckles of the index finger.

d. The thumb aids in imparting the spin by pushing up on the ball as the middle finger pulls down.

e. A pitcher's ability to develop a good curveball will be determined by his understanding and application of three important concepts:

1) The most effective curveball breaks down rather than sideways. Therefore, the fingers must be on top of the ball as it is released.

2) A sharp-breaking curveball is more effective than the "roundhouse." Therefore, the pitcher should concentrate on developing *rotation*.

3) Release the ball with as little effort as possible, says Warren Spahn, the former great pitcher for the Braves.

4. The Slow Curve:

a. Many pitchers find that a slow curve serves as a good change-up because it is easier for them to control than the change off the fastball.

b. Again, there are several methods of changing speeds on the curve:

1) The pitcher can jam the ball back into the "V" of the thumb and first finger.

2) He can hold the ball more loosely and take the fingertips off the ball as it is released.

3) He can merely "ease up" on the delivery.

c. The curve and slow curve must be kept down and away from the batter in order to be effective.

5. The Slider:

a. The slider has become a popular extra pitch mainly because it is relatively easy to control and it resembles the fastball as it approaches the hitter.

b. The action of the arm is identical to that used on the fastball. The break on the ball is attained by:

1) Applying almost all of the pressure on the ball with the middle finger, and

2) Twisting the wrist only slightly as in throwing a football or turning a door knob.

c. The slider is thrown hard with just enough spin to cause a slight but quick break in the same direction as the curve. (Ballplayers refer to the slider as a "nickel" curve.)

d. The slider is not recommended for the young, inexperienced pitcher. This pitch is hard on the throwing arm and may lead to an injury if the boy is not physically mature. Also, working on the slider has been known to inhibit the development of a good curveball.

6. The Screwball:

a. The screwball breaks in the opposite direction of the curve. However, the break is slower and not nearly as pronounced. The value of the screwball lies in the fact that it gives the lefthanded pitcher, for example, a pitch that will break away from the right-handed batters.

b. The screwball is released with an inside-out twist of the wrist and hand, almost opposite to that used on the curveball. Instead of the thumb being brought from the bottom up, it is brought from the top down and the ball is released between the third and fourth fingers. The rotation of the ball is counter-clockwise rather than clockwise as it is on the curveball.

c. Most younger pitchers should avoid working with the screwball because it is delivered with an unnatural motion and could contribute to an arm injury. However, for the fairly mature pitcher who cannot throw very hard and needs another pitch to stay in the game, the screwball might prove to be very valuable. Carl Hubbell, the former New York Giant lefthander, is probably the most famous exponent of the screwball. His best pitch was the screwball, particularly against righthanded batters. The screwball gave him a pitch that would break away from the righthanded hitter. Juan Marichal, a righthanded pitcher, uses the screwball in the same way against lefthanded hitters.

7. The Sinker:

a. The sinker is thrown mainly by the side-arm pitcher and, if kept low, can force the batter to hit the ball into the ground.

b. The method of throwing the sinker is somewhat like that used in throwing the screwball:

1) As the arm comes forward the first and second fingers are behind the ball as they would be on the fastball.

2) When the ball reaches a position opposite the ear, it is turned over by an inward and downward rotation of the hand.

3) At this point considerable pressure is applied by the first finger and the ball is released between the second and third fingers.

c. The action of the sinker may be improved by spreading the fingers slightly.

d. For most pitchers the sinker would not be worth the time and effort required for its development. However, it is presented here with the side-arm pitcher mainly in mind. The side-armer will have difficulty throwing a down-breaking curveball, and the sinker could fill the void.

Control

1. Control is the greatest of pitching assets. A pitcher may have an exceptional fastball and curve, but if he cannot control his pitches, he will not be effective.

2. Good control takes on a different meaning as a pitcher progresses from youth baseball into college and professional ball. The young pitcher can be satisfied with being able to keep the ball in the strike zone. But the more mature pitcher will find that to be effective he must develop an ability to hit the corners and keep the ball low.

3. There are psychological as well as physical reasons why a particular pitcher may be having difficulty with his control. The condition may be the result of a flaw in his delivery:

a. He may not be keeping his eyes on the target throughout his delivery. Many pitchers develop the bad habit of watching the hitter rather than the catcher's glove. Others take their eyes completely off the target during the initial part of the windup and do not pick up the target until the ball is released.

b. A pitcher may not be following through properly. The pitcher who does not bend his back upon releasing the ball will find that his pitches will "take off" on him.

c. He may be striding improperly. The stride foot should hit the ground in line with home plate or slightly to the left. The pitcher may also be striding too far and, therefore, landing on the heel rather than the ball of the foot. Landing on the heel may "jar" the motion and cause the throw to be erratic.

4. A weakness in the pitching motion would be relatively easy to correct. Finding the solution to a psychological flaw may be a different matter entirely:

    a. Control is a product of constant practice and is not a natural ability. Some pitchers simply lack the determination to work on their control. A pitcher should be working on his control every time he throws a baseball. He should never throw unless he is throwing to a target. He should avoid throwing batting practice unless he has a catcher to throw to. Otherwise, where would he aim the ball?

    b. A pitcher's inability to concentrate may be the source of his control problems. One of the best pitchers I have had the privilege of coaching was an excellent control pitcher until he got into a jam. Then, the pressure of the situation distracted him and he wouldn't be able to find the plate. This boy later become one of the best collegiate pitchers on the West Coast, but only after he had licked an emotional problem which prevented him from concentrating under pressure. The boy who is bothered by a lot of little things while he is taking his windup will not be able to concentrate on just pitching. Among the factors that bother some pitchers are the weather (wind), the mound, the fans or perhaps even being overly conscious of a particular part of the delivery. Needless to say, a pitcher can afford to think of only one thing once he has started his windup: *The catcher's target.*

5. One reason for a lack of control for some pitchers is poor conditioning. The pitcher who tires easily will not be able to put the ball where he wants it for nine innings. The legs as well as the arm must be in top physical condition. If a pitcher's legs become "rubbery" and weak during the later stages of a game, he has only himself to blame. Pitching a full game is an exhausting task and pitchers must prepare themselves for it with an extensive program of hard running.

6. Regardless of their cause, continuous problems with control will eventually breed a lack of confidence. The more a pitcher loses his confidence, the more his control will suffer. His inability to get the ball over the plate will become more and more of a barrier and can develop into an obsession in itself. For this reason, a young pitcher must experience some successes along the way. He should

not be expected to hit the corners and keep the ball low until he has demonstrated an ability to get the ball over the plate. He needs to take one step at a time, and he needs constant encouragement.

Pitching Strategy

No pitcher can overpower every hitter. Pitching becomes a science once the athlete has mastered the basic fundamentals and can put the ball where he wants it. The pitcher who can call upon a variety of pitches in a given situation and feel confident in his ability to throw the pitch that a particular batter is least likely to hit with authority, will be a winner.

The strategy a battery will use in a particular ball game will be partly determined by their knowledge of the *strengths and weaknesses of each opposing hitter*. This information may be available through scout reports and past experience. Gathering information on the opposition can be overdone. I recall preparing my team for one important game by giving them an extensive rundown on the strengths and weaknesses of each opposing hitter. When the game got underway, my sophomore pitcher became so concerned about pitching to spots that he couldn't find the strike zone. He failed to finish the first inning, and we never were in the ball game—thanks to me and my big league strategy! Normally, however, the amount of information a battery will have to work with will be determined by their ability to study the hitters as the game progresses.

The *conditions* under which the game is being played also will be an important factor. The weather and the size and condition of the playing field may influence pitching strategy. For example, when he is pitching in a park where the fences are fairly close, he will have to be particularly conscious of keeping the ball down low in the strike zone. On an open field he can afford to come in higher with his pitches as the long fly balls that may result can be caught by the outfielders. In a park where one fence is much shorter than the others, a pitcher will usually try to keep the hitters from pulling the ball to that field. With a short leftfield fence, righthanded hitters would be pitched low and away.

Of course, the *game situation* will be a major factor. The score, number of outs, position of baserunners, if any, and the alignment of the defense will certainly influence the pitcher and catcher.

Strategy will also be influenced by the *"stuff"* the pitcher has going for him in that particular ball game. Perhaps his curve is not breaking. Even though the hitter at the plate is weak on curveballs, the battery may decide against giving him that pitch under the circumstances.

Any of the several techniques of strategy may be employed by the pitcher to keep the hitter off-balance:

1. He can select from a variety of different kinds of pitches.
2. He can vary the speed of the pitches.
3. He can throw the pitch to different areas of the strike zone.
4. He can change the interval between pitches.
5. He can throw his pitches from different angles of delivery.
6. He can throw his pitches in an intelligent and effective sequence.
7. He can make good use of the "brush back" and "waste" pitch.

Selecting the Kind of Pitch

1. The pitcher should find out which of his pitches are working best on a given day. He should merely "show" the hitter the pitch which is not working and force him to hit the one that is.

2. In a tight spot it is usually best to rely on one's best pitch regardless of the "book" on the hitter at the plate.

3. Generally speaking, the curveball and other breaking pitches will be more effective on damp, cloudy days as the density of the air will cause the ball to break more. (Don Larson of the Yankees, pitched his "perfect" World Series Game on such a day.) On hot, dry days the fastball may be more effective.

4. A pitcher should take advantage of his fastball late in the game when darkness is starting to set in. The same suggestion would apply in night games when the lighting conditions are poor.

5. The pitcher who is forced to throw a slick, new ball in a crucial situation should avoid throwing the curveball.

6. The batter may reveal weaknesses against certain kinds of pitches. For example, the pitcher usually should:

    a. Throw inside fastballs to hitters who stand close to the plate or are slow bringing the bat around.

    b. Throw high fastballs to hitters who have a tendency to upper-cut.

c. Throw curveballs to hitters who stride away from the plate.

d. Throw change-of-speed pitches to hitters who overstride or lunge at the ball.

Varying the Speed of the Pitch

1. A pitcher should not try to put everything into every pitch. By taking a little off the fastball, for example, he will find that:

a. He will have better control.

b. The pitch will have more "stuff."

c. The hitter's timing may be impaired when the pitcher wants to use his best fastball in a crucial situation.

Throwing Pitches to Different Areas of the Strike Zone

1. Undoubtedly, the most consistently effective pitch in baseball is delivered in the area of the batter's knees. This is true for several reasons:

a. The low pitch cannot be hit with a level swing, thus making solid contact with the ball much less likely.

b. The low pitch is below the batter's line of vision, thus making it much more difficult for him to follow.

c. The low pitch is usually beat into the ground or popped in the air. The defense has a better chance to field these kinds of batted balls than they do line drives hit off pitches above the belt.

2. The pitch should always be down with runners in scoring position or when there is a possibility of a double play. A ground ball is wanted in this situation. A ball hit in the air may fall in between the outfielders and the drawn-in infield.

3. If the batter is bunting, the pitch should be high. This strategy may induce the batter to pop the ball up and possibly result in a double play.

4. A particular batter may reveal weaknesses against pitches in certain areas of the strike zone:

a. Pitch a hitter who uppercuts high and inside.

b. Pitch a hitter who chops down on the ball low.

c. Keep the ball low and away against hitters who try to pull everything and hitters who "step in the bucket."

d. Throw low and inside to a batter who strides in toward the plate.

5. A pitcher should not concern himself with hitting the corners unless he is ahead in the count. He should get ahead of the batter and try to get him out on a minimum number of pitches. The percentage of batters who hit safely with two strikes is quite small.

Changing the Interval Between Pitches

Some pitchers have found that they are able to disturb the batter's timing by purposely varying the time interval between one pitch and the next. This can be accomplished in a variety of ways:

1. One method amounts to nothing more than simply varying the time interval between the completion of one delivery and the start of another. On one pitch the pitcher takes 15 to 20 seconds before delivering the ball and on the next pitch he begins his delivery almost as soon as he receives the ball from the catcher. Of course, this technique can be used with either the full windup or stretch deliveries.

2. When the full windup delivery is being used, the pitcher can also vary the point in the delivery at which the hands are brought together:

a. On one pitch the hands are brought together behind the head.

b. On the next pitch the hands come together at the forehead.

c. On the next pitch the hands come together at the chest.

3. Almost the same principle can be exercised from the stretch delivery:

a. The pitcher takes his stretch, looks at the runner, then looks home and throws.

b. On the next pitch, he takes his stretch looking home, looks to first and then looks home again to throw.

c. Occasionally, he takes his stretch looking at the runner, looks home, looks back at the runner, and finally looks home again to throw.

4. As a general rule, a pitcher should take more time between pitches with a nervous batter at the plate and work rapidly on an especially calm hitter or one who waves his bat in pronounced fashion. (Former big-leaguer Pumpsie Green can verify the effectiveness of this technique. In his first trip to the plate in the majors he had to face one of the real "hitter haters" and best pitchers in the league in Early Wynn. As Pumpsie recalls it, Wynn simply stared at him for what seemed like five minutes before he delivered the first pitch. Nervous to begin with, Pumpsie was almost petrified by the time the ball was on its way.) The idea on the latter type of hitter being to catch him before he is set for the pitch.

Throwing Pitches from Different Angles of Delivery

1. A pitcher who has the ability to control all of his pitches from his natural delivery can contribute to his effectiveness by learning to throw from another angle.

2. He should use this technique sparingly and only under certain conditions:

a. For example, the righthanded pitcher can use the side-arm pitch to good advantage against a righthanded batter who has a tendency to "bail out" (that is, step back on inside pitches). The lefthanded pitcher could use the same pitch to lefthanded batters.

b. Some side-arm pitchers come over the top occasionally to make a particular type of pitch more effective. The screwball and curve are two pitches that have proved to be more effective from this angle.

The Sequence of Pitches

1. Generally speaking, a pitcher's success with a batter will be determined by his ability to get that batter to hit his (the pitcher's) pitch. In order to accomplish this, the pitcher and catcher must think along with the hitter and, in fact, think a couple of pitches ahead of him. They must learn to set up the hitter for the pitch they think has the best chance of getting him out.

a. A change-of-speed pitch will always be more effective if it is preceded by a fastball.

b. Conversely, a fastball appears faster and has a better chance of getting by the hitter if it is set up with a slower pitch.

c. A high and inside fastball is a perfect set-up pitch for the curve thrown down and away from the hitter.

d. The pitcher who can control his curve well enough to throw it when he is behind in the count is usually a successful pitcher. Most hitters look for a fastball in this situation.

e. If a pitcher goes to a full count on a batter using one pitch, he should come in for the pay-off with a different pitch.

The "Brush Back" and "Waste" Pitches

1. The brush back and waste pitches are not thrown for a strike, but they do have a purpose:

a. The brush-back pitch is used to keep the batter from "digging in" at the plate. The ball is aimed high and inside but not with the intention of hitting the batter. Its purpose is simply to get the hitter leaning back on his heels so that he will be less likely to wade into balls on the outside of the plate.

b. A waste pitch is delivered just outside of the strike zone but close enough that the batter *may* go after it. Of course, a pitcher should not use such a tactic unless he is ahead in the count. A waste pitch in the area of the hitter's strength is particularly effective. Another good place for a waste pitch is below the knees.

Fielding Responsibilities

1. The pitcher becomes a fifth infielder once he has delivered the pitch.

2. On pop flies the pitcher should:

a. Take any balls in the area of the mound and home plate that cannot be reached by an infielder or the catcher.

b. Call out the name and point to the player who has called for any pop fly in the infield.

3. Whenever there is a runner on first base, the pitcher must not deliver the pitch until the shortstop indicates to him who will be covering second base if the ball is hit back to the mound. If the ball does come back to the pitcher in this situation he:

a. Fields the ball and turning toward the glove hand, throws the ball shoulder high and about one stride to the fielder's side of the base.

b. If the pivotman is already to the bag, the throw is made directly to him. If the pivotman is late getting to the bag, the pitcher should take an extra step toward second base and then throw.

4. The pitcher must also be adept at fielding bunts:

a. The *righthanded pitcher:*

1) Fields bunt down the third baseline by trying to get in front of the ball, jamming the right foot in the ground, pivoting to the left and making the throw to first, second or third bases. He may have to pivot to his right to throw to third if the ball is on the line.

2) Fields bunts down the first baseline with his toes parallel with the line. He throws to first from that position and to second and third by pivoting to the left.

b. *The lefthanded pitcher:*

1) Fields bunts down the third baseline with his back to right-field. He pivots to the right to throw to second or first base.

2) Fields bunts down the first baseline by trying to get in front of the ball, jamming his left foot into the ground and pivoting to the right to throw to first, second or third. He may have to pivot to the left to throw to first if the ball is on the line.

5. The throw after fielding a bunt is usually overhand. The fielder usually has time to take a slide step in the direction of the throw for added momentum. The throw should never be made off-balance.

6. The pitcher must also learn to cover first base on balls hit to his left:

a. He should break in that direction automatically.

b. The path he takes to cover first depends upon the distance the ball is fielded from the bag:

1) On a ball hit to the first baseman playing fairly close to the bag, the pitcher takes a circular route and receives the ball while he is running parallel with the line. He should take the first baseman's throw before reaching the bag, then step on the bag and then slow down quickly and look for another play.

2) On a ball hit deep behind the baseline to the first baseman or second baseman, the pitcher goes directly to the bag and stops. If time permits, he stations himself at the bag and takes the throw as a first baseman would.

7. The pitcher covers home plate whenever the pitch gets by the catcher and a runner is on third base.

   a. He should help the catcher locate the position of the ball by pointing to it and shouting directions.

   b. He then takes a position at home plate with the feet parallel with the third baseline.

   c. Taking the catcher's throw, he tags the runner with a sweeping action and with the back of the glove facing the runner. The throwing hand is kept well out of the way.

11

Catching

A catcher can be the most important defensive player on the team. Although good pitching is generally acknowledged as the essential defense ingredient, an outstanding catcher can literally "make" a pitching staff. If pennants are rarely won without pitching, pennants are *never* won without exceptional catching.

Aside from his handling of pitchers, the catcher is the only player who faces the entire field of play. He is in a position to direct most of his team's crucial defensive plays. His ability to make quick and intelligent decisions in these situations makes him a vital cog in the entire defensive effort.

Qualifications

The catcher must be an *intelligent* athlete. He must have the mental capacity to remember how each batter has been handled during the course of a ball game.

The catcher must be a *good student of the game*. He must have an ability to analyze hitters for weaknesses. He must "know" his pitchers thoroughly, and he must understand completely the defensive responsibilities of his own position and those of the other eight players on the field.

A catcher must have a *good throwing arm*. He should be capable of throwing to any base quickly and accurately.

A catcher must have *good agility*. His greatest responsibility is receiving pitches, and the ability to catch pitches of all kinds will require some complicated footwork and body movements.

A catcher must have *good hands*. A catcher does not simply catch the ball, he receives it. That is, he catches the pitch in such a manner that it will look good to the umpire.

The catcher must be a *"hustler."* He will set the tempo for the entire team. If the catcher represents a hustling, alert, and aggressive brand of play, more than likely his teammates will approach their responsibilities in much the same way. One of our best teams was "quarterbacked" by a catcher who had an ability to hustle and little else. He compensated for his weaknesses by working twice as hard as the rest of the squad, and his teammates rewarded him for his efforts by electing him captain.

The fundamentals of catching are extremely important. The catcher will handle the ball during the course of a game more than any other player, with the possible exception of the pitcher.

The Signal Position

1. The position the catcher assumes to give the signal for various pitches should be comfortable, and it should provide a good shield for the signal:

a. The catcher squats behind the plate so that the heels are together and the knees point down the baselines.

b. The back is straight.

c. The right forearm extends down into the crotch, with the elbow against the hip.

d. The glove hangs loosely over the outside of the left knee to ·further shield the signals.

2. Of course, the catcher plays an important part in determining defensive strategy by the manner in which he handles his signal responsibilities. Every catcher should read the part of Chapter 10 that deals with pitching strategy. The various types of signals that a catcher will use will be discussed in Chapter 19 on defensive communication.

The Receiving Position

1. The catcher shifts into a receiving position that will allow him to hold his mitt as a good low target for the pitcher and at the same time enable him to move quickly to receive all types of pitches:

a. The feet are well apart, with the right leg slightly to the rear of the left. The taller the catcher the wider and more staggered his stance.

b. The knees are bent and facing straight ahead.

c. The rear end is below the level of the knees but not so low that the catcher's mobility is restricted.

d. The glove is held well away from the body and just above the knees. The face of the glove should be "open" and perpendicular to the ground.

e. The throwing hand is held in a position where it can quickly grip the ball once it enters the glove. Acceptable techniques include:

1) Wrapping the fingers around the thumb of the glove.

2) Holding the hand just behind the glove.

3) Holding the hand to the right of the glove with the backs of the fingers facing the flight of the ball and the thumb protected in a loose fist. If a foul tip hits the back of a finger there seems to be less chance of serious injury as the fingers can bend upon impact.

2. The receiving position should be assumed as close to the plate as possible but not so close that the catcher's glove "tips" the bat on the swing.

Catching Pitched Balls

1. Without a doubt the most important skill a catcher can possess is an ability to catch all types of pitched balls.

2. Pitches above the waist are handled with the fingers pointing up, and those below the waist are caught with the fingers pointing down.

3. The ball should be met firmly and as close to the strike zone as possible. At the same time, however, the glove should not be so rigid that the ball is constantly popping out of the pocket.

4. Receiving "close" pitches:

a. A good catcher can be valuable to his pitcher simply by the way he receives pitches that *might* be strikes. Generally speaking, the catcher wants to "ease" each close pitch in the direction of the belt buckle as he catches it. This is done by:

1) Catching the low pitches by extending the knees slightly and flicking the wrist and glove upward (fingers down).

2) Catching pitches at the top of the strike zone by flicking the wrist and glove down. On this pitch a catcher wants to be careful not to extend the knees any more than he has to.

3) Catching pitches on the inside or outside corner by merely "holding" the glove. The umpire will align the back of the glove with the edge of the plate and probably give the pitcher the benefit of any doubt.

b. On all close pitches, the techniques used by the catcher to make the pitch look good should be executed *as* he catches the ball and not after the ball is caught.

5. Receiving low pitches in the dirt:

The most difficult pitch for a catcher to receive is the low pitch in the dirt. A catcher should anticipate the low pitch whenever possible. On a curveball, for example, the catcher can begin to turn the glove over so the fingers point down as soon as the ball is released. As a general rule, he should try to catch balls that bounce high with the chest protector and those that bounce low with the glove.

a. The ball hitting directly in front of the plate is blocked by dropping forward on both knees.

b. The ball to the right or left of the plate is blocked by stepping out and forward with the foot nearest the ball and dropping to that knee.

c. If the ball is to the extreme right or left, the catcher steps out and drops to the near knee, pivots and crosses over with the far leg and dives for the ball.

d. On all balls in the dirt the catcher wants to keep the body facing the pitch, the shoulders "hunched in" and the glove protecting the hole between the legs.

e. He should be aggressive as he scoops forward and up on the ball. The chin is kept on the chest to protect the Adam's apple, and the eyes are on the ball.

Shifting to Throw

The secret to throwing from behind the plate is footwork. A catcher must be able to shift his body into a position in front of the ball as he receives it. This is important because it enables him to throw quicker. If he catches the ball from a throwing position, he will not waste valuable time reaching for the ball and bringing it back to throw. By being in front of the ball as he receives it, the catcher is also in a better position to handle his particular type of glove. A catcher's glove is not designed to make one-handed stabs as is a first baseman's.

1. Shifting to throw to third base:
    a. If the pitch is inside to a righthanded batter, the catcher:
    1) Steps to his left with the left foot to meet the ball.
    2) Then brings the right foot back behind the left.
    3) Throws from behind the hitter as the stride is made toward third with the left foot.

b. If the pitch is outside to a righthanded batter, the catcher:

1) Steps to meet the ball with the right foot.

2) Then throws from a position in front of the hitter as he strides toward third with the left. Taller catchers may find that they can throw over a short batter's head.

c. Of course, with a lefthanded batter at the plate the catcher has an unrestricted target to throw to. His footwork on the different pitches would be much the same as in a or b.

2. Shifting to throw to second base:

a. On a pitch over the plate, the catcher:

1) Takes a short step with the right foot to meet the ball.

2) Strides toward second base with the left to throw.

b. On an outside pitch to a righthanded batter and an inside pitch to a lefthanded batter, the catcher:

1) Steps out and forward at about a 45 degree angle with the right foot to receive the pitch.

2) Then steps toward second with the left to throw.

c. On an inside pitch to a righthanded batter and an outside pitch to a lefthanded batter, the footwork can be somewhat more

complicated. If the pitch is caught outside of the strike zone, the catcher:

1) Steps out and and forward with the left foot to catch the ball.

2) Then steps toward second with the right foot.

3) Then steps toward second with the left to throw.

d. On pitches that are not very far inside he does not have to make the initial step with the left foot to meet the ball:

1) He simply catches the ball with the weight on the left foot.

2) Then shifts the weight back over the right foot as he takes a short step forward with that foot.

3) Then strides toward second base to throw.

4. Shifting to throw to first base:

a. With a righthanded batter at the plate, the catcher has an unrestricted target. If the pitch is inside:

1) He meets the ball with a step to the left with the left foot.

2) Steps toward first with the right.

3) Then steps forward with the left again to throw.

b. On a pitch over the plate, his footwork amounts to no more than receiving the pitch with a short step forward with the right foot and stepping toward first with the left to throw.

c. With a lefthanded batter at the plate, his footwork becomes more complicated. On an inside pitch he may have to step toward the pitch with the right foot and throw from behind the batter.

d. If the pitch is outside to the lefthanded batter, the catcher:

1) Steps to meet the ball with the left foot.

2) Then steps forward with the right.

3) He then steps toward first with the left, in front of the hitter, to throw.

5. The catcher's footwork has been presented here in a step-by-step manner so that it can be analyzed. However, once the footwork has been learned it should be gradually speeded up to the point that it almost becomes a single movement.

Throwing Action

1. Good footwork will place the catcher in a balanced position to throw, but he still has to get the ball to the base. Unfortunately, a strong arm may or may not make a boy an effective throwing catcher. Throwing from behind the plate requires quickness and accuracy more than it does a rifle arm. (I coached one boy whose arm was so strong that he could throw accurately to second base from his knees. However, he never became a good throwing catcher because he would not take the time to learn how to shift to meet the ball and get rid of it quickly.)

2. The fundamentals of throwing for a catcher are much the same as for any other position:

a. A catcher should learn to grip the ball *across* the seams as it enters the glove.

b. The glove and ball are brought straight back to the throwing position behind the ear.

c. He uses a snap overhand delivery for most throws.

1) The fingers should be on top of the ball.

2) The elbow up.

3) The left shoulder pointed in the direction of the throw.

d. The throw is not made with a "pushing" action. The arm does not come down and around in a circular arc, but the wrist does follow a normal pattern.

3. Some throws to first base can be delivered more quickly if the catcher uses a side-arm motion.

4. The low pitch may present the catcher with a unique problem if he has to get rid of the ball quickly. The best way to do this is to drop the left shoulder down and throw over the top from a semisquat position.

5. All throws should be delivered *as* the catcher is coming out of his crouch and not after he has assumed a standing position.

Fielding Bunts and Slow-Hit Balls

1. On obvious bunt situations the catcher may alter his stance slightly by placing the right foot farther back than usual. This will give him a better start after the ball. Also, he should stand slightly more erect in order to be in a better position to receive a high pitch.

2. Pursuing a bunt or slow-roller, the catcher tries to position his body so that his feet are in line with the expected throw:

   a. To throw to first base on a ball down the first baseline or in front of the plate, the catcher approaches the ball from the left and fields it with his back toward leftfield.

b. To throw to first base on a ball down the third baseline, the catcher:

1) Approaches the ball from the right, fields the ball with his back toward rightfield and pivots to his left to make the throw.

2) Or, approaches the ball from the left, fields the ball with his back toward the third-base dugout and pivots clockwise to throw. This latter method will allow the catcher a better view of his throwing alternatives but may also encourage him to throw off-balance.

c. To throw to second base, the catcher approaches all bunts from the left and fields the ball with the back toward third.

d. To throw to third base, he fields the ball with his back toward the leftfield foul line.

3. The catcher should call for any bunt he can reach with a reasonable effort. If another player fields the ball, the catcher has the responsibility for telling that player where to throw.

4. To field a bunt or slow-roller, the catcher blocks the roll of the ball with the glove, scoops it into the throwing hand, and takes a short slide step onto the right foot to throw.

5. He should throw side-arm from a semicrouch position when he has to hurry but should throw overhand whenever time permits.

Catching Foul Tips and Pop Flies

1. The secret to being able to catch foul tips is to assume a receiving position as close to the batter as possible. The catcher should also be sure that he reaches for the ball and does not pull his glove back as he catches it.

2. The location of the pitch will usually indicate the direction a foul ball will take:

a. Inside pitches are usually fouled toward the batter's side of the plate.

b. Outside pitches are usually fouled to the opposite side.

3. An understanding of the aerodynamics of batted balls will also help the catcher to field pop flies:

a. Balls hit behind home plate will have a tendency to curve back toward home plate.

b. Balls hit out in front of the plate will curve away from the catcher and toward the infield.

4. The catcher pursues a pop fly by:

a. First discarding his face mask by catching the chin pad with the thumb.

1) On balls near the plate, he should locate the ball and then throw the mask away from that area.

2) On balls hit a considerable distance away, the catcher throws the mask behind him as he starts for the ball.

b. Once he has determined where the ball should land, he should run to that spot as fast as possible. He should not try to get there just as the ball comes down.

c. Whenever possible, the catcher should try to catch a pop fly with his back to the infield, so that the ball will be curving toward him.

d. If he has to field the ball curving away from him, he aligns the ball directly over the head to compensate for the curve.

e. The ball should be pursued with the arms at the sides.

5. To field a pop fly, the catcher either: (a) brings the glove up to a position high on the chest with the little fingers together, or (b) catches it as an outfielder would with the thumbs together.

6. A catcher should always allow an infielder to call him off of a pop fly. The catcher's glove is less adapted to catching fly balls than are those used by infielders.

Covering Home Plate

1. On tag plays:

a. The catcher stands with his left foot on the plate, close to the third-base corner, and his right foot comfortably spread and to the right of the plate.

b. As he receives the throw he turns to his left and brings the right knee down to the ground.

c. With the ball held firmly in the "meat" hand, he sweeps the glove down in front of the third-base corner of the plate and tags the runner with the back of the glove. The ball is held in the glove with the throwing hand.

d. He should bring the ball and glove high in the air immediately after the tag to prevent the runner from knocking the ball out of his hand.

e. If the runner is a "dead duck," the catcher tries to avoid contact with the runner. He remains on his feet, moves up the line and tags the runner. If the runner tries to run him down, he merely pivots backward and away from him as he makes the tag. (My catcher of a few seasons back—all 150 pounds of him— learned this the hard way. Never one to back down to an opponent, he challenged a 200-pound baserunner when he had time to simply tag him and get out of the way. The baserunner ran right over my catcher, knocked the ball out of his hands and scored. I commended him for his courage if not for his intelligence.)

f. If the throw is off target, the catcher should go get the ball and then dive for the runner as he crosses the plate.

g. If the throw comes to the catcher on an "in-between" hop, he backs up and tries to catch the ball over the plate.

h. On all tag plays, the catcher should let the throw come to him rather than reaching for the ball. He should stay low and, if necessary, block the ball with his body.

2. On force plays (with the bases loaded):

a. The catcher stands behind the plate facing the fielder who is making the throw.

b. If the throw is right at him, he:

1) Steps forward to meet the ball by placing the right foot on the plate.

2) Pivots and strides toward first with the left to throw.

c. If the throw is to his left, the catcher:

1) Steps in that direction with the left foot to meet the ball, dragging the right foot across the plate.

2) Then jump shifts (pivots in the air) to the right to make the throw to first if there is a play there.

d. On a throw to his right, the catcher:

1) Steps toward the ball with the right foot, dragging the left toe across the plate.

2) Then pivots to the right and strides toward first with the left foot to throw.

12

Playing First Base

Teams have been known to place a good hitter but poor fielder at first base, their thinking being that the defensive responsibilities of this position may not be as demanding as they are at some other positions. Perhaps the extreme example of this occurred back in the early fifties in the Pacific Coast League. One team had a first baseman who was extremely slow (he weighed close to 300 pounds) but was one of the best hitters in the league. In fact, this particular first baseman was so slow that opponents sometimes had their second baseman field his bunts on the first-base side of the infield!

The teams that have subscribed to this theory have usually suffered for it. During the course of a season, the first baseman will be involved directly in more plays than any other player with the exception of the pitcher and catcher.

Qualifications

Above all, a first baseman must have *good hands*. He must be capable of fielding batted and thrown balls of all kinds. Former Dodger great, Gil Hodges, was said to have been a great fielding first baseman because he had an ability to receive throws with "soft" hands.

A first baseman must also have *good agility*. An awkward boy could never perform the complex footwork and body movements required of the position.

A first baseman must have *good defensive instincts*. Because he will handle the ball on a great many plays, the first baseman must have an ability to do the right thing at the right time. His good judgment on crucial plays will be essential to his team's success.

A first baseman should have *good size*. It only stands to reason that a taller boy will be able to reach more throws without having to take his foot off the bag.

Field Positions

Each game situation calls for the first baseman to assume a basic position in relation to the bag. The position called for in a particular situation is designed to place the player in the best location for the play he is most likely to have to make.

These positions are not absolutes and are intended only to eliminate some of the guesswork for younger players. A player should be encouraged to deviate from these basic positions whenever he has a logical reason to do so.

The positions are located initially by pacing off a certain number of steps from the bag. Once the player has gone through this a couple of times he should be able to position himself without measuring the distances.

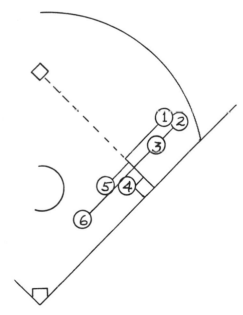

POSITION	DISTANCE FROM BAG	GAME SITUATION
⚹1	5 steps off, 8 back	Righthanded batter and no baserunners
⚹2	3 steps off, 9 back	Lefthanded batter and no baserunners
⚹3	3 steps off, 4 back	Runner on first, second unoccupied, but runner not likely to steal
⚹4	On the bag	Runner on first, second unoccupied
⚹5	4 steps off, 2 in	Lefthanded batter, sacrifice expected with runner on 2B Or, important runner on third
⚹6	3 steps off, 8 in	Righthanded batter, obvious sacrifice situation with a runner on second

Covering First Base

1. The first baseman breaks for the bag as soon as he sees that the batted ball will be fielded by another infielder. He should not try to locate the bag and watch the ball at the same time.

2. He assumes a position in front of the bag, facing the expected throw, with the heels apart and in contact with the edge of the base.

3. He determines the accuracy of the throw before shifting the feet or beginning the stretch.

4. On throws directly to the bag:

a. The righthanded first baseman places his right foot on the bag and stretches with the left.

b. The lefthanded first baseman places the left foot on the bag and stretches with the right.

5. On throws to his extreme right:

a. The righthanded first baseman places the right foot on the bag and crosses over in the direction of the throw with the left.

b. The lefthanded first baseman places the left foot on the bag and stretches with the right.

6. On throws to his extreme left:

a. The righthanded first baseman places the right foot on the bag and stretches with the left.

b. The lefthanded first baseman places the left foot on the bag and crosses over in the direction of the throw with his right foot.

7. On throws from the home-plate area: The left foot is placed on the bag and the right foot is placed well down the baseline toward second base. The first baseman faces home plate and gives an exaggerated target, away from the approaching runner.

8. On throws from foul territory on the first-base side of home plate: The right foot is placed on the bag and the left extends well into foul territory. Again, the first baseman gives a good target away from the approaching runner.

9. On throws high and wide to the left: The first baseman leaves the bag, catches the ball one-handed and tags the runner with his glove hand as he goes by.

10. The first baseman should try to catch high throws without leaving the bag:

a. The righthanded first baseman steps back on top of the bag with the right foot and reaches for the ball with the left hand.

b. The lefthanded first baseman steps back on top of the bag with the left foot and reaches for the ball with the right hand.

c. On extremely long throws that have started a downward arc, the first baseman can step back into foul territory with the foot on the glove side and catch the ball behind the bag.

11. Whenever possible, the ball should be caught with both hands. However, adeptness at catching the ball with only the glove hand is important because it allows for a greater reach. (Willie McCovey of the Giants catches almost everything with just the glove hand.)

12. The first baseman should always leave the bag to catch a throw he cannot reach otherwise.

13. For his own protection, a first baseman must learn to use as little of the bag as possible, and he should develop the habit of taking his foot off the bag as soon as possible after he has received the throw.

14. First basemen are *expected* to be able to field low throws in the dirt. The techniques for making this play are presented in the chapter on defensive fundamentals (Chapter 9).

Holding a Runner on Base

1. With a runner on first base and second base unoccupied, the first baseman takes his ⚹4 position on the bag:

a. The righthanded first baseman stands with his feet almost parallel with the first-base foul line. His upper body faces the pitcher.

b. The lefthanded first baseman can bring his right foot up closer to the corner of the bag nearest to the pitcher and face more toward home plate.

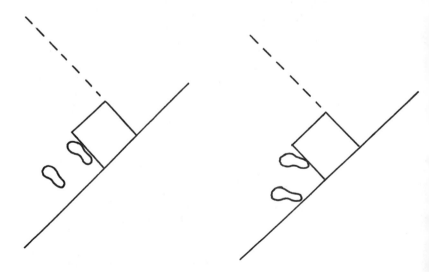

2. To make the tag:

a. The righthanded first baseman brings the tag down hard with the thumb side of the glove.

b. The lefthanded first baseman sweeps across and tags the runner with the little finger side of the glove (see photo on page 39).

c. The tag is made aggressively and to the rightfield corner of the base. The first baseman should not delay the tag to find the runner but let the runner come to the ball.

3. If the pitcher throws to the plate, the first baseman:

a. Breaks off the bag by taking a cross-over step with the left foot, a step with the right foot, and then a quick shuffle step toward second base to face the batter.

b. Charges in to cover balls on the first-base side if the batter squares around to bunt.

4. If the first baseman decides or receives instructions to take his ✗3 position behind the runner, he must make sure that the pitcher knows that the bag is not being covered. Otherwise, the pitcher just might attempt a pickoff throw to first and either throw the ball away or balk when he sees that the bag is uncovered.

Basic Fielding Plays

1. Fielding Bunts:

a. The first baseman is responsible for bunts on the first-base side which the catcher and pitcher cannot reach (see Chapter 17 for specific assignments).

b. He should attempt to field the ball with his feet already in position to throw to the most desirable base:

1) The righthanded first baseman should approach the ball from the left to throw to third base and from the right to throw to second or first base.

2) The lefthanded first baseman should approach the ball from the left to throw to all bases.

c. He should call for the ball, if he is in the best position to field it, and listen for the catcher's instructions on where to throw.

d. Unless the ball has stopped rolling, it should be fielded with both hands.

2. Feeding the Pitcher Covering First Base:

a. The first baseman should pursue any ground ball that goes by the pitcher and cannot be fielded by the second baseman:

1) If he fields the ball deep and wide of the bag, he should wait for the pitcher to get to the bag, then throw overhand directly to the base.

2) If he fields the ball near the bag, he should toss it underhand to the pitcher well before he reaches the bag. This throw is executed with a stiff wrist. That is, the hand is stopped when the ball is released rather than allowing it to follow through.

3) If the ball is dribbled just beyond the pitcher's reach, the first baseman flips it backhand to the pitcher covering.

3. Throwing to the shortstop covering second base:

a. The first baseman's throw to second base should be directed in such a manner that there is little chance the ball will hit the baserunner:

1) If the ball is fielded in front of the baseline, the throw should be directed to the third-base side of second base.

2) If the ball is fielded behind the baseline, the throw should be directed to the rightfield side of the bag.

b. The lefthanded first baseman can execute the play by simply fielding the ball and stepping toward second with the right foot to make the throw.

c. The same play for the righthanded first baseman can be somewhat more difficult:

1) If the ball is right at him or to his left, he fields the ball, then jump shifts in a clockwise direction to make the throw to second.

2) If the ball is hit to his extreme left, he fields the ball with the glove hand, turns to his left, plants the right foot and throws directly overhand to second.

Relay and Cut-off Assignments

1. The first baseman is the cut-off man on all throws from the outfield into the plate except:

a. When a sharp line drive is hit to leftfield and he does not have time to get over to the cut-off position.

b. When his attempt to field a batted ball makes it impossible for him to get back to the cut-off position.

2. The first baseman takes his cut-off position about 50 feet in front of home plate and in line with the fielder. This distance

will vary somewhat depending upon the strength of the fielder's
throwing arm.

a. With his back to the plate, the first baseman holds both
hands high over his head and allows the catcher to verbally align
him with the ball and the plate.

b. As the ball approaches he positions his feet in such a
manner that the ball can be relayed with a minimum of footwork
after the catch.

c. The catcher will call for him to cut the ball off and relay
it to a particular base, let it go through to the plate, or simply
cut it off and hold onto it (see Chapter 17).

d. If the catcher does instruct the first baseman to let the ball
go through, the first baseman should fake a cut-off as the ball
goes by to keep the trailing runner(s) from taking a big turn.

Special Plays and Responsibilities

1. The first baseman should knock a bunt or topped ball that rolls foul farther out of play to prevent it from spinning back into fair territory.

2. Because he is relatively close to the batter, the first baseman will have to field some extremely hard-hit ground balls. His first concern should be to keep the ball in front of him. This can be accomplished by either:

a. Dropping down on the knee on the throwing side to block the ball.

b. Or by squatting in front of the ball with the heels together.

3. Whenever the first baseman can make a play himself, he should wave off the pitcher coming over to cover. Depending on the closeness of the play, he can tag the base in any one of three ways:

a. He can simply approach the bag along the baseline and tag the base with the inside foot.

b. On a close play he can avoid a collision with the runner by either sliding into the base, or

c. Diving for the bag and touching it with the ball in the throwing hand.

4. The first baseman should always check to see where the second baseman is playing a particular batter. If he knows where the second baseman is playing, he will be in a better position to judge whether he should attempt to field a ball hit to his right.

5. Occasionally, a first baseman will field a ground ball near the bag with less than two outs. As a general rule, he should:

a. Tag first and then throw to second if he fields the ball within two steps of the bag or moving in that direction. In this case, he should be sure to shout "tag him" to the man covering at second as the force is eliminated as soon as the batter is retired.

b. Throw to second base if he fields the ball more than two steps from the bag or if he is moving toward second as he fields the ball.

c. Of course, these suggestions should not be accepted as absolute rules. There will be times when getting the out is more important than retiring a lead runner or attempting a possible double play.

6. The first baseman has the major pop-fly responsibility on all balls hit in the area of his position and down the baseline toward home plate. He should be particularly aggressive in calling off the catcher when he can reach the ball with a reasonable effort. A catcher's glove is not particularly adapted to catching pop flies, and balls hit toward first base are curving away from the catcher and toward the first baseman.

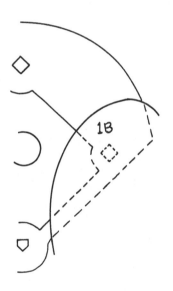

13

Playing Second Base

A player is often selected to play second base purely on the basis of his defensive ability. It is quite common at all levels of play to find second basemen who are able to remain in the line-up even though they are hitting in the low .200s. In fact, coaches have been known to place their best infielder at second base rather than at shortstop. They have found that, particularly with younger players, even the righthanded batters hit more balls to the right side than they do to the left.

Qualifications

Contrary to the belief of some, a second baseman must have a *strong throwing arm*. Even though many of his throws will be short, the second baseman's responsibilities in relay situations and in making the double play require a good arm.

The second baseman must have *good range*. With the first baseman having to remain on or close to the bag in many situations, the second baseman is left with a huge area to cover.

The second baseman must have *quick hands*. He will become the pivotman on most double-play situations, and he must have an ability to catch and get rid of the ball quickly.

Most good second basemen are *complete ballplayers*. They must be able to perform a variety of plays, and they are usually willing to spend the time it takes to learn the finer elements of the game. Not long ago we had a second baseman who represented this quality in every respect. Not even a good natural athlete, this boy had grown up with a bat and ball in his hand and had made himself into a sound high school ballplayer.

Field Positions

In each game situation, the second baseman should be able to place himself in the best location for the play he is most likely to have to make. These basic field positions are identified by pacing off the prescribed number of steps from second base. Once the player has gone through this procedure a couple of times, he should be able to position himself properly without measuring the distances.

POSITION	DISTANCE FROM BAG	GAME SITUATION
※1	4 steps off, 8 back	Righthanded batter and no baserunners
※2	6 steps off, 9 back	Lefthanded batter and no baserunners
※3	4 steps toward the batter (from ※1 or ※2 position)	Steal possibility, second baseman responsible for bag
		Double-play or double-steal situation (runners on first and third)
		Holding runner on second base with a righthanded batter at the plate
※4	8 steps off, 6 back	Sacrifice, second baseman must cover first base
※5	6 steps off, 2 toward batter	Runner on third, play to be made to the plate.

Basic Fielding Plays

1. Fielding a ground ball and throwing to first base:

    a. On a routine ground ball hit directly at him, the second baseman:

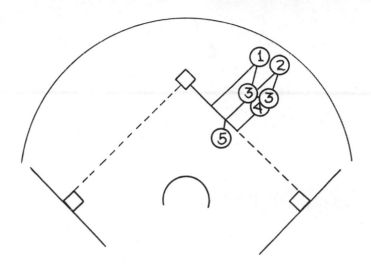

1) Receives the ball in his normal fielding position.

2) Takes a short step forward with the right foot to catch the weight of the body.

3) Makes a side-arm throw to first as he strides in that direction with the left foot.

b. On balls hit to his extreme right, the second baseman:

1) Moves over to a position in front of the ball if possible; otherwise, he reaches across the body to backhand the ball.

2) Comes to a sliding stop against the inside of the right foot.

3) Comes up throwing by bringing his rear up underneath him and striding with the left foot toward first.

4) On some plays he will not have time to get set and will have to jump in the air to make the throw.

5) Occasionally, he will have time to crow-hop toward first before throwing.

6) In either case, the throw is usually made directly overhand.

c. On balls hit to his extreme left, the second baseman:

1) Angles his approach toward rightfield in an effort to get in front of the ball.

2) Fields the ball with the glove hand.

3) Brings the right foot around behind the left to catch the weight of the body.

4) Then makes a side-arm throw to first as he steps in that direction with the left foot.

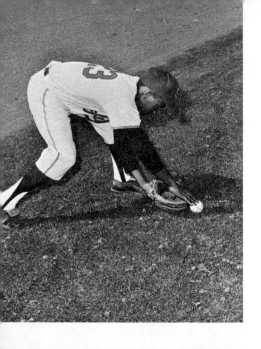

d. On a slow *bouncing* ground ball, the second baseman:

1) Charges in and fields the ball with both hands.

2) Flips the ball underhand to first as the right foot hits the ground and the body moves toward home plate.

e. On a slow-*roller,* the second baseman:

1) Approaches the ball from the left.

2) Scoops up the ball with the throwing hand only (the thumb on top and the first two fingers underneath).

3) Flips the ball underhand to first while moving toward the plate.

2. Fielding a ground ball and throwing to second base for a force out or to start a possible double play:

a. On a ball hit at him but 20 feet or more from the base, the second baseman:

1) Fields the ball in the normal position.

2) Makes a jump shift to his right and throws to second with a three-quarter delivery.

b. On a ball hit at him but less than 20 feet from the base, the second baseman:

1) Fields the ball in the normal position but with the right foot slightly further to the rear.

2) Pivots the upper body toward second and makes a three-quarter, short-arm throw to the base without straightening up or moving the feet.

c. On a ball hit to his right and within 10 to 15 feet of the bag, the second baseman:

1) Fields the ball in the normal position and flips the ball underhand to the shortstop.

2) In executing this throw, the arm is stopped as the ball is released with a stiff wrist and the glove remains out of the way so it does not hide the ball.

d. On a ball hit within 10 to 15 feet of the bag, in the baseline or in front of the baseline, the second baseman:

1) Fields the ball and flips it backhand without turning to face the shortstop. (I have heard people remark that the infielder who flips the ball backhand like this is showing off, trying to

make an easy play look difficult. I disagree—this is the easiest way to make the throw.)

e. On a ball hit to his extreme left, the second baseman:

1) Fields the ball with the glove hand.

2) Turns to his left and allows the weight to land on the right foot.

3) Throws overhand to second as he strides in that direction with the left foot.

f. All throws to second base should be directed at the short-stop's chest and to his glove side.

Covering Second Base

Whenever the second baseman is responsible for covering the bag, whether it be a steal situation or a double play situation, he must move in to his ⚹3 position so he will be able to get to the bag in time to take the throw in a balanced position.

1. On tag plays:

a. The second baseman normally covers second base on steal attempts when there is a righthanded batter at the plate and on throws from the outfield when the shortstop is the relay man.

b. As the play develops he races to get to the bag as quickly as possible, straddles it and waits for the throw with the upper body facing the throw:

1) On close plays when the runner and ball arrive at the same time, he sweeps down with the glove, tags the runner, and brings the glove high in the air.

2) On plays when the ball arrives well ahead of the runner, he brings the glove down to a position in front of the base and allows the runner to slide into the ball.

c. There are several important tips for making either kind of tag:

1) The player making the tag should not reach for the ball but let it come to him.

2) Once he has the ball he should watch for the runner's lead foot.

3) He should always make the tag with the ball in the glove hand and keep the throwing hand out of the way.

4) The tag should be made with the back of the glove facing the runner so the wrist can bend with the impact.

2. On double-play pivots:

a. The second baseman normally covers the bag on double-play situations when the ball is hit to the left side of the infield. To avoid confusion on balls hit back to the pitcher, the short-stop is usually given the responsibility of signaling before the pitch which of them should cover.

b. The approach to the bag is important. The second baseman should:

1) Race to get to the bag as soon as possible.

2) Try to approach the bag in line with the expected throw.

3) Slow down almost to a stop about one yard behind the bag so the feet can be shifted quickly if the throw is off line.

c. The *straddle* is one of a number of pivots used by second basemen. Because it is easy to execute, it is highly recommended to the young player. Many professional second basemen also use this pivot on plays that allow them time to stop before taking the throw. (This pivot is highly recommended by former Yankee great Bobby Richardson.)

1) The player straddles the bag with the right foot on the left-field side.

2) He relays throws to his right by dragging the left foot

across the bag as he catches the ball and then strides toward first with left again to throw.

3) He relays throws directly at him by merely dragging the right foot across the bag as he throws.

4) On throws to the extreme left, he steps with the left foot to catch the ball, dragging the right foot across the bag, then plants the right foot in front of the bag and strides with the left to throw.

d. Occasionally, the second baseman will be late getting to the base and will not be able to stop before taking the throw. The *cross-over pivot* is usually used under these circumstances. This technique enables the second baseman to get out of the way of the runner and also gives him the extra momentum to put something on his throw. A few years ago we had a boy who played an excellent second base but had a difficult time making the relay throw on the double play. We had taught him the straddle pivot, but he simply could not get any velocity on his throws to first base. Another coach, a former infielder himself, suggested that he experiment with the cross-over pivot. The result was amazing. The cross-over pivot allowed him to make the throw while he was moving toward first base, as opposed to throwing from a standing position.

1) On this pivot the second baseman approaches the bag as much in line with third base as possible and steps on the bag with the left foot.

2) He then crosses over toward home plate with the right foot as he receives the throw.

3) The relay throw is made as the left foot comes off the bag and strides toward first base.

e. The *rocker pivot* is used by many second basemen when the throw is late in arriving and the runner is close to second base. The straddle pivot would not be appropriate under these circumstances because it leaves the pivotman in a position where he can be easily upset by a sliding runner.

1) To execute the rocker pivot the second baseman waits for the throw from a position about one step behind the bag on the rightfield side.

2) As he receives the ball he steps on the edge of the bag with the left foot.

3) He then rocks back on the right foot and strides toward first base with the left to make the throw.

f. In executing each of these pivots, it is important that the second baseman learns to relay the throw as quickly as possible:

1) He should catch the ball with both hands so the ball can be transferred to the throwing hand with a minimum of delay.

2) He should deliver the ball from where he catches it.

3) He should use a quick short-arm delivery rather than a big windup.

g. The pivotman can usually avoid being injured by a runner trying to break up the double play by simply jumping in the air as soon as he releases his throw to first base. The slider may knock the second baseman's feet out from underneath him, but he will also provide him a good cushion to land on.

h. The pivotman should never make an unnecessary throw to first base. If he sees that he has no play on the runner there, he should hold onto the ball.

i. If the second baseman fields the ball within 5 feet of second, he should make the play unassisted. He calls the shortstop off, tags the base and makes the throw to first using the easiest footwork possible.

j. Occasionally, the second baseman will be covering the bag on a possible double play, and he will see that the fielder will not be able to get the ball to second base in time for the force out. If this situation develops, the second baseman should yell "first base" so the fielder can direct his throw there without looking to second first.

Relay and Cut-off Assignments (see Chapter 17)

1. The second baseman normally becomes the relay man on all singles to the rightfield side of second base:

a. He races out to a position about 50 feet from second base and in line with the ball and the bag.

b. Both hands are extended into the air to provide an obvious target for the outfielder.

c. As the ball approaches, he adjusts the position of his feet so that he will be able to relay the throw with a minimum of footwork.

d. He then listens for the shortstop to tell him whether to cut the throw off and relay it, or let it go through.

2. On extra-base hits most teams use a "double cut-off." If a

possible extra base hit is hit to the leftfield side of second base, the second baseman serves as the backup man for the shortstop:

a. He covers second base until he sees that the batter-runner has at least a double. He then races out to a position about 25 feet behind the shortstop (who has already gone out for the relay).

b. If the throw from the outfielder to the shortstop is on target, the second baseman simply tells the shortstop where to throw the ball.

c. If the throw from the outfielder cannot be fielded cleanly by the shortstop, the second baseman tells him to "let it go" and he makes the play himself.

3. On extra-base hits to the rightfield side of second, the second baseman becomes the relay man and the shortstop serves as the back-up man:

a. The second baseman goes out for the relay as he would on a single, but in this case he aligns himself with the ball and home plate.

b. With his hands in the air, he listens for the shortstop's directions on where to throw.

c. If the throw is on target, he simply makes the relay. If the throw is not on target, the shortstop will tell him to let it go.

4. Some teams prefer not to use the double-relay system. In this case the procedure on extra-base hits is the same as that used on singles. For example, the second baseman would remain at second on an extra-base hit to leftfield and only the shortstop would go out and line up with the ball and third or home plate.

Special Plays and Responsibilities

1. Because most of his throws will be short, the second baseman's first concern in fielding a hard-hit ground ball is to get his body in front of the ball. Even if he can only knock the ball down, he may still have time to recover and make a play to first or second base. This can be accomplished by either:

a. Dropping down on the knee on the throwing side to block the ball.

b. Or by squatting in front of the ball with the heels together.

2. Occasionally, the second baseman will field a ground ball in the baseline with a runner on first with less than two outs. If the runner stops to avoid his tag, he should throw to first to get the batter, and the first baseman can throw back to second to complete the double play.

3. On ground balls hit into the hole to his left, the second baseman should call the first baseman off if he (the second baseman) can make the play. This will free the first baseman to cover the bag.

4. The second baseman normally covers first base on sacrifice-bunt situations that require the first baseman to leave the bag to field the ball:

a. He assumes his #4 position and watches the batter for the first possible indication that he is bunting.

b. If the batter does square around, the second baseman races over to cover the bag. If he has time, he should approach the bag parallel with the baseline and take the throw facing home with the left foot on the bag and the right extended out toward second.

5. The second baseman is responsible for pop flies hit in the area of his position and from behind second base all the way over to the rightfield line:

a. On any pop fly hit behind the infield on the rightfield side, he should race back for the ball as if he were the only fielder available to make the play. He should not give up on the ball until he hears an outfielder call him off.

b. He has priority over the first baseman on balls hit behind first base, which the first baseman would have to field with his back to the infield. The second baseman has a better angle on the pop-up behind first, and since he normally plays deeper than the first baseman he usually can get to the ball just as quickly.

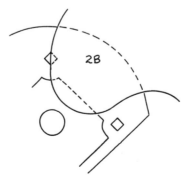

14

Playing Third Base

Third base is called the "hot corner," and whoever gave the position that name knew what he was talking about. The third baseman is usually positioned closer to the batter than any other infielder. A lot of hard-hit ground balls and line drives come his way, some of them hard enough to go right through him if he fails to get his glove up in time. A good third baseman can be worth the price of admission to a ball game all by himself.

Qualifications

A third baseman must have *quick hands*. Although his range does not have to be as great as that of the shortstop or second baseman, he must be able to react fast enough to spear balls that come within his reach.

A third baseman must have *courage*. On balls hit hard and right at him, the third baseman must be willing to block the ball with his body, even if he cannot field it cleanly.

A third baseman must have a *strong arm*. He must be capable of throwing accurately from one corner of the infield to the other.

A third baseman must be particularly *calm under pressure*. Because of his close proximity to the plate, the third baseman will often field a ground ball before the batter has covered very much of the distance to first base. The very fact that he has so much time to make the play will add pressures that many infielders find difficult to overcome. I coached one boy who simply was not cut out to be a third baseman. He would make a great play fielding the ball but would invariably throw the ball away trying to get it to the first baseman, especially when he had plenty of time. We moved him over to shortstop and he became an all-league infielder.

Field Positions

For reasons that we have discussed in previous chapters, each infielder must be able to position himself in the best location for the play he is most likely to have to make. The third baseman can identify these basic field positions by measuring from the third-base bag the distances prescribed below:

POSITION	DISTANCE FROM BAG	GAME SITUATION
⚓1	5 steps off, 6 back	Righthanded batter and no baserunners
⚓2	7 steps toward first base (from ⚓1)	Lefthanded batter and no baserunners
⚓3	4 steps off, 2 in	First batter in the inning, possible drag bunt
		Sacrifice-bunt situations
		Play at the plate
		Possible double steal
⚓4	On the bag	Important runner on third, possible squeeze or steal home

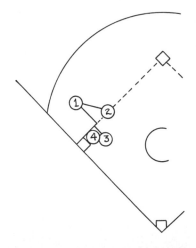

The third baseman may choose to adjust his basic position for a number of reasons. For example, with two outs and no runners on base, he should play closer to the foul line to minimize the chances of the ball being hit down the line. A base hit to the third baseman's right is usually a double. One to his left is usually a single. With two outs, the defense is most concerned about preventing the batter from getting into scoring position.

Basic Fielding Plays

1. Fielding bunts and slow-hit balls:

a. With a runner on first base, the third baseman is normally given the assignment of fielding bunts on the third-base side that cannot be reached by the pitcher or catcher (see Chapter 17).

b. With a runner on second base, the third baseman does not leave his position near the bag unless the ball is bunted past the pitcher (see Chapter 17).

c. Whenever he has time, the third baseman should field a bunt or slow-hit ball in the following manner:

1) Circle around behind the ball so the body is moving toward first base.

2) Field the ball wth both hands.

3) Take a short step forward with the right foot and stride with the left toward first to throw.

d. If he has to hurry a throw to first and the ball is bouncing, the third baseman:

1) Charges in and fields the ball with both hands.

2) Flips the ball underhand to first as the right foot hits the ground and the body is still moving toward the plate.

e. If he has to hurry a throw to first and the ball is *rolling,* the third baseman:

1) Approaches the ball from the left.

2) Scoops up the ball with the throwing hand only (the thumb on top and the first two fingers underneath).

3) Flips the ball underhand to first.

f. If he has to hurry a throw to first and the ball is *not* moving, the third baseman:

1) Approaches the ball from the left.

2) Reaches down and "plucks" the ball with the throwing hand as the right foot hits the ground.

3) Delivers the ball with an underhand throw to first base.

g. Whenever the third baseman has to make a throw to first while his body is still moving toward the plate, he should aim the ball to the left of the first baseman. Throws have a natural tendency to break to the right when they are thrown in this manner.

2. Fielding a solidly hit ground ball and throwing to first base:

a. On a routine ground ball hit directly at him, the third baseman:

1) Receives the ball in his normal fielding position.

2) Takes a short step forward with the right foot to catch the weight of the body.

3) Makes an overhand throw to first as he strides in that direction with the left foot.

b. On a ball hit to his extreme right, the third baseman:

1) Moves over to a position in front of the ball if possible; otherwise, he reaches across the body to backhand the ball.

2) Comes to a sliding stop against the inside of the right foot.

3) Takes a side step or "crow-hop" onto the right foot again if he has time.

4) Strides toward first with the left to make an overhand throw.

c. On a ball hit to his extreme left, the third baseman:

1) Moves over to a position in front of the ball or spears the ball with the glove hand.

2) Brings the right foot around behind the left to catch the weight of the body as it falls toward second base.

3) Strides toward first with the left foot to make a three-quarter overhand delivery in that direction.

3. Fielding a ground ball and throwing to second base for a force out or to start a double play:

a. On a ball hit directly at him or to his right, the third baseman:

1) Fields the ball in his normal fielding position.

2) Crow-hops toward second to give the second baseman time to get to the bag.

3) Delivers the ball with a snap overhand throw as he steps toward second with the left foot.

b. On a ball hit to his left, the third baseman:

1) Moves over in front of the ball or spears it with the glove hand.

2) Crow-hops toward second if he has time.

3) Delivers the ball side-arm to second base as he strides in that direction with the left foot.

c. On all throws to second base the third baseman should try to hit the second baseman chest high and on the glove side.

Covering Third Base

1. On tag plays:

a. The third baseman takes throws from the catcher with the feet straddling the bag and the upper body facing home plate. He should be particularly careful not take his eyes off the ball before he catches it on this play.

b. He takes throws from the outfield in the same position but leans to one side to give the thrower a good target away from the baserunner.

c. The third baseman executes the tag in the same manner as any other infielder. (See Chapter 9 for the description of this fundamental.)

2. On force plays:

a. Races to the bag and takes a position with the heels in contact with the home-plate and second-base sides of the base.

b. If the throw is right at him, he catches the ball with the left foot on the bag, transfers the weight to the right foot and looks for a chance to throw the batter out at first base.

c. If the throw is off target, he shifts his feet and stretches for the ball like a first baseman (see Chapter 12).

Relay and Cut-off Assignments (see Chapter 17)

1. The third baseman has cut-off responsibilities on throws into the plate in just two situations:

a. On sharp line drives to leftfield that do not allow the first baseman enough time to assume the cut-off position.

b. Whenever the first baseman's attempt to field a batted ball makes it impossible for him to get back to the cut-off position.

2. The third baseman takes his cut-off position about 50 feet in front of home plate and in line with the ball. This distance will vary somewhat depending upon the strength of the outfielder's throwing arm:

a. With his back to the plate, the third baseman holds both hands high over his head and allows the catcher to verbally align him with the ball and the plate.

b. As the ball approaches he should adjust his feet in such a manner that the ball can be relayed without being adjusted after the catch.

c. The catcher will call for him to cut the ball off and relay it to a particular base or let it go through to the plate.

d. If the catcher does instruct him to let the ball go through, he should fake a cut-off as the ball goes by to keep any trailing runners from taking a big turn.

Special Plays and Responsibilities

1. The third baseman should always try to keep a hard-hit ball in front of him, even if he cannot field it cleanly. (I had one third baseman who rarely caught a ground ball. He was more like a backstop than a third baseman, but he usually got his man.)

a. With his feet well apart and the knees bent, his "ready" position should be particularly low to the ground.

b. Although he should make an effort to field all ground balls in his regular fielding position, there will be balls to his extreme right or left which he will only have time to dive for. On such plays, the third baseman may have to make the throw from his knees.

2. As a general rule, the third baseman should try for any ball he can reach to his left. It is a lot easier for him to make the throw than it would be for the shortstop who is moving away from a play at first or second base.

3. Since many ground balls get to the third baseman well before his receiver has a chance to get to the bag, he should learn to delay his throw by looking at the ball and taking an extra step before throwing.

4. The third baseman should check the slope of the third baseline on the fields where he plays to determine how a ball along the line will be likely to roll. He should knock a bunt or topped ball which rolls foul farther out of play to prevent it from spinning back over the line into fair territory.

5. When the opposing team is attempting to sacrifice a runner from second to third, the third baseman is presented with one of his most difficult plays (see Chapter 17):

a. He assumes his ⚒3 position in front of the line but remains alert for a fake bunt and steal attempt.

b. If the batter is successful in bunting the ball down the third baseline, the third baseman holds his position until he sees whether the pitcher will be able to field the ball.

c. If the pitcher does field the ball, the third baseman retreats to cover third. If the ball goes by the pitcher, the third baseman must rush in and field the ball and make the play to first base.

6. With less than two outs and two or more runners on base, the third baseman is faced with a decision as to where he should make the play if a ground ball should come to him:

a. With runners on first and second, the third baseman:

1) Steps on third and throws to first if the ball is hit within two steps of the bag or he fields it moving toward third.

2) Throws to second base to start the double play if the ball is hit to his left or more than two steps from the bag.

b. With runners on first and third, the third baseman:

1) Throws to the plate on slow-hit balls if the runner tries to score. Otherwise, he throws to first.

2) Throws to second base on sharply hit balls directly at him or to his left.

3) Throws to home or first on balls hit to his right unless the runner on first and the batter are slow enough that there is still a double-play possibility.

c. With the bases loaded, the third baseman should make the easiest and quickest throw to get the double play:

1) He should throw to second base on balls hit to his left.

2) He should throw home on balls hit directly at him.

3) He should either throw home or step on third and throw to first on balls hit to his right or those he fields close to the bag.

d. The above rules would be influenced by the number of outs and the importance of the runner on third. For example, with no outs and the winning run on third base, the third baseman would have to throw home, even if the ball were hit to his left.

7. The third baseman has the major pop-fly responsibility on all balls hit in the area of his position and down the baseline toward home plate. He should be particularly aggressive in calling off the catcher when he can reach the ball with a reasonable effort. A catcher's glove is not particularly adapted to catching pop flies and balls hit toward third base are curving away from the catcher and toward the third baseman.

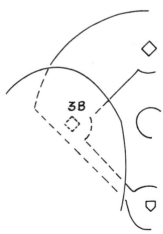

15

Playing Shortstop

Playing shortstop calls for more all-around defensive ability than any other position. A coach will usually fill this infield position, then look for candidates for the others. To be even adequate defensively, a team must have a good shortstop. In fact, a great shortstop can transform a fair defensive team into a good one, simply because he will be involved in a large percentage of key defensive plays. One season it became obvious to me that we had two good ballplayers and that was about it. Both of them pitched and both of them were good infielders. I decided to play one at short and pitch the other on Tuesdays and have them switch positions on Friday. We simply were not going to go anywhere as a team unless we filled those two positions with our best athletes.

Qualifications

A shortstop must have *good speed*. He must be capable of covering more ground than any other infielder.

A shortstop must have a *good arm*. He must be able to make throws from the edge of the outfield grass on balls hit into the hole. The shortstop is also a key relay man on most extra-base hits.

A shortstop must have *good, quick hands*. His responsibilities on ground balls and as the pivotman in many double-play situations call for a good glove and an ability to get rid of the ball quickly.

A shortstop must be particularly *consistent* in his performance. There are athletes with great natural abilities who cannot do the job at shortstop. Their great abilities enable them to make an occasional spectacular play, but they do not have the consistency to *always* make the routine plays.

A shortstop must be *at his best under pressure*. Because he will have to make so many difficult plays, the shortstop is bound to be involved in many pressure situations. This quality in our shortstop of a few seasons back really saved us in one game. We were playing the game we had to win to stay in the running for the championship and were losing to a team that didn't belong on the same field with us. Just before we came to bat for the last time, our shortstop came up with a fantastic play to keep the score close. I am convinced to this day that his great play inspired our team to rally and win the game in the last inning.

Field Positions

The shortstop must also be able to locate himself in the best possible position for the play he is most likely to face. He can learn these basic positions by pacing off a prescribed number of steps from the bag.

POSITION	DISTANCE FROM BAG	GAME SITUATION
※1	7 steps off the bag toward third, 8 back	Righthanded batter, and no baserunners
※2	3 steps off, 9 back	Lefthanded batter and no baserunners
※3	4 steps toward first base from ※1 or ※2	Runner on first, possible steal or sacrifice
		All double-play situations that call for the SS to cover second
		Runners on first and third, possible double steal
※4	2 steps off, 1 back	Sacrifice, runner on second or first and second
※5	7 steps over, 2 in	Runner on third, play at the plate

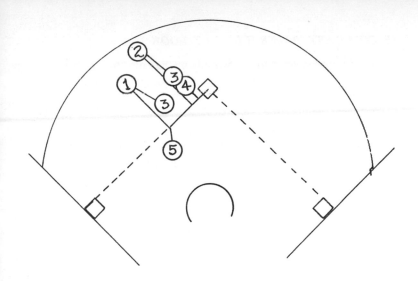

Basic Fielding Plays

1. Fielding a ground ball and throwing to first base:

   a. On a routine ball hit directly at him, the shortstop:

   1) Moves in quickly on the ball from an angle as much in line with first as possible.

   2) Fields the ball in the normal fielding position.

   3) Takes a short step forward with the right foot or a crow-hop with both feet if there is time.

   4) Throws to first with a three-quarter or overhand delivery as the left foot strides in that direction.

   b. On a ball hit in the "hole" to his right, the shortstop:

   1) Moves over to a position in front of the ball if possible; otherwise, he reaches across the body to backhand the ball.

   2) Comes to a sliding stop against the inside of the right foot.

3) Straightens up and throws all in one motion by bringing the rear foot up underneath him and striding toward first with the left foot.

4) Occasionally, the shortstop will have time to take a slide step toward first before making the throw.

5) The throw must be directly overhand for maximum carry.

c. On a ball hit to his extreme left, the shortstop:

1) Moves over to a position in front of the ball if possible; otherwise, he spears the ball with the glove hand.

2) Brings the right foot around behind the left to catch the weight of the body as it moves toward rightfield.

3) Makes the throw to first using a three-quarter delivery and striding in that direction with the left foot.

d. On a slow hit ball, the shortstop:

1) Charges in and fields the ball with both hands.

2) Makes the throw to first as the right foot hits the ground.

3) The throw can be made underhand, side-arm or overhand, depending upon the amount of time he has and how high the ball bounces.

2. Fielding a ground ball and throwing to second base for the force out or to start a double play:

a. On a ball hit directly at him or to his right, the shortstop:

1) Moves into a position in front of the ball.

2) Simply makes a quick side-arm throw to second from the fielding position.

3) If the ball is hit to his extreme right, he may find it necessary to straighten up and throw overhand.

b. On a ball hit to his left and within 10–15 feet of the bag, the shortstop:

1) Fields the ball and flips it underhand to second. This throw is executed with a stiff wrist and the arm is stopped as the ball is released. The glove hand is held well away so as to not impair the second baseman's view of the ball.

c. On balls hit to his extreme left and behind second base, the shortstop:

1) Spears the ball with the glove hand.

2) Transfers it to the right hand and flips it backhand to the second baseman without turning around.

d. All throws to second base should be directed at the second baseman's chest and to his glove side.

3. Fielding a ground ball and throwing to third to retire a runner trying to advance to that base:

a. The shortstop fields the ball, then makes a jump shift to his right and throws the ball side-arm to third.

b. The throw should be to the leftfield side and well away from the approaching runner.

Covering Second Base

1. Whenever the shortstop is responsible for covering the bag, whether it be a steal situation or a double-play situation, he should move into his ✗3 position so he will be able to get to the bag in time to take the throw in a balanced position.

2. On tag plays:

a. The shortstop normally covers second base on steal attempts when there is a lefthanded batter at the plate and on throws from the outfield when the second baseman is the relay man.

1) On a steal attempt, he races to the bag and straddles it with the left foot on the rightfield side, the right on the third-base side, and the upper body facing the throw.

2) His position at the bag on a throw from the outfield is much the same. However, he may have to adjust the feet slightly if the ball is approaching from center field.

b. Once he has received the ball, the tag is executed in the manner we have already described in detail for the second baseman in Chapter 13.

3. On double-play pivots:

a. The shortstop normally covers the bag on double-play situations when the ball is hit to the rightfield side of the infield. To avoid confusion on balls hit back to the pitcher, the shortstop is usually given the responsibility of signaling who will cover.

b. His approach to the bag on the double play is important.

1) He should get to the bag as quickly as possible.

2) He should angle his approach so that he is almost in line with first base when he receives the throw.

3) He should slow down almost to a stop about one step behind the bag, then continue across the bag in accordance with the direction of the throw.

c. The shortstop uses an *outside pivot* on throws originating from the first or second baseman playing behind the baseline:

1) From a position behind the bag, on the leftfield side, he steps across the bag and to the left with the left foot to catch the ball.

2) At the same time dragging the right toe across the center-field corner of the bag.

3) Then shifts the weight to the right foot and steps toward first with the left to throw.

d. The shortstops will normally use an *inside* pivot on throws originating from the first baseman playing in front of the baseline or from the pitcher:

1) From the same position behind the bag, he steps across the bag with the right foot into the infield to take the throw.

2) At the same time he drags the left toe across the leftfield corner of the bag.

3) He then strides toward first with the left to make the throw.

e. In executing each of these pivots it is important that the shortstop learns to relay the throw as quickly as possible:

1) He should catch the ball with both hands so that it can be transferred to the throwing hand with a minimum of delay.

2) He should deliver the ball from where he catches it.

3) He should use a quick short-arm delivery rather than a big windup.

f. If the shortstop fields the ball within 5 feet of second, he should make the play *unassisted*. He calls the second baseman off, tags the base and makes the throw to first using the easiest footwork possible.

g. To avoid being injured by a sliding baserunner, the shortstop leaps into the air after releasing the throw and allows the runner to slide under him.

h. The throw should be directed at first base. He should not try to throw over or around an approaching runner.

i. If there is no play at first, he should always hold onto the ball rather than take the chance on throwing it away.

Relay and Cut-off Assignments (see Chapter 17)

1. The shortstop normally becomes the relay man on all singles to the leftfield side of second base:

a. He races out to a position about 50 feet from second base, in line with the ball and the second-base bag.

b. Both hands are extended into the air to provide an obvious target for the outfielder.

c. As the ball approaches, he adjusts the position of his feet so that he will be able to relay the throw with a minimum of additional footwork after the catch.

d. He then listens for the second baseman to tell him to cut it off and make a throw or let the ball go on through.

2. The shortstop also becomes the relay man on a single to rightfield with a runner on first. Since the throw will be to third, the shortstop stations himself about 50 feet from that base and lines up with the ball. In this case, the third baseman will tell him whether or not to cut the ball off.

3. On extra-base hits most teams use a "double cut-off." If the ball is hit to the rightfield side of second, the shortstop serves as a backup man for the second baseman:

a. He covers second base until he sees that the batter-runner has at least a double. He then races out to a position about 25 feet behind the second baseman (who has already gone out for the relay).

b. If the throw from the outfielder to the second baseman is on target, the shortstop simply tells the second baseman where to throw the ball.

c. If the throw from the outfielder cannot be fielded cleanly by the second baseman, the shortstop tells him to "let it go" and he makes the relay throw himself.

4. On extra-base hits to the leftfield side of second, the shortstop becomes the relay man and the second baseman serves as the backup man:

a. The shortstop goes out for the relay as he would on a single, but in this case, he aligns himself with the ball and home plate.

b. With his hands in the air, he listens for the second baseman's directions on where to throw.

c. If the throw is on target, he simply makes the relay. If the throw is not on target, he lets it go through to the second baseman.

5. Some teams prefer not to use the double-relay system on extra-base hits. In this case, the procedure is much the same as that used on singles. For example, the shortstop would remain at second on an extra-base hit to rightfield and only the second baseman would go out and line up with the ball and third or home.

Special Plays and Responsibilities

1. A shortstop's success in fielding ground balls will depend largely upon his ability to develop several important skills:

a. He must learn to charge all but the extremely hard-hit ground balls. Unlike the third baseman, who plays close to the batter, and the second baseman, who has a short throw to first, the shortstop cannot afford to wait for the ball to come to him.

b. He must learn to get an "angle" on the ball. That is, he should try to approach the ball in line with the throw. Almost all of his throws will be for a good distance and fielding the ball while moving in the direction of the throw will help him to get his body into the throw.

c. He must develop exceptionally sure hands. Only rarely does a shortstop have time to recover a "bobbled" ground ball and still throw out the runner at first.

2. The shortstop is responsible for pop flies hit in the area of his position and from behind second base all the way over to the leftfield line:

a. On any pop fly hit behind the infield on the leftfield side, he should race back for the ball as if he were the only fielder available to make the play. He should not give up on the ball until he hears an outfielder call him off.

b. The shortstop has priority over the third baseman on balls hit behind third, which the third baseman would have to field with his back to the infield. He not only has a better angle on the ball, but he can usually get to the ball just as quickly since he normally plays deeper than the third baseman.

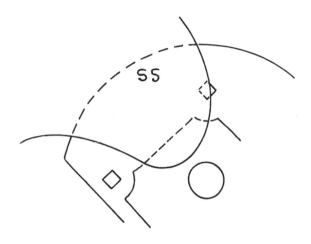

16

Playing the Outfield

In youth league baseball, a boy is often assigned to an outfield position simply because there just is not any place else to put him. Even on many high school teams a good hitter but poor fielder will be used in the outfield simply because outfielders normally do not receive as many fielding opportunities as do the other positions.

There are two general weaknesses to this theory. In the first place, an error by an outfielder is usually more costly than a misplay by an infielder. If a shortstop boots a ground ball, the batter usually ends up on first base. If an outfielder boots a ground ball, the batter will get at least two bases and maybe more.

The other factor that must be considered is the level of competition. Even if a young team could afford to play a weak fielder in the outfield, teams at higher levels definitely could not. The boy who wants to play the outfield in college or professional baseball must have defensive ability equal to that of any other player. As Lefty Gomez once put it, "I owe my pitching success to clean living and a fast outfield."

Qualifications

An outfielder must have an exceptional amount of *self-discipline.* Because the ball does not come his way very often, an outfielder can get into the habit of letting his mind wander. An outfielder must be just as alert to what is going on as any other player, and he must discipline himself to keep his mind on the game.

An outfielder must have *good speed*. Although this requirement is particularly important in the case of a centerfielder, it is also true of the left- and rightfielders. There is a lot of open space from one foul line to the other, and a slow outfielder can create quite a gap in a team's defense.

An outfielder must have a *strong arm*. Needless to say, outfielders have to be able to throw farther than any other player, and a weak throwing arm would be a severe handicap.

Field Positions

1. Normally, an outfield will shift as a unit so that there will not be any large gaps between them:

a. For a righthanded hitter: the leftfielder shades the line; the centerfielder moves to left-center, and the rightfielder plays relatively shallow in right-center.

b. For a lefthanded batter: the rightfielder shades the line; the centerfielder moves to right-center, and the leftfielder plays relatively shallow in left-center.

2. Any of several additional factors may cause an individual outfielder to modify his basic position:

a. He should alter his position slightly depending upon the strength and direction of the wind. By throwing some grass in the air or checking the flag he can tell whether he should:

1) Play deeper than usual if the wind is blowing out (toward him as he faces the infield).

2) Play closer to the infield if it is blowing in.

3) Move over a few steps in the direction it is blowing if there is a cross-wind.

b. The type of hitter at the plate may influence an outfielder's position:

1) He will play deeper with a long-ball hitter at bat.

2) He will play more toward the line for a hitter who pulls to his field.

3) He will play closer to the infield for a "punch" hitter.

4) He will play straight-away for the batter who hits to all fields.

c. The game situation will influence an outfielder's position:

1) He should play the hitter a little deeper and more to pull if the pitcher is behind in the count.

2) He will look for a hitter with two strikes on him to hit with less power and more toward his opposite field.

3) With two outs, the outfielder will always play deeper than usual.

d. The pitcher will influence the position of his outfielders:

1) An outfielder will look for the hitters to pull the ball more against a curveball pitcher and hit to the opposite field more against a hard thrower.

2) Whenever possible, the pitch signals should be relayed to the outfielders so that they can adjust their position accordingly.

Fielding Ground Balls

1. An outfielder should learn to field ground balls as though he were playing in the infield. In fact, Ty Cobb suggested that outfielders ought to work out in the infield occasionally, in order to develop their ability to field ground balls.

2. The particular technique he will use to field the ball will depend upon the game situation, how hard the ball is hit, and whether or not he will have to make a throw after fielding the ball:

a. An outfielder should field all hard-hit balls with the knee on the throwing side down on the ground (see Chapter 9).

b. He should field medium-hit balls on one knee if he is playing on a rough field.

c. Otherwise, he should field medium-hit, bouncing ground balls in the regular manner (see Chapter 9).

d. When a throw must be made after the catch an outfielder can field a *rolling* ball by scooping it up with the glove hand only. If the ball is bouncing, however, he should use the regular fielding position.

Fielding Fly Balls

1. Once an outfielder has determined his field position for the hitter at the plate he must concentrate on getting a jump on the

ball if it is hit in his direction. The fundamentals for pursuing a batted ball are described in Chapter 9.

2. An outfielder must develop proficiency in catching all kinds of fly balls. On *line drives* he must learn to:

a. Stay relatively low in going after the ball so that he has a good visual angle to judge whether or not he should try to make the catch.

b. Approach balls hit to either side at an angle so that he will have a better chance of intercepting them.

3. On *doubtful* or *diving* catches he must learn to:

a. Play it safe if his team is ahead in the early innings and gamble when his team is behind, especially in the late innings.

b. There are two accepted methods of making the diving catch:

1) The outfielder dives for the ball, then doubles up and rolls as he hits the ground.

2) Or he may merely dive for the ball and catch it while sliding forward on his stomach.

4. On balls hit *directly over his head:*

a. The left- and rightfielder should turn toward the foul line as batted balls tend to curve toward foul territory.

b. The centerfielder will turn in the direction the wind is blowing if there is a cross-wind. The left- and rightfielders should also turn in the direction of the wind if it appears to be strong enough to affect the normal curvature of the ball.

c. On extremely long fly balls:

1) The outfielder quickly estimates where he thinks the ball will come down and races after it with his back to the infield.
2) He looks for the ball and raises the glove to make the catch only when he reaches the estimated point of interception.

d. Occasionally an outfielder will turn the wrong way for a ball. Hoping to catch the ball over his left shoulder, he finds that the ball has drifted too far to his left. This situation is best handled by turning all the way around to the right, taking the eye off the ball for an instant, then catching the ball over the right shoulder.

5. On balls hit into the sun:

a. Older players make good use of the flip-type sun glasses on balls hit in the sun field. However, learning to use sun glasses requires some practice, and the younger player is better off without using them unless he has had considerable experience.

b. If the outfielder is not using sun glasses, he should:

1) Use the glove to shield the sun if the sun is on the glove side.
2) Use the throwing hand to shield the sun if the sun is on that side.

c. If the eyes become bothered by the sun on extremely high fly balls, it will help to quickly glance at the ground and then back at the ball.

6. An outfielder must learn to play fly balls hit near or off the fence:

a. Before a game begins he should study the area of the fence behind his position in an attempt to predetermine how a batted ball would rebound off the fence.

b. During the game, he should always be aware of the location of the fence in relation to where he has positioned himself for each hitter.

c. In attempting to field a fly ball near the fence, an outfielder should first go to the fence, locate the ball, then break off the fence to make the catch. This will keep him from having to watch the ball and the fence at the same time.

Throwing

1. The secret to throwing from the outfield, aside from having a strong arm, is to develop an ability to get rid of the ball quickly. And the key to getting rid of the ball quickly is to catch the ball moving in the direction of the throw.

2. An outfielder should try to avoid taking more than one step after fielding the ball (described here for a righthanded player):

a. If he catches the ball as the left foot hits the ground, he should take another step with the right foot and then throw.

b. If he catches the ball as the right foot hits the ground, he should throw immediately off of that foot.

c. On extremely long throws into the plate, once he has his weight on the right foot, he takes a hop step onto the right foot again before throwing.

3. An outfielder should always throw directly overhand. Even a three-quarter delivery will result in considerable curvature on the ball by the time it reaches its destination.

4. Throws to a cut-off man are always aimed high, between the cut-off man's arms or at his face. If the cut-off man has a backup man, as he would on extra-base hits, an outfielder should always overthrow, but never underthrow the cut-off man.

5. Throws that remain on a low trajectory will always travel faster than those that have a high trajectory. In fact, if an outfielder is throwing to a base and does not have a cut-off man to aim at, he should throw the ball in on one bounce. If he feels he can make the throw on a line, without bouncing it, he may do so.

6. An outfielder should always be aware of the percentages involved in making an attempt to throw out a runner. For example, with the tying run at the plate and a runner on second base, an outfielder would not want to make a throw into the plate on a single unless he knows he can throw out the runner trying to score. In this situation, if he does not get the runner at the plate, the batter, representing the tying run, may be able to advance into scoring position on the throw into the plate.

7. A neighboring outfielder will normally tell the player fielding the ball where to throw.

8. Of course, as a general rule an outfielder should always throw ahead of the runner. This rule should not be taken too literally, however. I was working with a particularly young group of boys once and an opposing player hit a long ball over the head of my centerfielder. As he retrieved the ball, the batter-runner was rounding third base. To everyone's amazement, my outfielder threw the ball to first base instead of home and the runner scored easily. I

approached him about it when he came off the field and he said, "But coach, you said to always throw one base ahead of the runner!"

Fly-Ball Priorities

1. Certain outfielders have precedence over other fielders under certain conditions:

a. All outfielders have priority over infielders on medium-distance fly balls that the outfielder could reach with a reasonable effort.

b. On balls hit between two outfielders, the player who would be in the best position to make the throw would have priority.

c. The centerfielder has priority on all fly balls that he can reach when there is some doubt as to who will have the easiest throw.

d. Additional conditions that may modify these basic priorities are:

1) The sun: If possible, an outfielder looking into the sun should allow another player to call him off.

2) The strength of the fielder's arm: Everything else being equal, the outfielder with the strongest throwing arm should be allowed to make the play.

17

Defensive Game Situations

There are a number of defensive situations that will arise again and again during the course of a baseball season. These situations occur with such frequency that a team must have a predetermined method of coping with them. The team that is able to consistently present a co-ordinated effort in defensing these situations will allow its opponents a minimum of scoring opportunities. (I know of one coach who does not allow a bat on the field during the first five days of practice each spring. His teams learn their defensive assignments first, then they begin working on other phases of the game.)

Every player on the field has an assignment on every batted ball. Unfortunately, situations do not always occur in competition exactly as they will be described on these pages. These are only the basic plays. The ability of a team to adjust to less common situations is largely a matter of player attitude. Aside from knowing his basic responsibilities, a player must *want* to be in on every play. He must think ahead and he must work hard to be in the right place at the right time.

The methods presented here show one of several ways a team might co-ordinate its defense. No system alone will guarantee success. As long as each of the nine individuals operates as part of a unit working together and in a logical manner, almost any approach will be effective.

Pitcher Covering First-Base Situations

1. Ground ball to the first baseman, short throw to the pitcher covering first base:

a. The *pitcher* takes a circular route to the bag so that he is running parallel with the baseline when he crosses the bag. He should take the first baseman's throw, touch the bag with the right foot, and then stop quickly, turn in toward the infield and look for another play.

b. The *catcher* yells for the pitcher to "cover" on any ball hit to the right side. He then backs up the throw to first if a play at the plate does not appear likely.

c. The *first baseman* fields the ball and flips it underhand to the pitcher before he gets to the bag. He waves the pitcher off if he can make the play unassisted.

d. The *second baseman* calls the first baseman off the ground ball if he can reach it himself. Otherwise, he backs up the play.

e. The *third baseman* covers third and the *shortstop* covers second.

f. The *rightfielder* must back up the throw to first.

g. The *leftfielder* and *centerfielder* back up a possible throw to second.

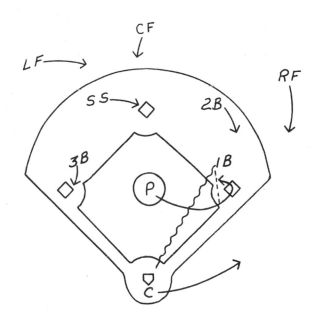

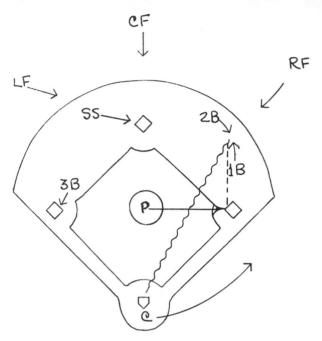

2. Ground ball between first base and second base, long throw to the pitcher covering first base:

a. The *pitcher* breaks in a direct line for first. He stops at the bag, if he has time, and takes the throw as a first baseman would.

b. The *catcher* yells "cover" and backs up the play.

c. The *first baseman* breaks over to field the ball unless the second baseman calls him off. If the second baseman calls for the ball, he covers first base. If he has to field the ball, he waits for the pitcher to reach the bag, then makes an overhand throw to first base.

d. The *second baseman* calls off the first baseman if he is able to field the ball. Otherwise, he backs up the play.

e. The *third baseman* covers third and the *shortstop* covers second.

f. The *rightfielder* backs up the play at first and the *left-* and *centerfielders* look for a possible play at second.

Bunt Situations

1. Runner on first base, sacrifice bunt:

a. The *pitcher* delivers the ball high in an effort to cause a pop-up. He then becomes responsible for any ball bunted in front of him. If the catcher has to cover third, the pitcher covers home.

b. The *catcher* is responsible for fielding any short bunts in front of the plate. If he does not field the ball, he directs the throw by shouting "second" or "first." If the third baseman fields the bunt, the catcher must cover third.

c. The *first baseman* assumes his ※4 position on the bag, then breaks in to field any bunts on the right side. If another player fields the ball, he returns to the bag.

d. The *second baseman* takes his ※4 position and breaks over to cover first. If the first baseman is able to get back to the bag, the second baseman backs up the throw.

e. The *third baseman* takes his ※3 position and fields any bunts to the pitcher's right. He should return to third base as soon as possible in case the runner attempts to come all the way around.

f. The *shortstop* covers second base.

g. The *rightfielder* backs up a possible throw to first; the *centerfielder* backs up any throw to second; and the *leftfielder* backs up third in case of a throw there.

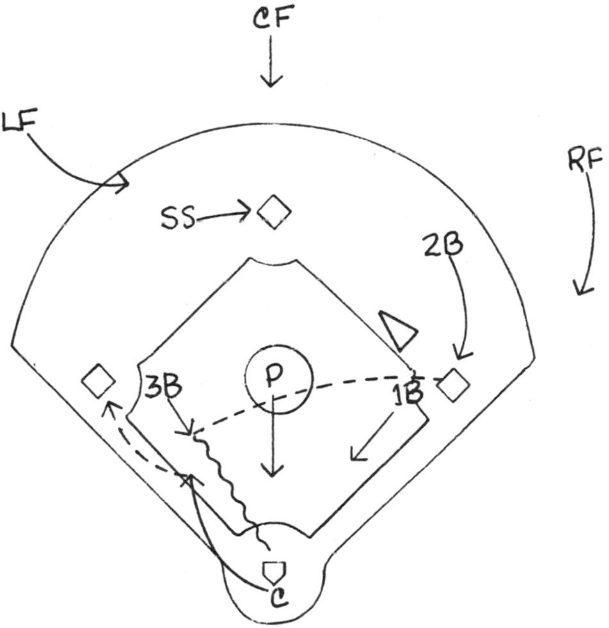

2. Runner on second base, or first base and second base, sacrifice bunt:

a. Again, the *pitcher* will try to force a pop-up by delivering the pitch high. To prevent the runner on second from getting a good lead, the pitcher throws to the plate just as the shortstop breaks the runner back. (Feints covering second base to get the runner leaning in that direction.) Immediately upon delivering the pitch, the pitcher breaks to his right and fields any ball he is able to reach on that side.

b. The *catcher* fields short bunts or directs the throw of another fielder.

c. The *first baseman* takes his ⚡5 position with a lefthanded batter and his ⚡6 position with a righthanded batter. As the batter squares to bunt, he breaks in to field any ball bunted on the right side.

d. The *second baseman* takes his ⚡4 position and breaks over to cover first as the batter squares around to bunt.

e. The *third baseman* takes his ⚡3 position and holds that position until he sees who will be fielding the bunt. If the catcher, pitcher or first baseman is able to field the ball, the third baseman covers third to take a possible throw. If the pitcher is unable to field a bunt down the third baseline, the third baseman breaks in and fields the ball and makes the throw to first.

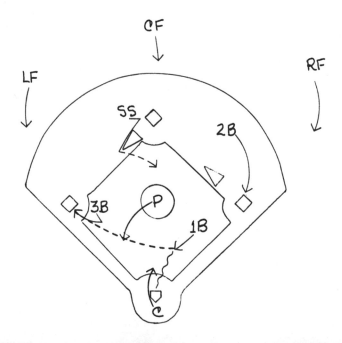

f. The *shortstop* assumes his ⚹4 position behind the runner. When the pitcher is ready to pitch, he breaks into the bag to move the runner back, then breaks back to a fielding position on the baseline as the pitch is delivered. The shortstop must field any ball bunted through the area of the mound as the pitcher is breaking to his right. Otherwise, he covers second base.

g. The *leftfielder* backs up a possible throw to third, the *centerfielder* backs up any throw to second, and the *rightfielder* backs up any throw to first.

3. Runner on second base or first base and second base, sacrifice bunt:

a. Younger players may find it difficult to defense the sacrifice with a man on second in the manner described under ⚹2. This method requires a great deal of practice and places much responsibility on the pitcher. We feel that it is the best way to defense the play under most circumstances. However, here are two other ways in which the play may be executed:

1) Have the shortstop cover third and allow the third baseman to come in and field bunts on his side. The pitcher covers the middle portion and the first baseman covers the first baseline. The runner on second must be kept close as the shortstop will have to outrun him to third.

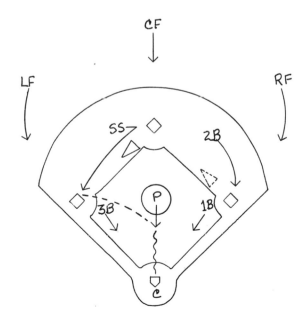

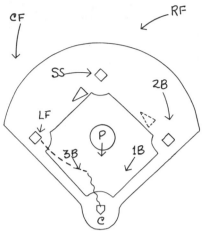

2) Many coaches like to use a five-man infield in this situation. They bring one of their outfielders in to cover third. The third baseman takes a position almost halfway to the plate on the third-base side. The shortstop covers second and the second baseman covers first. The first baseman takes his #6 position. The remaining two outfielders split the outfield area. Of course, the five-man infield would be used only when the defense is certain the batter is bunting and/or an extremely weak hitter is at the plate. The objective of this strategy is to *force* a weak hitter to swing away and, hopefully, strike out.

4. Runner on third base, or first base and third base, sacrifice bunt (safety squeeze):

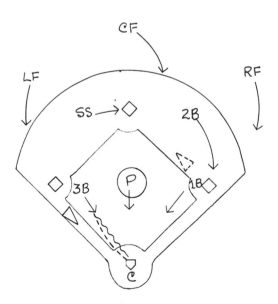

a. With just a few exceptions, the responsibilities in this situation are the same as those with a runner on only first base.

b. The *pitcher, first baseman* and *third baseman,* of course, look first for a play at the plate if the ball is bunted.

c. The *catcher* leaves home plate only if he feels he can field the ball and tag the runner trying to score.

d. The *third baseman* must keep the runner close at third.

e. If the runner does not try to score on the bunt, they should look for him to try to score on the throw to first.

5. Runner on third base, or second base and third base, suicide squeeze:

a. The first objective of the defense in this situation is to prevent the batter from bunting the ball.

b. The *pitcher* takes his windup watching the runner on third. If the runner breaks for the plate, the pitcher throws an automatic pitchout. If the runner does not commit himself early, the pitcher throws for a strike. He then fields any ball bunted in front of him.

c. The *catcher,* listening for "here he comes" from the bench, readies himself for a possible pitch-out. If the runner on third does not leave early, and the batter does bunt the ball safely, the catcher directs the throw to the appropriate base. The catcher

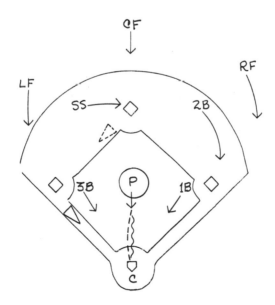

should not field the ball unless he can get back in time to tag the runner.

d. The *first baseman,* from his ⚹5 position, breaks in to field balls bunted on the first-base side.

e. The *second baseman,* from his ⚹4 position, breaks over to cover first if the batter squares around.

f. The *third baseman,* from his ⚹3 position, charges in to field any bunt on the third-base side.

g. The *shortstop* covers second base.

h. The *leftfielder* backs up a possible throw to third, the *centerfielder* backs up any throw to second, and the *rightfielder* backs up any throw to first.

Double-Play Situations

1. Runner(s) on first, first and second, first and third, or bases loaded, ground ball to the left side of the infield:

a. The primary defensive objective in this situation is to get the double play the easiest way possible.

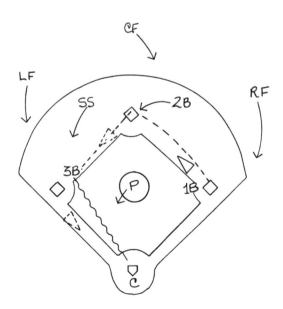

b. The *pitcher* must check with the shortstop to see who is covering second base, before he pitches. He tries to keep the ball low so the hitter will hit it into the ground. On a ball hit back to him, he throws home if the bases are loaded. With runners at first and second, he should throw to third if he fields the ball going in that direction; otherwise, to second. With runners on first, or first and third, he should try for the double play by throwing to second.

c. The *catcher* reminds the pitcher to keep the ball down. When the ball is hit he takes a position behind the plate and waits for a possible throw. If the bases are loaded, he looks for a chance to relay the ball to first for a double play.

d. The *first baseman* takes the position appropriate for the situation, then covers first. If the first throw goes to the plate, he should give the catcher a good inside target for the relay throw to first.

e. The *second baseman* checks with the shortstop for the base-covering assignment. He takes his ⅜3 position and covers second as the ball is hit to the left side.

f. The *third baseman* takes his ⅜3 position. If the ball is hit to him he throws home, steps on third and throws to first, or throws to second, depending on the location of the baserunners and where he fields the ball. (See details under special plays for third basemen.) If the ball is hit to the pitcher or shortstop, the third baseman covers third.

g. The *shortstop* gives the signal for the base-covering assignment. He then assumes his ⅜3 position. If the ball is hit to him, he throws to second to start the double play. If the ball is hit to the pitcher, he covers second or backs up a possible throw to second, depending on who has the assignment.

h. Each of the *outfielders* backs up the base appropriate for the play and his area of responsibility.

2. Runner(s) on first, first and second, first and third, or the bases loaded, ground ball to the right side of the infield:

a. Primary defensive objective: get the double play the easiest way possible.

b. The *pitcher's* responsibilities are basically the same as for a ball hit to the left side. However, he must remember to break over to cover first on balls hit near the first baseman. If the first

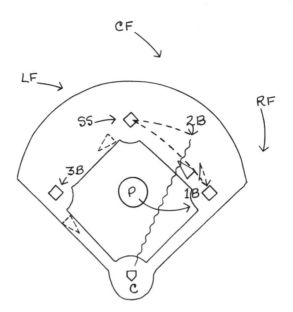

baseman throws to second to start the double play, the pitcher may have to take the return throw from the shortstop.

c. The *catcher's* responsibilities are the same as on a ball hit to the left side.

d. The *first baseman* takes his #4 or #5 position, depending on the situation. If the ball is hit directly to him with the bases loaded, he should throw home, then cover first for the catcher's return throw. If the ball is hit to his left, he should touch first base, then throw to second for the possible double play. Retiring the batter first eliminates the force at second. Therefore the first baseman should yell "tag him" to the player taking his throw at second base. If the ball is hit to the pitcher or second baseman, the first baseman merely covers first base.

e. The *second baseman* takes his #3 position and makes sure of the base-covering assignment by checking with the shortstop. If the ball is hit to him he throws to second base to start the double play. If the ball is hit to the pitcher, he covers second or backs up a possible throw to second, depending on who has the assignment.

f. The *third baseman* simply covers third base.

g. The *shortstop* takes his #3 position and relays the base-covering signal. If the ball is hit to the second baseman or the first baseman, he covers second base. If the ball is hit to the pitcher, he covers second or backs up a possible throw there, depending on who has the assignment.

h. Each of the *outfielders* backs up a base, depending on the expected play and his own area of responsibility.

Steal Situations

1. Runner on first base, steal:

a. The primary objective of the defense in this situation is to retire the runner at second base.

b. The *pitcher* must check with the shortstop to see who is covering second. He then concentrates on keeping the runner close at first. When he does throw to the plate he should get rid of the ball quickly, using a low, flat stride if he is righthanded. Upon releasing the ball, he should step to the side to give the catcher a clear view of second.

c. The *catcher* should anticipate obvious steal situations and call for a pitchout if the count on the batter will allow it. On throwing to second, the catcher should concentrate on getting rid of the ball with a minimum of footwork.

d. The *first baseman* holds the runner on first from his ⚹4 position and yells "there he goes" when the runner takes off.

e. The *second baseman* checks with the shortstop for the base-covering assignment. He would be in his ⚹3 position if he were

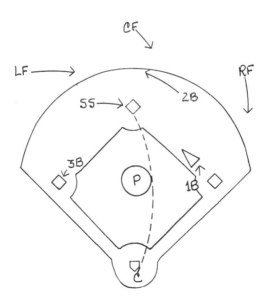

covering second. When the runner breaks, he covers second base or backs up the throw, depending on who has the assignment.

f. The *third baseman* covers third.

g. The *shortstop* gives the signal for the base-covering assignment. He takes his ✗3 position if he is covering the bag. When the runner breaks for second he either covers the bag or backs up the throw, depending on who has the assignment.

h. The *leftfielder* and *centerfielder* should back up the play at second base. The *rightfielder* should be alert to back up first in case a run-down situation develops.

2. Runner(s) on second base or first base and second base, steal:

a. The primary objective of the defense in this situation is to retire the runner attempting to steal third.

b. The *pitcher* must keep the runner close at second and get rid of his pitch quickly.

c. The *catcher* should look for this play in a bunt situation with the batter faking a bunt to draw the third baseman off the bag. The catcher's first concern is the runner trying for third, but he should throw to second if the lead runner gets too big a jump.

d. The *first baseman* moves down the line toward second in case a rundown play develops.

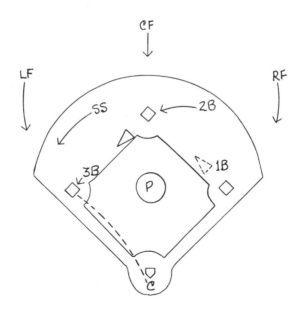

e. The *second baseman* checks with the shortstop for the base-covering assignment if there is also a runner on first. He must keep the runner close at second from his ⚓3 position if a right-handed batter is at the plate. When the runners break he covers second base as the shortstop will be backing up third.

f. The *third baseman* must not be too quick to charge in if the batter squares around to bunt. He should remind the shortstop to let him know if the runner on second breaks for third. When the runner does break, the third baseman covers third.

g. The *shortstop* relays the base-covering signal. He is responsible for keeping the runner close if a lefthanded batter is at the plate. He must yell "there he goes" if the runner breaks for third. He then backs up the throw to third from a position well behind the bag.

h. The *leftfielder* backs up the throw to third, and the *centerfielder* and *rightfielder* back up a possible throw to second base.

3. Runners on first base and third, early double steal:

a. See Chapter 7 for the intent of the offense on this play.

b. Normally, the primary objective of the defense on this play is to retire either baserunner before the runner on third has a chance to score. However, there may be occasions when the defense will be willing to give up a run to get an out. If this is the case, the defense would concentrate their efforts on the runner between first and second and forget about the runner on third.

c. When the *pitcher* hears the first baseman yell that the runner is going he steps back off the rubber, arm-fakes a throw to third to hold the runner there, then throws the ball to the second baseman in the baseline about one-third of the way to first. If the runner on third is more than a third of the way home when he fakes to that base, the pitcher should forget about the runner going to second and concentrate on the runner off third. He can do this by throwing immediately to third instead of making a fake. Or he can fake a throw to third, fake again to second base, and then make a play on the runner trying to score. The pitcher backs up home once he is rid of the ball.

d. The *catcher* covers home plate.

e. The *first baseman* yells "there he goes" when the runner breaks for second, then shortens up toward second for a possible rundown.

f. The *second baseman* takes his ⚹3 position and moves up to the baseline as the runner breaks for second base. If the pitcher throws the ball to him, he starts running the baserunner back toward first. He either tags the runner or throws home depending on the shortstop's instructions.

g. The *third baseman* covers third base.

h. The *shortstop* should be in his ⚹3 position before the play develops. When the runner on first breaks for second, he covers second and then follows the second baseman as he begins to run the baserunner back to first. The shortstop must keep an eye on the runner on third. If that runner breaks for the plate, the shortstop yells for the second baseman to throw "home."

i. Each of the *outfielders* backs up the base in front of him.

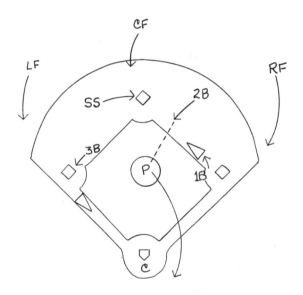

4. Runners on first and third, regular double steal:

a. See Chapter 7 for the offensive purpose of this play.

b. Primary objective of the defense: Retire the runner trying to score, or retire the runner going to second before the lead runner is able to cross the plate (if there are two outs).

c. Most teams are prepared to use any one of several different methods to defend this play. The catcher will normally signal for one of the following:

1) The catcher throws through to second base.

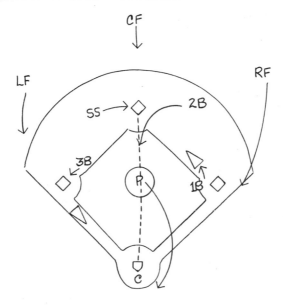

2) The catcher fakes a throw to second and attempts to pick the runner off at third.

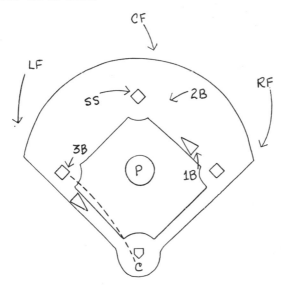

3) The catcher throws the ball back to the pitcher, who then attempts to pick the runner off third.

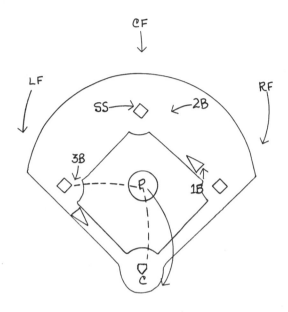

d. The *pitcher* simply delivers the ball as quickly as possible and steps to the side to give the catcher a good view of second if the throw is going through. Or he receives the catcher's throw and throws to third base for the pickoff attempt if option ✕3 is in effect. Whichever the case, he then backs up home in case a rundown develops.

e. The *catcher* gives the signal for one of the three options when the first and third situation first develops. He should anticipate the play and call for a pitchout whenever possible. On option ✕1, the catcher must quickly check the runner's lead at third before throwing to second. If the runner is more than a third of the way home, he should fake a throw to second and throw to third.

f. The *first baseman* yells "there he goes" as the runner leaves and then shortens up toward second in case of a rundown.

g. The *second baseman* and *shortstop* will usually use one of two methods of handling the throw, which is directed through to second base:

1) Many young teams use the *cut-off* method. Both players take their ⚡3 positions. With a righthanded batter at the plate, the second baseman breaks into a position halfway between the mound and second base just as the runner on first breaks for second. The shortstop covers second base. With a left-handed batter at the plate these assignments may be reversed. If the runner on third breaks for the plate, the cut-off man intercepts the catcher's throw and makes the play on the runner trying to score. If the runner on third does not break for the plate, the cut-off man allows the throw to go through to the shortstop (or second baseman), who is covering second base, and he makes the tag on the runner coming from first.

Some coaches prefer to simplify the play for the cut-off man by predetermining whether or not the throw is to be intercepted, regardless of the actions of the runner on third base. This procedure is recommended for pre-high school and most high school aged athletes. The cut-off man can concentrate on the ball without having to watch the runner on third as well. 2) More mature players can make the play without the use of a cut-off man. Either the shortstop or the second baseman handles the play himself, depending on who is given the base-covering assignment. With a righthanded batter at the plate, the second baseman will break over to a position about 2–3 steps in front of second base as the runner on first breaks for second. The shortstop will watch the runner on third at the same time he backs up the throw. If the runner on third breaks for the plate, the shortstop yells "home" and the second baseman takes the throw from the catcher and throws home. If the runner on third does not break, the shortstop yells "tag him," and the second baseman steps back toward the bag as he takes the throw and tags the runner coming in to second base.

If the runner on third remains there, and the runner going to second holds up to get caught in a rundown, the shortstop and second baseman handle the situation exactly as they would in an early steal. One player runs the baserunner back toward first and the other follows him and tells him when to throw home.

h. The *third baseman* covers third base.

i. Each of the *outfielders* backs up the base in front of him.

5. Runners on first and third, long-lead double steal:

a. See Chapter 7 for the offensive theory behind this play.

b. The objective of the defense, of course, is to retire the runner trying to score, or retire the runner on first before the runner off third has a chance to score (provided there are already two outs).

c. If the *pitcher* notices the exaggerated lead of the runner on first, he should step back off the rubber and make the play exactly as he would in the early steal. If he throws to first, he should immediately backup home in case a play develops there.

d. The *first baseman* takes the throw from the pitcher and upon seeing that the runner has remained off the bag, he quickly checks the runner on third and then throws the ball to the second baseman in the baseline. If the runner on third is already more than a third of the way toward home, the first baseman makes the play on him. If he throws the ball to the second baseman, he should follow his throw toward second to put a "pinch" on the runner in the rundown.

e. The *second baseman* moves up to the baseline and takes the throw from the first baseman. From this point on his responsibilities are the same as those in the early steal.

f. The *third baseman* covers third.

g. The *shortstop* covers second, then follows the second baseman on the rundown and tells him when to throw "home."

h. Each of the *outfielders* backs up the base in front of him.

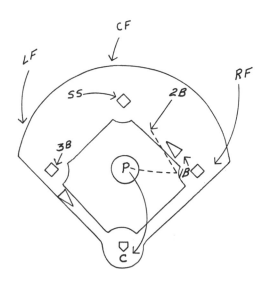

Rundown Situations

1. If a baserunner is caught in a rundown *between first base and second,* the first objective of the defense is to force him to start running to one base or another.

a. If the first baseman has the ball, he chases the runner toward second. If it becomes obvious that he will not be able to run him down himself, he throws the ball to the second baseman (or shortstop) as soon as:

1) The runner is actually "sprinting" toward second.

2) The runner has gone more than halfway to second base.

b. If the second baseman (or shortstop) has the ball, he chases the runner back to first and either:

1) Runs him down and tags him out.

2) Throws the ball to the first baseman when he yells "now."

c. When a runner is being chased toward him, the first baseman takes a position inside the baseline and about 10 feet from the bag:

1) As soon as the runner gets to within 10 feet of him, the first baseman calls for the ball by yelling "now."

2) He then tags the runner as he runs by.

THE COMPLETE BASEBALL PLAY BOOK

d. In addition to these primary responsibilities:

1) The pitcher should cover first base and be the backup man for the first baseman.

2) The shortstop (or second baseman) should cover second base and be the backup man there.

2. If a baserunner is caught in a rundown between *second base and third,* the same basic procedure is applied:

a. If the shortstop (or second baseman) has the ball, he chases the runner toward third. If it becomes obvious that he will not be able to run him down himself, he throws the ball to the third baseman as soon as:

1) The runner is actually "sprinting" toward third, or

2) The runner has gone more than halfway to third base.

b. If the third baseman has the ball, he chases the runner back toward second and either:

1) Runs him down and tags him out.

2) Throws the ball to the shortstop (or second baseman) when he yells "now."

c. When a runner is being chased toward him, the shortstop (or second baseman) takes a position inside the baseline and about 10 feet from the bag:

1) As soon as the runner gets to within 10 feet of him, the shortstop calls for the ball by yelling "now."

2) He then tags the runner as he runs by.

d. In addition to these primary responsibilities:

1) The pitcher should cover third base and be the backup man for the third baseman.

2) The second baseman (or shortstop) should cover second base and be the backup man there.

3. The baserunner caught *between third base and home* is handled in much the same way:

a. If the third baseman has the ball, he chases the runner toward home. If it becomes obvious that he will not be able to run him down himself, he throws the ball to the catcher as soon as:

1) The runner is actually "sprinting" toward home.

2) Or the runner has gone more than halfway to home plate.

b. If the catcher has the ball, he chases the runner back toward third and either:

1) Runs him down and tags him out.

2) Throws the ball to the third baseman when he yells "now."

c. When the runner is being chased toward him, the third baseman takes a position inside the baseline and about 10 feet from the bag:

1) As soon as the runner gets to within 10 feet of him, the third baseman calls for the ball by yelling "now."

2) When he has the ball he tags the runner as he runs by.

d. In addition to these primary responsibilities:

1) The pitcher should cover home and be the backup man for the catcher.

2) The shortstop (or leftfielder) should cover third base and be the backup man there.

4. There are a few *general rules* that apply to rundown situations between any two bases:

a. Both of the defensive players involved in the play should stay on the inside of the baseline so that they do not have to throw the ball over the runner.

b. The player chasing the baserunner carries the ball in the throwing hand, high and out in front of the body so that he can either tag the runner or make a quick overhand throw to another player.

c. Generally, it is not a good idea to "fake" a throw in a rundown situation because the player waiting for the ball becomes just as confused as the runner. However, if the player chasing the runner is just about to tag him, he might slow him down enough to do so by making a quick fake throw.

d. If the baserunner gets by the tag man, that player should get out of the way and allow the ball to go through to the player covering the base.

e. Whenever there are other runners on base, those players handling the rundown should reduce the distance between them to allow for a quicker tag.

f. Whenever a runner is stranded halfway between two bases and the ball is not in the hands of a player on either of those bases, the player with the ball should run right at the runner and make him commit himself to one base or another.

g. Whenever possible, the tag should be made with the runner moving in the direction of the base he came from.

Relay and Cut-off Situations

It might be easier for the player to accept his cut-off responsibilities as being important if he has a better understanding of the rationale behind them. Basically, there are two reasons for having a relay man stationed between the fielder and the player covering the base on a throw from the outfield. In the first place, it is just possible that the ball can be relayed faster and more accurately than it can be thrown by one player. On an extremely long throw, an outfielder would have to deliver the ball with a high trajectory in order to have it reach its destination. Generally speaking, the higher the ball is thrown, the slower it will travel and the more difficult it will be to control.

The second reason for using the relay system is probably the most important of the two. More often than not, the throw into a base or home plate will not be in time to retire the lead runner. If the throw is allowed to go through to the base or home, the batter and any other trailing runners will probably be able to advance an extra base on the throw. If a relay man is in position, he can cut off the throw as soon as he sees there is no play on the lead runner and can throw quickly to other bases. The trailing runners are thus forced to hold their places, and if the hit is a single, a double play situation has been created.

1. No baserunners, a single is hit to the leftfield side of second base:

    a. Primary objective of the defense: prevent the batter-runner from advancing to second base.

    b. The *pitcher* takes a circular route behind the runner to first base and looks for a possible pickoff throw if the runner takes a big turn.

    c. The *catcher* backs up first base.

    d. The *first baseman* backs up the leftfielder's throw to second.

    e. The *second baseman* covers second base and tells the shortstop to either cut the throw off or let it come through to him.

    f. The *third baseman* covers third.

    g. The *shortstop* takes the cut-off position about 50 feet from second base and in line with the ball. He either cuts off the ball or lets it go on through, depending on the second baseman's instructions.

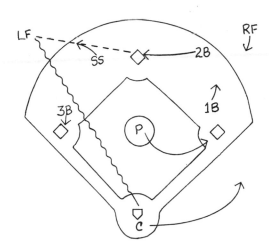

h. The *leftfielder* fields the ball and aims his throw at the shortstop's face.

i. *The centerfielder* either fields the ball and makes the throw to second or backs up the leftfielder if he fields the ball.

j. The *rightfielder* backs up the throw to second.

2. No baserunners, single to the rightfield side of second base:

a. Primary objective of the defense: prevent the batter-runner from advancing to second base.

b. The *pitcher* circles in behind the runner and covers first.

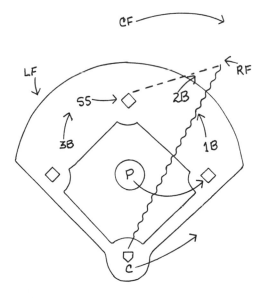

c. The *catcher* backs up a possible throw to first.

d. The *first baseman* goes for the ball and then remains off the bag to lure the runner into taking a big turn.

e. The *second baseman* takes the cut-off position about 50 feet from second and in line with the ball. He either cuts off the throw or lets it go, depending on the shortstop's instructions.

f. The *third baseman* backs up the throw to second base.

g. The *shortstop* covers second and tells the second baseman to either cut off the throw or let it come through to him.

h. The *leftfielder* backs up the throw to second base.

i. The *centerfielder* either fields the ball and makes the throw to second or backs up the rightfielder if he fields the ball.

j. The *rightfielder* either fields the ball and throws it to the cut-off man or backs up the centerfielder if he fields the ball.

3. Runner on first base, single to rightfield; or runners on first and second, fly ball to rightfield:

a. Defensive objective: prevent the lead runner from advancing to third or prevent the batter, or runner, on first from taking second on the throw to third.

b. The *pitcher* backs up third base from a position well behind the bag.

c. The *catcher* covers home plate.

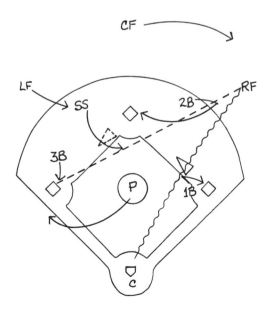

d. The *first baseman* covers first and checks to see that the runner there does not leave early if he tags up on a fly ball.

e. The *second baseman* covers second base and checks to see that the runner there does not leave early if he tags up on a fly ball.

f. The *third baseman* covers third and tells the shortstop to either cut off the ball, cut it off and throw to second or let it come on through to him.

g. The *shortstop* takes the cut-off position about 50 feet in front of third and in line with the ball. He either cuts off the ball and looks for a play at second or lets the ball go through, depending on the third baseman's instructions. If he does let the ball go through, he should fake a cut-off and throw to second to slow down the trailing runner.

h. The *leftfielder* backs up a possible throw to second.

i. The *centerfielder* backs up the rightfielder and tells him where to make the throw.

j. The *rightfielder* fields the ball and makes the throw to third or second, depending on the centerfielder's instructions.

4. Runners on first and second, single to leftfield; or runners on second and third, fly ball to leftfield:

a. Defensive objective: if possible, prevent the lead runner from scoring; otherwise, prevent the trailing runners from taking an extra base on a throw to the plate.

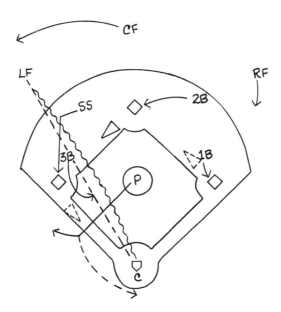

b. The *pitcher* runs to a point in foul territory halfway between third and home. He then backs up third or home as the play develops.

c. The *catcher* covers home plate and lines up the third baseman in the cut-off position. He directs the play on a throw into the plate by telling the third baseman to either cut it off and relay it to a particular base or let it come on through to home plate.

d. The *first baseman* covers first base if the ball is hit sharply to left. However, if the third baseman's attempt to field the ball makes it impossible for him to get back to the cut-off position, the first baseman must take the cut-off position.

e. The second baseman covers second and makes sure the runner there does not leave too early on a fly ball.

f. The *third baseman* takes the cut-off position about 50 feet from home and in line with the ball. He either cuts off the throw and relays it or lets it go through, depending on the catcher's instructions. If he does let it go through, he should fake the relay to keep the trailing runners from taking a big turn.

g. The *shortstop* covers third base. On a fly ball, he should check to see if the runner leaves early if he tries to advance after the catch.

h. The *leftfielder* fields the ball and makes the throw to the plate only if he has a good chance of retiring the runner there. Otherwise, he throws the ball in to second.

i. The *centerfielder* backs up the leftfielder and tells him where to make his throw.

j. The *rightfielder* backs up a possible throw in to second.

5. Runners on first and second, single to center- or rightfield; or runners on second and third, fly ball to center- or rightfield:

a. Defensive objective: if possible, prevent the lead runner from scoring; otherwise, prevent the trailing runners from advancing an extra base on the throw to the plate.

b. The *pitcher* runs to a point in foul territory halfway between third and home. He then backs up third or home as the play develops.

c. The *catcher* covers home plate and lines up the first baseman in the cut-off position. He directs the play on a throw in to the plate by telling the first baseman to either cut it off and relay it to a particular base or let it come on through to the plate.

d. The *first baseman* takes the cut-off position about 50 feet in front of home plate and in line with the ball. He either cuts off the ball and relays it or lets it go on through, depending on the catcher's instructions. If he does let it go through, he should fake a cut-off to keep the trailing runners from taking a big turn.

e. The *second baseman* covers first base. On a fly ball he checks to see that the runner tagging up does not leave early.

f. The *third baseman* covers third and lines up the shortstop in his cut-off position. If the throw is made to third, he tells the shortstop to either cut it off, relay it or let it come on through.

g. The *shortstop* takes the cut-off position about 50 feet from third base and in line with the ball. If the throw comes to him, he either cuts it off, relays it or lets it go on through, depending on the third baseman's instructions. If he does let it go through, he should fake a cut-off to keep the trailing runners from taking a big turn.

h. The *leftfielder* backs up the play if the ball is hit to centerfield. Otherwise, he backs up a possible throw to second base from rightfield.

i. The *centerfielder* either fields the ball and throws to home, third or second, or backs up the rightfielder and tells him where to throw the ball.

j. The *rightfielder* either fields the ball and throws to home, third or second, or backs up the centerfielder and tells him where to throw the ball.

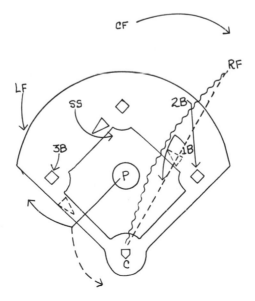

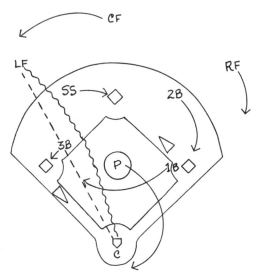

6. Runners on first and third, fly ball to leftfield, centerfield or rightfield:

a. Defensive objective: if possible, prevent the runner on third from scoring after the catch. Otherwise, prevent the runner on first from taking second base on the throw to the plate.

b. The *pitcher* backs up home.

c. The *catcher* covers home, lines up the cut-off man and tells him to cut the throw off, relay it or let it come through.

d. The *first baseman* takes the cut-off position about 50 feet in front of home and in line with the ball. He either cuts off the throw, relays it or lets it go through, depending on the catcher's instructions. If he allows the throw to go through, he should fake a cut-off and throw to discourage the runner on first from trying for second.

e. The *second baseman* covers first and watches for the runner to leave early.

f. The *third baseman* covers third and watches for the runner there to leave early.

g. The *shortstop* covers second base.

h. The *leftfielder* either fields the ball and throws to home or second, backs up the centerfielder if he fields the ball or backs up a possible throw to second if the rightfielder fields the ball.

i. The *centerfielder* either fields the ball and throws to home or second or backs up the left- or rightfielder and tells one of them where to make the throw.

j. The *rightfielder* either fields the ball and throws to home or second, backs up the centerfielder and directs his throw if he fields the ball, or backs up a possible throw to second base if the leftfielder fields the ball.

k. Many teams will use this situation to advantage on a short pop fly behind the infield by having the runner break for the next base as soon as the ball is caught. For example, the runner on first breaks for second to force the defense to play on him there. Of course, as soon as the throw does go to second, the runner on third can score easily. Or the runner on third can make a bluff for the plate on the catch to draw a throw there. Then the runner on first goes to second and the lead runner can return to third. The best way to defense these tactics is to use the pitcher as a cut-off man. The player fielding the ball doesn't throw to second or home. He throws to the pitcher in the cut-off position in front of the plate, and the pitcher relays the ball if he sees an opportunity to do so.

7. Runner on first or no baserunners, extra-base hit to the leftfield corner:

a. Defensive objective: possibly prevent a lead runner from scoring or the batter from going to third or home.

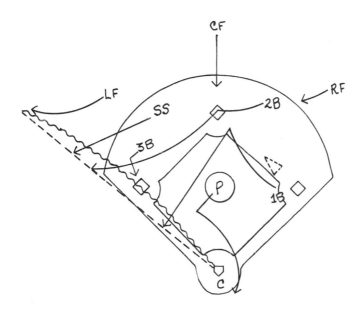

b. The *pitcher* backs up third or home as the play develops.

c. The *catcher* covers home and tells the cut-off man to either cut it off, relay it or let it come on through.

d. The *first baseman* watches to see that runner touches first base. With a runner already on first, he immediately takes the cut-off position in front of home and in line with the throw. If not, he trails the batter-runner down to second base and looks for a possible pickoff there. If the runner goes on to third, the first baseman breaks in to his cut-off position in front of home in case of a play at the plate.

e. The *second baseman* covers second until he sees that the batter has a sure double. Then, he drifts over in the direction of the shortstop to retrieve a possible loose ball and to direct the shortstop's relay throw.

f. The *third baseman* covers third.

g. The shortstop takes the relay position on the leftfield line and listens for the second baseman's direction on where to make the throw.

h. The *leftfielder* fields the ball and throws immediately to the cut-off man.

i. The *centerfielder* covers second base if it is not being covered by the first or second baseman.

j. The *rightfielder* backs up a possible throw to second.

8. Runner on first base or no baserunners, extra-base hit to left or left-center:

a. Defensive objective: possibly prevent the runner on first from scoring or the batter from going to third or home.

b. The *pitcher* runs to a point in foul territory halfway between third and home and then backs up the throw as the play develops.

c. The *catcher* covers home and directs the cut-off man to cut off the throw, relay it or let it come on through.

d. The *first baseman* watches to see that the runner touches the bag. With a runner already on first, he immediately takes the cut-off position in front of home and in line with the throw. If not, he trails the batter-runner down to second and looks for a possible pickoff there. If the runner goes on to third, he breaks in to his cut-off position in case of a play at the plate.

e. The *second baseman* covers second until he sees that the batter has a sure double. Then, he goes out and lines up as the backup man about 25 feet behind the shortstop. If the outfielder's throw to the shortstop is accurate, he tells the shortstop where to throw. If the throw is not on target, the second baseman yells "let it go" and he makes the throw himself.

f. The *third baseman* covers third.

g. The *shortstop* takes the relay position in line with the ball and home plate and listens for the second baseman's directions on where to make the throw. If the ball is off target and the second baseman shouts "let it go," he lets the ball go through to the second baseman to make the relay.

h. The *leftfielder* fields the ball and throws to the cut-off man or backs up the centerfielder if he fields the ball.

i. The *centerfielder* fields the ball and throws to the cut-off man or backs up the leftfielder if he fields the ball.

j. The *rightfielder* backs up a possible throw to second base.

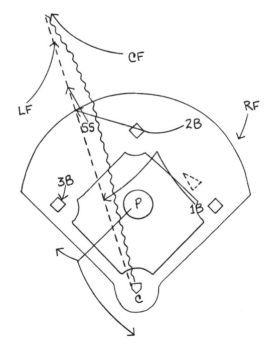

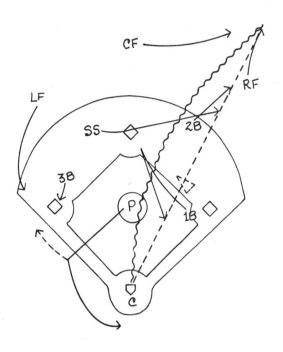

9. Runner on first or no baserunners, extra-base hit to right or right-center:

a. Defensive objective: possibly prevent the runner on first from scoring or the batter from going to third or home.

b. The *pitcher* runs to a point in foul territory halfway between third and home, then backs up the throw as the play develops.

c. The *catcher* covers home and directs the cut-off man to cut off the throw, relay it or let it come on through.

d. The *first baseman* watches to see that the runner touches the bag. With a runner already on first, he immediately takes the cut-off position in front of home and in line with the throw. If not, he trails the batter-runner down to second in case of a pickoff there. If the runner goes on to third, he breaks in to his cut-off position in case of a play at the plate.

e. The *second baseman* takes the relay position in line with the ball and home plate and listens for the shortstop's directions on where to make the throw. If the ball is off target and the shortstop shouts "let it go," he lets it go through to the shortstop so he can make the throw.

f. The *third baseman* covers third.

g. The *shortstop* covers second until he secs that the batter has a sure double. Then, he goes out and lines up as the backup man about 25 feet behind the second baseman. If the outfielder's throw is accurate, he tells the second baseman where to throw. If the throw is not on target, he tells the second baseman to "let it go" and he makes the throw himself.

h. The *leftfielder* backs up a possible throw to second base.

i. The *centerfielder* fields the ball and throws to the cut-off man or backs up the leftfielder if he fields the ball.

j. The *rightfielder* fields the ball and throws to the cut-off man or backs up the centerfielder if he fields the ball.

10. Runner on first or no baserunners, extra-base hit to the right-field corner:

a. Defensive objective: possibly prevent the runner on first from scoring or the batter from going to third or home.

b. The *pitcher* runs to a point in foul territory halfway between third and home and then backs up the throw as the play develops.

c. The *catcher* covers home and directs the cut-off man to cut off the throw, relay it or let it come on through.

d. The *first baseman* checks to make sure the runner touches the bag and then breaks in to take the cut-off position in front of home plate.

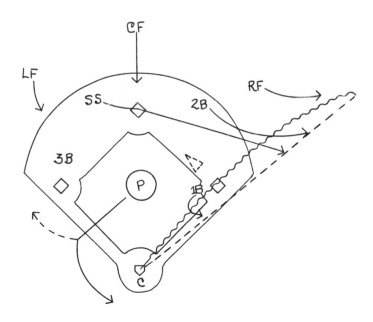

e. The *second baseman* takes the relay position on the rightfield line and listens for the shortstop's directions on where to throw.

f. The *third baseman* covers third and lines up the shortstop with the ball and third. He then instructs the shortstop to either cut it off or let it come on through if the throw is made to third base.

g. The *shortstop* covers second base until he sees that the batter has a sure double. He then drifts into the cut-off position in line with third. It is the shortstop's responsibility to tell the second baseman where to throw the ball.

h. The *leftfielder* backs up a possible throw to second.

i. The *centerfielder* covers second base in case of a pickoff play there.

j. The *rightfielder* fields the ball and throws to the second baseman in the relay position.

It should be noted that many teams do not assign their cut-off responsibilities in the same manner that we have described on these pages. Particularly with younger athletes, coaches have found that their cut-off man is more likely to be where he is supposed to be if the same infielder handles that responsibility on all throws into the plate. For example, some teams assign the first baseman to the cut-off responsibility on every play as opposed to having him share the responsibility with the third baseman. Little League coaches will often give their pitchers the cut-off assignment. Of course, at that level the pitcher is likely to be the team's best player. Why not make the most of his ability?

18

Defensive Plays

There are a number of ways in which the defensive team can go on the offensive, so to speak, and lure its opponent into a trap. Preplanned plays on defense are limited to various kinds of pickoff plays. They can be initiated by the defensive team once the situation for a particular play presents itself.

The extent to which a team might utilize pickoff plays varies somewhat depending on the coach or manager's philosophy. Alvin Dark, former manager of the Giants and A's and now the manager of the Cleveland Indians, claims that pickoff plays are not worth the time that must be spent to perfect them. Dark's philosophy is shared by a number of other major league managers but not all of them. Generally speaking, however, plays of this sort do tend to be more effective at the high school level and below. I have seen more than one team bail itself out of a potentially disastrous inning by executing an unexpected pickoff play.

The plays presented here repesent just a few of the many different plays that teams have used successfully.

1. Runner on first base, sacrifice situation, catcher to first-base pickoff:

    a. Defensive strategy: anticipating that the batter is sacrificing, lure the baserunner into leaning toward second to give the catcher an opportunity to pick him off first.

    b. The righthanded *pitcher* throws a curveball pitch-out and the lefthander a fastball. In either case, the pitch must be well outside the strike zone. If a rundown play develops, the pitcher covers first base.

c. The *catcher* signals for the pitch-out, then for the pickoff play. He then receives the pitch and makes the quick throw to first if he has a good chance of getting the runner.

d. The *first baseman* acknowledges the catcher's signal from his ⚹4 position on the bag. As the pitcher starts to throw home, the first baseman breaks off the bag toward home as he would to field a bunt. On approximately his fourth step, he pivots quickly and returns to the bag and takes the catcher's throw.

e. The *second baseman* should anticipate a rundown and move up to the baseline as the throw is made by the catcher to first base.

f. The *rightfielder* must be alert for the pitch-out signal and break in behind first base to back up the play.

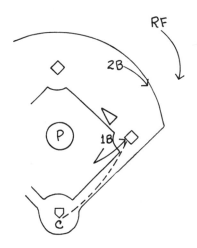

2. Runner on second base, pitcher to shortstop pickoff:

a. Defensive strategy: the shortstop attempts to get between the runner and second base to take the pitcher's throw for the pickoff.

b. The *pitcher* takes the pickoff signal from the shortstop. He then takes his stretch looking toward home, then looks back to second. When he sees "daylight" between the runner and the shortstop he pivots and throws to second base. The throw should be aimed at the third-base side of the bag and about knee high. The pitcher should not throw if he has no play on the runner.

c. The *second baseman* should disregard the runner to lure him into taking a bigger lead. When the pitcher wheels around to throw, the second baseman should back up second base.

d. The *third baseman* should look for a rundown play to develop.

e. The *shortstop* sets up the play on previous pitches by allowing the runner to take longer and longer leads. He signals for the play and looks for the pitcher's return signal. As the pitcher takes his stretch, looks home and then toward second, the shortstop breaks over to take the throw.

f. The *centerfielder* must be alert for the pickoff signal and be ready to back up second base.

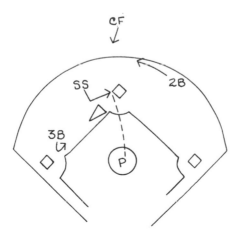

3. Runner on second base or first base and second, pitcher to second baseman pickoff:

a. Defensive strategy: the second baseman covers the bag for the pickoff as the runner starts to regain his lead following a fake pickoff by the shortstop.

b. The *pitcher* takes the pickoff signal from the shortstop and gives the return signal. He comes to his set position looking at home plate, then looks back to second base as the shortstop breaks in behind the runner. He then looks home again and pivots and throws to second when the *catcher drops his target*. He should not throw to second unless he has a play there.

c. The *catcher* takes his regular receiving position but drops his glove rather abruptly when he sees "daylight" between the runner and the shortstop.

d. The *second baseman* takes the signal from the shortstop and acknowledges it. He ignores the runner on previous pitches to set up the play. He breaks over to cover second when he sees that the shortstop is directly in front of the runner as he returns to his position.

e. The *third baseman* remains alert for a possible rundown.

f. The *shortstop* relays the pickoff signal before the pitcher takes his stretch. As the pitcher comes set, he breaks in to the bag and then returns to his position by running in *front* of the runner.

g. The *centerfielder* looks for the signal and is alert to back up second base as the throw is made.

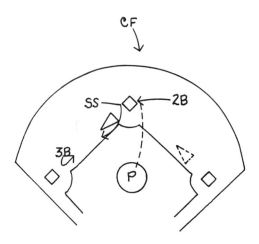

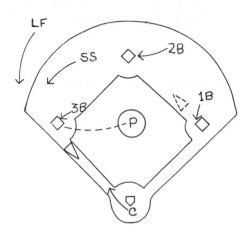

4. Runner on third base or first base and third, pitcher to third baseman pickoff:

a. The *defensive strategy* on this play calls for the righthanded pitcher to use the same advantage in throwing to third as the lefthander does in moving to first.

b. The *pitcher* takes the signal from the third baseman and goes into his stretch watching the runner on first or the runner on third. He looks home abruptly, then quickly throws to third using a motion much like the lefthander would to first (see Chapter 10).

c. The *third baseman* would normally be in his ⚡3 position for this play. He gives the pickoff signal and waits for the pitcher to return it. He then watches the pitcher take his stretch. The instant the pitcher looks to the plate the third baseman breaks back to the bag and takes the throw. With a runner also on first base, he must be alert for a play at second if that runner attempts to advance on the pickoff.

d. The *leftfielder* must be aware that the pickoff is on and break in to back up third base on the play.

General Comments Regarding Pickoff Plays

As we mentioned before, the plays we have described here represent only a few of the many pickoff plays that have been used successfully. We have confined our presentation to these because they are relatively easy to execute.

One of the more popular plays which we did not make mention

of has the second baseman sneaking over behind the runner to take the throw at first in a sacrifice situation. The first baseman charges in to field the bunt to lure the runner farther off the bag.

Lou Boudreau and Bob Feller used to make the *count* play at second base work for them in many a tight situation. Both players would begin counting on a prearranged signal. Boudreau (the shortstop) would break for second on the count of two and Feller (the pitcher) would pivot to throw on the count of three. The play was effective because Feller was able to ignore the runner on second right up until he turned to throw.

These and other pickoff plays can be effective, but many coaches question their worth because of the practice time it takes to perfect them. To be executed correctly and safely, the play must be practiced many times before it should be used in game competition. The players involved must learn to act out their parts, and the timing must be exact. Otherwise, the play becomes more of a liability than a help.

Our feeling is that pickoff plays should be used but only to the extent that they are needed. A team that has weak pitching, for example, might have more justification for spending practice time on pickoff plays than would a team that has an exceptional mound staff. Why take a chance on throwing the ball away if the pitcher has a good chance of striking out the batter?

19

Communication on Defense

Effective communication is equally as important on defense as it is on offense. Nine defensive players are spread out over a large area yet each must be aware of the intentions of the other.

Defensive instructions are communicated visually and/or verbally. They may originate from the bench or from specific players on the field. The signals that will be presented here represent the *kinds* of signals that most teams use. However, almost any signal will be effective as long as every player on the team can easily interpret its meaning.

Visual Signals

1. Signals that originate from the bench:

a. The coach or manager of the team will want to be able to adjust the *individual position* of his players:

1) He can move a player back by using a one-arm motion with the palm facing the player.

2) He can bring a player in by using a one-arm motion with the back of the hand facing the player.

3) He can move a player to the right or left by pointing in that direction.

b. The coach or manager may also want to set his *infield alignment* for a particular situation:

1) He can tell his infield that he wants them to play in for a

play at the plate by holding both arms up with the back of the hands toward the field.

2) He can tell his infield that he wants them to play back for the runner at first by holding both arms up with the palms of the hands facing the field.

3) He can tell his infield to play at double-play depth by crossing both arms in front of him.

4) He can tell one side of the infield to play back and the other in by holding one arm in the air with the palm away and the other with the palm toward him.

c. The coach or manager can tell his pitcher and catcher to give a batter an *intentional pass* by simply pointing to first base.

d. He can warn a particular player to *hold a runner on a base* by holding up a clenched fist.

e. He can indicate to a player to put on a *pickoff play* by picking at his shirt.

2. Signals that originate with the pitcher:

a. The pitcher must be able to tell his catcher that he wants him to *change the pitch signal*. Pitchers will normally use one of the following to shake off their catcher's signal:

1) Simply shake the head.

2) Clench the glove several times.

3. Signals that originate with the catcher:

a. Under normal conditions, with no runners on second base, the catcher will use the following as *pitch signals:*

1) Fastball—one finger.

2) Curve—two fingers.

3) Change-up—three fingers.

4) Any other pitch—four fingers.

b. With a *runner on second base,* the same signals can be used but they must be disguised somewhat. (I will never forget one game when we were able to capitalize on our opponent's failure to disguise their pitch signals. We had the bases loaded and the runner on second relayed the signal back to the batter, our shortstop, who hadn't gotten an extra-base hit all season. He "muscled up" on the pitch and knocked it out of the park for a grand-slam home run!) The catcher will give a series of three-digit signals. One signal will be on and the other two will be dummy signals. The signal that will be "on" during a particular game is decided upon by the team beforehand. Therefore, if the catcher had announced before the game that the second signal would be the live signal, a series consisting of one finger, one finger again, then three fingers, would be calling for the pitcher to throw his fastball.

c. The catcher may also want to signal for the *location* of a particular pitch. This signal normally follows the signal for the type of pitch and should always be given when a fastball has been called for. (Change-of-speed pitches are almost always thrown down and away.)

1) Low and outside—palm down and away from batter.
2) Low and inside—palm down and toward batter.
3) High and outside—palm up and away from batter.
4) High and inside—palm up and toward batter.

d. The catcher must also be able to signal for a *pitchout*. Two of the more common pitch-out signals are:

1) Extending a clenched fist over the right knee.

2) Flashing the pitch signal twice. For example, if the catcher wants a fastball pitch-out, he simply flashes one finger twice in quick succession. For a curveball pitch-out, he would do the same using two fingers.

e. The catcher must also indicate the kind of defense to be used in a double-steal situation (see defense for regular double steal). As soon as a first and third situation develops, the catcher may use one of the following signals to tell his teammates what he plans to do if the opposition attempts a regular double steal:

1) Grabbing the front of the face mask means that he will be throwing the ball through to second base.

2) Crossing the chest protector with the throwing hand means that he will fake a throw to second and attempt a pickoff at third.

3) Rubbing the right hand down the right thigh means that he will throw the ball back to the pitcher.

f. The catcher may also want to signal an infielder that he wants to throw to a particular base to attempt a *pickoff*. Any number of signals can be used for this, but here are some which have been used effectively:

1) To signal for a pickoff attempt at first base, the catcher can simply pick up some dirt with his throwing hand and toss it in that direction.

2) To signal for a pickoff attempt at second base, he can press his glove to the ground between his legs.

3) To signal for a pickoff attempt at third base, he can press his glove to the ground outside his left heel.

4. Signals that originate from an infielder:

a. Some teams like to have the second baseman and shortstop relay the *pitch signal* to the outfielders to aid them in getting a jump on the ball:

1) The fastball signal can be relayed by placing the right hand behind the back, with the palm of the hand pointing down.

2) A curve or change-of-speed pitch can be relayed with the palm of the hand parallel with the belt.

3) A pitchout can be relayed using a clenched fist.

b. The shortstop is normally responsible for designating who will be *covering second base* on a double-play ball back to the pitcher or an attempt to steal second base:

1) He can indicate that the second baseman is covering the bag by opening the glove so the thumb is pointing toward second.
2) He can indicate that he will be covering the bag by showing the pitcher the back of the glove (so the thumb is pointing to him).

c. The second baseman should return the base-covering signal by:

1) Hiding the face with the glove and opening his mouth if the shortstop is covering (as if he were mouthing the word "you").
2) Hiding the face with the glove and closing his mouth if he is covering (as if he were mouthing the word "me").

d. Each infielder will normally initiate the *pickoff play* for which he is primarily responsible. A few of the signals more commonly used for pickoff plays are:

1) The infielder takes his glove off.
2) The infielder picks at his pant leg.
3) The infielder may tug at his belt.

5. Signals that may originate from any player:

a. The number of outs:

1) Fist—no outs.
2) One finger—one out.
3) Two fingers (first and last fingers)—two outs.

b. A *return signal* to acknowledge the reception of a signal for a particular pickoff play:

1) Touch the cap.
2) Repeat the pickoff signal (such as taking the glove off).

Verbal Communication

1. A team should have an *alert* signal to bring a player's attention to the fact that a visual signal is being given. For example, the second baseman may want to give the pitcher the pickoff signal but is unable to get the pitcher to look his way so the visual pickoff

signal can be relayed. Some of the "alert" signals that have been used effectively are:

a. Call the player by his last name, rather than his first name.

b. Or, a team may decide to use a somewhat "catching" phrase such as:

1) "Shake it up."
2) "Get the big one."
3) "Take a look."

2. Verbal communication is vitally important when more than one player is in a position to make a particular play. The players involved must make the appropriate call *loud* and *clear* and in some instances, repeat it several times:

a. On a fly ball or ground ball between two or more players, the player in position to make the play should shout "mine."

b. If another player has a better angle on the play and wants to call the other(s) off, he shouts "mine" too, but repeats the call several times.

c. Once it becomes obvious that a particular player will make the play, and that player has already called for the ball, the other players in the area should call out the fielder's last name.

d. It is important that a player not call for the ball until he is certain that he can make the play.

3. A defensive team must also understand each other on relay and cut-off plays:

a. The player covering the base to which a throw is being made will normally shout:

1) "cut, no play" if he wants the cut-off man to intercept the throw and hold it.

2) "cut, first base" (second base, third base or home) if he wants the cut-off man to cut it off and relay it to a particular base.

3) "let it go" or "leave it" if he wants the ball to come on through. Some teams will have the receiving player remain quiet if he wants the cut-off man to let the ball go through.

20

Training and Conditioning

Philosophy

It is in this vital area of training and conditioning that most baseball players lag well behind athletes in other sports. Although Rogers Hornsby used to refuse to attend moving pictures because he was afraid they would tire his eyes, his case is certainly the exception rather than the rule among baseball players. There appears to be a prevailing attitude among ballplayers that they can attain a satisfactory state of physical condition by simply going out and playing the game. In fact, it is not unusual to find a veteran professional player sporting a "pot belly" from spring training right on through the regular season.

Actually, there are at least five good reasons why the baseball player should be as much concerned about his physical readiness to play as any other athlete:

1. If there are sports in which the athlete can play himself into shape, baseball is certainly not one of them. For the most part, baseball calls for short bursts of physical exertion and by its nature does little to prepare the athlete for more exhausting situations. Yet, those exhausting situations will occur for some players in most ball games. A pitcher may find himself facing the toughest part of his opponent's batting order following an inning in which he spent most of his time running the bases. Or, another player may spend a busy day in the field and then have to leg-out a triple late in the game. Only the extremely well-conditioned athlete will have the stamina to perform at his best when these situations arise.

2. The well-conditioned athlete is less susceptible to injuries. It stands to reason that the tired player will have slower reactions and will be less able to co-ordinate the movements of his body. The hitter who literally drags himself up to the plate late in the game is not only less likely to hit the ball but also more likely to get hit by a wild pitch. Minor injuries such as muscle pulls and joint sprains are also more likely to occur if the athlete is not properly conditioned.

3. Only the well-conditioned athlete will have the vitality to perform every play to the limit of his ability. The player who is in shape "feels" like hustling. He is eager to back up plays and perform other essential but often neglected responsibilities simply because they do not tire him. He finds that the only time he really has to pace himself is between innings when he is sitting on the bench.

4. A well-planned and conscientiously followed conditioning program can help an athlete improve upon his natural abilities. The degree to which a boy is able to develop baseball skills is influenced by his strength, speed, reaction time, agility, flexibility and, to some extent, endurance. A weakness in any of these areas may prove to be a real handicap to an aspiring ballplayer. A sound conditioning program could improve that weakness. The slow runner may not become a fast runner but he may become a better runner.

5. Conditioning is becoming more and more important to all athletes as our manner of living becomes increasingly sedentary. The young athlete of the 1920s did not have to resort to extensive conditioning programs simply because his daily chores were enough to keep him in shape. Today's athlete has few duties of a physical nature and rarely walks anywhere. Yet the physical requirements of the game are the same. The modern ballplayer must make a special effort to attain the same level of fitness that was almost a by-product of living forty years ago.

Off-Season Training

The fall and winter months provide the dedicated player with an opportunity to improve any weakness he may have in his basic athletic abilities. Although the weakness will certainly vary with the individual, there appears to be one area in which most of today's athletes have the greatest need. Physical fitness test scores indicate that American boys are lacking in upper body strength.

This fact should be particularly disconcerting for baseball players. Almost every baseball skill is performed to some extent with the muscles of the upper body. The ability to hit with authority and throw effectively cannot be developed without strength. For this reason, most young players should seriously consider weight training as an off-season conditioning program. Research has failed to support the claim of many old-timers that weight training is harmful for baseball players because it leads to muscle-boundness. In fact, numerous studies have shown that there is a definite improvement in some baseball skills when a player's strength is significantly increased.

Of course, like anything else, weight training can be harmful if it is not done properly. (I made the mistake of recommending weight training to one particularly dedicated athlete of mine, and he became so infatuated with the muscles he was building that he gave up baseball and became a competitive weight lifter.) There are a few important principles that an athlete should completely understand before he undertakes a program in weight training:

1. Most authorities agree that weight training should be confined to the off-season. In the warmer climates where winter baseball is played, a boy should not be lifting weights at the same time that he is playing competitive baseball.

2. Weight training should not be looked upon as a cure-all for every baseball weakness. Weight training can improve strength and, to some extent, total body fitness, but these attributes alone will not make a boy a good baseball player. For this reason, it is advisable that the athlete use it in conjunction with other phases of training.

3. Basically, the athlete should strive to develop overall muscular strength and fitness. However, in selecting his exercise routine, he should also consider any specific muscular weaknesses he may have and the needs of his particular position.

4. The development of strength requires a high-resistance, low-repetition system. That is, the athlete's objective is to gradually increase the amount of weight he can lift on each exercise rather than the number of repetitions he is able to perform.

5. An on again-off again weight-training program will be of little or no value. The athlete who does not have the self-discipline to stay with a regular program will be wasting his time.

Procedure

1. The athlete sets up an every-other-day workout schedule. The entire training period should extend over a minimum of three months if anything is to be accomplished.

2. Prior to beginning each workout, the athlete should go through a series of warm-up exercises (see latter part of this chapter).

3. For the first few days the weight-lifting exercise should be done with a weight that can be lifted 12 to 15 times without undue strain. After a week, the transition should be made to the high-resistance, low-repetition system.

4. Normally, the athlete will set out to complete three sets of each exercise by going through his selected routine three times.

    a. For the first 4 to 6 weeks he should attempt to lift the same weight 10 times on the first set, 8 times on the second set, and 6 times on the third set.

    b. Later on he may choose to do 10 repetitions of each exercise on all three sets.

5. Once the athlete finds that he is able to perform an exercise more than the prescribed number of times (10–8–6), then additional weight should be added. On a bar bell exercise, add on 5 pounds at each end of the bar and on a dumbbell exercise, add on 2½ pounds.

6. At the end of each week, the amount of weight lifted on the third set should be recorded.

7. For maximum benefit, the following additional rules should be observed:

    a. A day's workout should be confined to as short a period of time as possible. The athlete should not take extended rests between exercise.

    b. The lifter should be inhaling when he is executing the exercise.

    c. The athlete should be careful to always use a correct lifting position to avoid injuries.

Suggested Exercises

The following weight-lifting exercises should be adequate for most baseball players. Since flexibility cannot be sacrificed for strength, the list includes a minimum of bulk-building exercises. The extremely weak boy may want to add more exercises to his workout program. The naturally muscular boy may want to use only a few of these exercises or confine his workout to just one or two sets of each exercise.

EXERCISE	STARTING POSITION	ACTION
1. Pullover	Back lying with arms extended overhead; bar bell grasped with both hands shoulder-width apart; bar on floor behind head.	a. Keeping arms straight, raise bar to vertical position. b. Maintain control of weight and lower to starting position.
2. Sit-up	Back lying; feet shoulder-width apart; knees flexed; feet held down by partner; disk weights or dumbbell held behind head.	a. Curl trunk upward and forward and touch left knee with right elbow. b. Return to starting position. c. Repeat again, touching right knee with left elbow.
3. Bench Press	Back lying on low bench; legs spread, lower legs flexed; feet planted firmly on floor; arms extended upward and vertical to floor; bar bell is handed to performer by partner; performer's hands spread well apart.	a. Lower bar until it touches chest. b. Extend arms and push bar upward to starting position.
4. Wrist Curl	Sitting in chair; feet on floor and shoulder-width apart; trunk leaning forward; back of forearms resting against front of thighs; wrists extended	a. Raise bar upward and backward as far as possible with a curling motion; the forearm remaining in contact with the thigh throughout.

EXERCISE	STARTING POSITION	ACTION
	beyond knees; bar bell grasped with reverse grip (palms up).	*b.* Lower bar back to starting position or lower if possible.
5. Lateral Raise	Standing; feet shoulder-width apart; trunk bent forward 90 degrees at the waist; arms extended downward; hands grasping dumbbells with palms facing inward.	*a.* Keeping arms straight raise dumbbells sideward to a position slightly higher than the shoulders. *b.* Return to starting position. *c.* Movement should be confined to the arms; there should be no upward movement of the body.

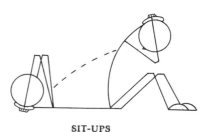

PULLOVER

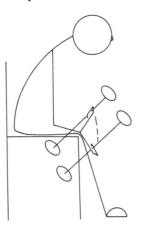

SIT-UPS

WRIST CURL

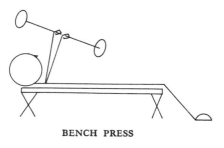

BENCH PRESS

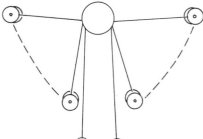

LATERAL RAISE

EXERCISE	STARTING POSITION	ACTION
6. Jump Squats	Standing; feet in striding position, the right foot well ahead of the left; arms extending down to either side; dumbbells in hand.	*a.* Reverse position of feet with a jumping action, allowing no more than a 45 degree bend at the knees.
7. Tricep	Standing; feet apart; bar bell positioned across the back of the neck and shoulders; the elbows pointing directly upward.	*a.* Press the bar to a full overhead extension, keeping the head slightly forward to avoid contact with the bar. *b.* Return to starting position.
8. Wrist Adductor	Standing; holding dumbbell (loaded on one end only) with one hand opposite the weighted end; the loaded end of the dumbbell pointing to the rear.	*a.* Allow the dumbbell to drop slowly in an arc until it points to the floor. *b.* Return it slowly to the original position. *c.* Repeat desired number of repetitions, then exercise opposite wrist.
9. Wrist Roll	Using a short piece of broom handle attached to about 5 feet of rope with a weight on the other end. Stand with the arms extended out in front, the hands gripping the broom handle at shoulder level, weight hanging to the floor.	*a.* Begin rolling the handle, winding the rope onto it and bringing the weight up to shoulder height. *b.* Then, unwind the rope and return the weight to the floor.

Immediately following each weight-lifting session the athlete should hang from a horizontal bar for 30 to 45 seconds to help reduce any tightening that may result from the exercises.

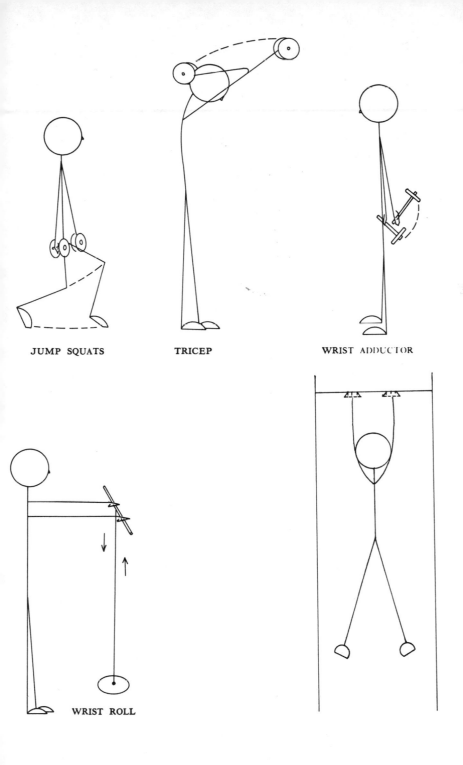

JUMP SQUATS   TRICEP   WRIST ADDUCTOR

WRIST ROLL

Related Sports

On weight-lifting days the athlete should also include one of the following sports activities in his workout schedule. These activities will contribute to total body fitness and will provide some enjoyment to the off-season program:

1. Handball	3. Basketball
2. Badminton	4. Squash

Skill Development

On days when the player is not scheduled to lift weights he should make an effort to improve his baseball skills. Of course, the extent to which this can be done will depend upon the weather, space and the availability of extra players. The activities presented here represent just a few of the low-organizational drills that can be used under very limited conditions. An imaginative athlete could devise additional drills depending on his own particular needs. For example, a friend of mine, a former infielder, said he spent most of his free time during the winter bouncing a baseball against his basement wall to improve his ability to field ground balls.

1. Bat Drill:
   a. The player assumes his regular batting stance.
   b. Using a bat with 8 to 10 ounces of lead in the end, he takes 10 swings holding the bat with only the top hand; 10 swings holding the bat with only the bottom hand; and finally, 10 swings holding the bat with both hands.
   c. The number of repetitions is gradually increased until he is swinging the bat from 75 to 100 times in all.
   d. If it is done properly, this drill will not only build arm and wrist strength but also improve batting fundamentals.

2. Batting Tee:
   a. A batting tee is constructed by inserting a short piece of hose over a broom handle and sticking the other end of the broom handle in a bucket of sand.
   b. A tennis ball or baseball is placed on the hose, and the batter assumes his batting stance alongside the tee.

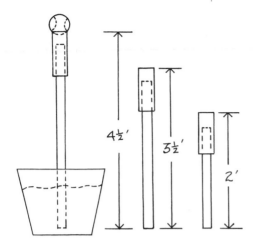

c. He then hits the ball off the tee into a rug or blanket hanging over a clothes line or a backstop or cyclone fence.

d. By changing his position in relation to the tee and by using broom sticks of different lengths, the player can work on hitting pitches in different areas of the strike zone.

3. Pick-ups:

a. Two players face each other about 10 feet apart.

b. One of them rolls the ball to one side and then to the other as his partner moves in a semicircle, picking up the ball and flipping it back underhand to the feeder.

c. As soon as one player has retrieved the ball 25 times, he becomes the feeder. The drill may be repeated as many as 4 times.

d. The participants may or may not use gloves.

e. This drill is of value as a conditioner and for developing fielding skills.

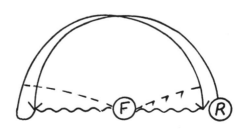

4. Two-man Pepper:

   a. Two players face each other about 15 to 20 feet apart.

   b. One is the batter, the other the fielder. The fielder lobs the ball to the batter who chokes up on the bat and hits the ball easily back to the fielder.

   c. The hitter concentrates on watching the ball hit the bat and the fielder concentrates on his glove work.

   d. The drill can be given a competitive element by awarding the fielder 2 points if he catches the ball on the fly and 1 point if he catches the ball on the ground. They exchange places when the fielder accumulates 15 points. If the fielder errs on a reasonable chance, he must start over. If the batter misses a good pitch completely, he must give up his turn at bat.

   e. Inexperienced players may find it easier to use two or more fielders.

5. Blanket Drill:

   a. An individual player can work on his sliding skills by using this indoor drill.

   b. Depending on their thickness, two to three blankets are folded in a 4-foot square. The blankets are then placed on a hardwood floor.

   c. The athlete can then practice sliding by jumping onto the blankets.

6. Fence Drill:

   a. Two players face each other about 15 feet apart. One is the batter the other is the feeder.

   b. The feeder flips the ball underhand to the batter who hits the ball into a high cyclone fence or backstop.

   c. The feeder should move the ball up and down to give the batter practice hitting pitches in different locations of the strike zone.

Preseason Training

As soon as regular team practices begin the player should discontinue his weight-training workouts. From this point on he must concentrate more on learning the skills of the game in preparation for actual competition.

Although conditioning should remain a primary concern, coaches

often find that they just do not have enough practice time available to do an adequate job of conditioning their squad and still teach the fundamentals. When this is the case conditioning becomes the responsibility of the individual player.

At this stage of the season training should include a great deal of running and at least twenty minutes of calisthenics a day. The following calisthenics are recommended for baseball players:

EXERCISE	STARTING POSITION	ACTION
1. Jumping Jack	Standing; feet together; arms at side.	*a.* Bring arms overhead and spread legs apart. *b.* Return to starting position.

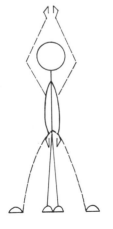

JUMPING JACK

EXERCISE	STARTING POSITION	ACTION
2. Toe Toucher	Standing; right leg crossed over to the left of the left leg.	*a.* Bend over at the waist and touch the ground in front of the feet 3–4 times. *b.* Return to starting position and perform the desired number of repetitions. *c.* Then cross the right leg over in front of the left and repeat the exercise.
3. Windup	Standing with feet about shoulder-width apart; right hand on hip, left hand at side.	*a.* Circle left arm, gradually increasing speed. *b.* Repeat the desired number of times and then do the same with the right arm.
4. Hill Climber	Regular push-up position except with right leg flexed at the knee and well up under the body.	*a.* Alternate leg positions. *b.* For maximum benefit, the stride should be long and gradually increased in speed.
5. Windmill	Standing; legs well apart; hands extended to either side.	*a.* Without bending the knees, touch the right toe with the left hand. b. Return to starting position. *c.* Then touch the left toe with the right hand.
6. Sit-up	Lying on back; knees flexed; hands clenched behind the head.	*a.* Sit up, touching right elbow to left knee. *b.* Return to starting position. *c.* Repeat, touching left elbow to right knee.

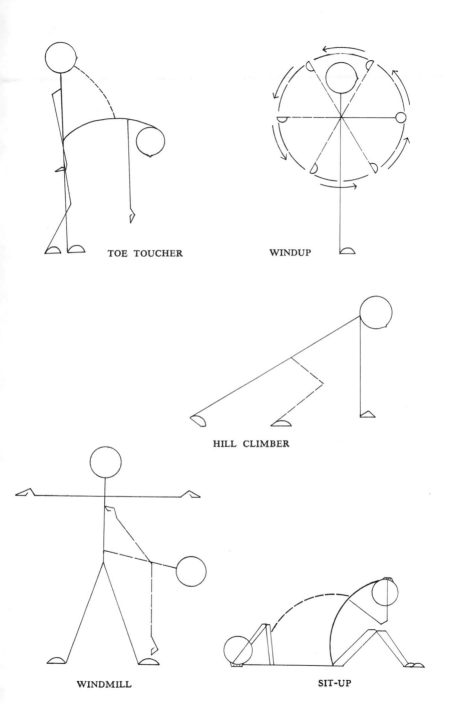

TOE TOUCHER

WINDUP

HILL CLIMBER

WINDMILL

SIT-UP

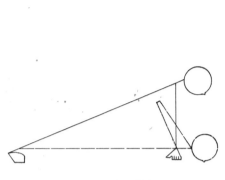

PUSH-UP   SHOULDER ROLL

EXERCISE	STARTING POSITION	ACTION
7. Push-up	Front; facing floor, body supported by extended fingers and arms; back straight.	*a.* Bend arms until the body is almost touching the ground. *b.* Return to starting position.
8. Shoulder Roll	Standing; arms extended to either side at shoulder level.	*a.* Rotate arms in a tight circle, gradually increasing the arc. *b.* Repeat until the arms become extremely heavy. *c.* Reverse directions, gradually increasing the arc again.
9. Kick-up	Standing; feet apart; arms at the sides	*a.* Kick right leg up to meet left hand as right hand swings backward. *b.* Repeat 10 times, then kick left leg up to meet right hand as the left hand swings backward.

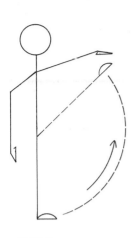

KICK-UP

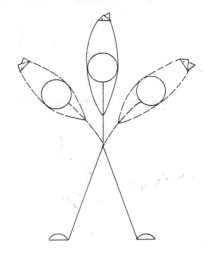

BODY BENDER

EXERCISE	STARTING POSITION	ACTION
10. Body Bender	Standing; feet shoulder-width apart; arms up over the head with the fingers interlocked and palms facing upward.	*a.* Keeping the knees straight, bend to the left. *b.* Return to starting position. *c.* Then bend to the right and return to starting position.

In-Season Training

Once the competitive season is underway, training becomes almost entirely a matter of keeping in shape and avoiding injuries. A player can usually keep himself in good playing condition by spending from five to ten minutes a day on calisthenics and continuing with a fairly vigorous running schedule.

As for avoiding injuries, there are some definite precautions which every baseball player should consider carefully:

1. He should warm up thoroughly before every practice or game. His warm-up routine should include stretching exercises, jogging and throwing. The time spent on each of these will depend on the individual player and the weather conditions.

2. He should learn to slide properly before competing and should never change his mind once he has started to slide.

3. If possible, he should wear a protective helmet on the bases as well as at the plate. In fact, wearing a helmet in the field during practice session is an extremely good idea.

4. He should never turn his back to a batter who is hitting at the plate (during batting practice).

5. He should warn another player who is attempting to field a ball near a fence or dugout.

6. As the on-deck hitter, he should never station himself in a position where he could be hit by a foul ball or a bat that slips out of the batter's hands.

7. During practice, he should never throw a ball to a teammate unless he is certain that player is ready to receive the ball.

8. He should not stand in front of a base to take a throw when a runner is sliding into the bag.

9. He should always call for a fly ball he is attempting to catch, whether it be in practice or game competition.

10. He should always wear clothes appropriate for the weather. For example, in cool weather, the undershirt should cover the elbow.

11. If he is a pitcher, catcher or an infielder, he should wear a cup to protect the groin area.

12. If he wears glasses, he should be sure that the lenses are unbreakable.

13. He should always wear some sort of sliding pads.

Treating Injuries

Some injuries are inevitable, and every player should know how to treat the minor ones when they do occur:

1. Sprained ankle, wrist or finger:

   a. Immediately wrap the injured area with a pressure bandage (elastic).

   b. Apply ice packs regularly for the first twenty-four hours, then switch to heat.

   c. Tape for protection when normal movements are resumed.

   d. Have the injury X-rayed if there is any chance of breakage.

2. Slide burns:

a. Shave the area surrounding the wound and clean it thoroughly with soap and water.

b. Coat the wound with a disinfectant and then with benzoin.

c. Apply a good ointment (zinc oxide) to a gauze pad and cover the wound with it.

d. Add more gauze pads for protection; change dressing daily.

3. Spike wounds:

a. Once the bleeding has been stopped, treat this type of wound in the same manner as a slide burn.

b. Consult a physician if stitches are needed and for a possible tetanus shot.

4. Charlie horse or muscle bruise:

a. Apply ice packs for the first twenty-four hours, then heat.

b. Massage the injured area slightly.

c. Protect the wound from further injury with a sponge "doughnut."

5. Sore arm:

a. Stop throwing activities immediately.

b. Apply heat by:

1) Holding it under a hot shower.

2) Applying a heat pack of analgesic balm covered with cotton and wrapped with an elastic bandage.

c. Persistent sore arms, particularly in the area of the elbow, should be referred to a physician.

6. Pulled muscle:

a. Wrap injury with tape, working from the bottom up.

b. Exercise injured area gradually until full movement can be resumed.

7. Blisters:

a. Finger blisters:

1) Pitchers should try to avoid blood blisters on the index finger by keeping their fingernails clipped and coating the area daily with tuf-skin (benzoin).

2) If a blood blister does form, it should be drained with a sterilized needle.

3) The wound should then be left open and sprayed regularly with benzoin to toughen the skin.

b. Foot blisters:

1) If unopened, simply cover the area with a bandage.

2) If open, cleanse thoroughly with a disinfectant and apply ointment and compress.

21

A Coaching Philosophy

Men find themselves coaching baseball under a variety of circumstances. There are the high school and college coaches who represent the "professionals" in the field. These people are hired by their communities to coach their teams and are usually well-trained to perform the task. But equally important in the player's development are the thousands of youth league coaches who use their own spare time to make a vital contribution to the game.

Regardless of whether he is a paid teacher or a volunteer worker, a coach's approach to his job should be basically the same. To be sure, he should regard baseball as an enjoyable recreational activity, but he should also realize that he is the key person in what can be a great learning experience for his players. His most important contribution will be in the skills he teaches and the character and qualities of citizenship that he encourages in the process. My club was competing in a practice game recently against a team coached by a man who had probably sent more boys to the big leagues than any other coach in the area. We won the game as a young pitcher of ours experienced one of his best days on the mound. The coach came over to congratulate me after the game, remarking that we were certainly the better team. He also said that my pitcher had been "telegraphing" his curveball throughout the game and that I might want to talk to him about it (he showed me how he was doing it) before the boy pitched again. I thanked him for the tip and asked him if he had given the information to his players during the ball game. He said he hadn't because he felt that his hitters would get their timing down faster if they did not know what pitch was coming. This coach has a reputation for being a great teacher of the game, and this incident illustrates one reason why he is held in such esteem. He likes to win, but he also wants his players to learn how to play the game. The coach who does not see his function as something of this sort needs to take a long hard look at his reasons for accepting the assignment.

Personal Qualities

Men have found success in coaching with vastly different personalities. Clearly, there is no *one* effective approach to coaching. As a general rule, a coach should be himself and should not pattern his behavior after another person who has been successful in the field. However, every good coach seems to possess certain qualities that the inexperienced coach would do well to develop within the limits of his own personality:

1. He has an overwhelming enthusiasm for the game and the part he plays in it. His players have the feeling that there just isn't anywhere he would rather be than out there on the field with them.

2. He has great confidence in his own coaching ability. He is not arrogant or conceited, but there is a certainty, almost boldness, that characterizes his decisions and actions.

3. He has a reputation for being a worker. He is almost constantly doing something or working with someone to make the whole situation just a little better. He is clearly willing to make the same personal sacrifices he expects from his team.

4. He is willing to be flexible in his relationship with his players. At times he may find it necessary to be hard, brutally frank, or even cruel toward an individual. On other occasions he may find that the player needs companionship, understanding and warmth.

5. He is extremely tough mentally. A coach is often the loneliest man in the world. Some of the decisions he must make are unpleasant, to say the least. Yet his job is not to try to please everyone but to do what is best for the individual on his team.

6. He has an ability to remain calm under pressure. The man who can accept a player's blunder or a poor decision by an of-

ficial, even when it occurs in a crucial situation, is better prepared mentally for the next important play. Disciplining players and debating umpires are part of his job, but the coach who has the poise to do this in a manner that shows respect for others will be more effective in the long run. A coaching friend of mine remarked that he still remembers being "dressed down" in front of everyone by his high school coach. He indicated that the experience had been enough to discourage him from ever wanting to do the same to one of his athletes, regardless of the circumstances.

7. He has the ability to be objective in his handling of game decisions. He makes every effort to resist being governed by his own or the fans' emotions.

8. He knows the game thoroughly and never passes up an opportunity to learn more. He is quite willing to accept a good suggestion from one of his players. He is not convinced that his way is always the right way.

9. He is a great competitor in his own right. Regardless of the circumstances, he never allows himself or any member of his squad to give up on a game until the last man is out.

10. He is able to see the real significance of daily happenings. He is capable of laughing, especially at his own mistakes. He is not a clown or an entertainer, but he is not afraid to let his players know that he is as human as they are.

Getting to Know the Players

A coach's relationship with his players represents the most important single element in coaching. He can know all there is to know about the game from a tactical standpoint, but if he is unable to communicate with the boys who play for him, his successes will be few indeed.

The degree to which a coach is able to establish rapport with his players is usually proportionate to his willingness to work for it. To begin with, he must make every effort to learn as much as possible about each of his players. The coach who is somewhat aware of the kinds of pressures a boy carries with him will be in a better position to deal with that boy's needs on the field. Here are some of the techniques that coaches have used to become better acquainted with their athletes:

1. Hold an individual conference with each boy at the beginning of the season. Discuss the boy's philosophy of baseball, his chances of making the team, his weaknesses and his strong points. Use this opportunity to make it clear to him that you would welcome his coming in and talking things over at any time during the season.

2. Make an effort to learn as much as possible about the boy's interests and activities other than baseball. In a school situation, check with teachers and counselors for information about a player's academic record.

3. Meet and talk with each boy's parents. (I talked with the mother of one boy and discovered that his recent indifference toward the game was probably due to his concern for his father who was about to undergo a serious operation. Needless to say, knowing this was crucial if I was going to be at all helpful to the boy, and yet he was not about to offer the information to me himself.) A coach may write or call the parents of his players and extend a personal invitation for them to attend a ball game. An even better and more revealing approach would be to arrange to visit each family in its own home.

4. During the season, take advantage of every possible opportunity to talk with a boy privately. If a player appears to be bothered by a personal problem, even if it does not apply to baseball, arrange a meeting with that boy and see if there is any way you can be of service to him.

5. Hold another conference with each boy at the end of the season. Discuss his success in relation to his capabilities and his plans for the future. Promise to try not to lose contact with a boy who has played his last season for you.

Team Morale

Baseball squads rarely achieve the degree of team spirit that is so characteristic of successful teams in other sports. The one-for-all-and-all-for-one attitude of a football team, for example, is seldom found among baseball players. This unfortunate situation exists for a number of reasons.

In the first place, baseball rules do not permit unlimited substitution, and no athlete likes to sit on the bench. A football or basketball coach can make spot substitutions and utilize boys with limited abilities in special situations. Their games are also controlled by a clock. When it becomes obvious that a game is won or lost, a coach can clear his bench and give his substitutes some playing time. A baseball coach really cannot be sure about the outcome of a game until the last man is out. The coach who wants to win will be reluctant to substitute unless he needs another player for a particular reason. He simply cannot afford to take his best players out of most ball games.

Another reason why morale is often low on baseball clubs is that players find it particularly hard to be objective about their own ability. There are so many skills by which a player's worth can be determined that a coach is often making an educated guess, at best, when he decides to play one athlete in front of another. The boy sitting on the bench sees his situation as being even more unjust if the athlete performing in his spot is playing anything but perfect baseball.

There is a third reason why baseball teams rarely establish much team spirit, and this reason is probably the one most responsible for the condition. For some unknown reason, baseball coaches just don't seem to care as much about developing a team atmosphere as do other coaches. Many baseball coaches become so wrapped up in teaching the skills of the game that they do little or nothing to promote *esprit de corps*.

It is our contention that team morale is vital to success in baseball, and it is an important part of the learning process. It is also our belief that a coach cannot expect morale to take care of itself. We have already discussed a couple of the inherent difficulties in achieving good morale on a baseball team. Therefore, baseball coaches in particular must work just that much harder to teach their players a concept of teamwork and respect for each other.

The following coaching principles have proven to be effective in developing a *team* atmosphere:

1. The key to good team spirit and hustle is based on one important element; namely, the fairness of the coach.

    a. It must be imprinted on the mind of every player that no one player is indispensable and that there is no such thing as a one-man team.

    b. Even the lowliest substitute should be made to feel that

THE COMPLETE BASEBALL PLAY BOOK

his role, small though it may be, is essential to the overall success of the team.

c. It is the coach's responsibility to make certain that the player who is producing is the one that plays. To rely on the strength of past performances and use a player who at present is incompetent, is unfair to another boy who is yearning to break into the line-up.

2. An atmosphere of togetherness is absolutely essential. A ball club should be encouraged to do everything as a group. They should associate with one another as much as possible when they are off the field; they should dress together in the locker room; above all, they should take the field together.

3. Short, carefully organized practice sessions are a must for squad morale. Baseball is notorious for long, drawn-out and boring practices. A short practice is more likely to leave a boy wanting to play some more. An extremely long and disorganized practice session is apt to drive a potentially good athlete right out of the game.

4. A coach should devise ways to give his players a psychological lift on certain occasions:

a. Provide them with chipped ice during a ball game being played on an extremely hot day.

b. Provide them with chewing gum before ball games.

c. Allow them to select and keep their own bats.

d. Make arrangements to provide them with a soft drink following each ball game.

5. A coach should look for athletes who appear discouraged and take the time to give that player some personal words of encouragement. The right word at the right time can do wonders for a boy's morale.

6. As much as possible, rivalries should be developed between players at each position. It is a well-known fact that the player who is being "pushed" will be more likely to play up to his potential.

7. Generally speaking, a boy should not be on the ball club unless he can help the team in some capacity. Perhaps a boy is a good baserunner but can do little else. He should be encouraged to perfect this particular skill, and his coach should have the courage to make use of it in competition. An athlete can be made

to feel that he is an important cog in the machine, but only if his particular skills are used when the opportunities arise.

A Word About Discipline

Team morale is almost always influenced by the way in which a coach handles the disciplinary problems that arise during the course of a season. No coach enjoys this part of his job, but players simply cannot always be allowed to do what comes naturally.

Here are some suggestions that may help the coach to function more effectively in this important capacity:

1. Meet with the squad early in the season with the express purpose of discussing discipline in general and establishing team rules:

   a. Discuss the need for controls of some kind.

   b. Ask the squad to set up its own rules.

   c. Provide each player with a written copy of the rules that the team agrees to follow.

   d. Discuss the responsibilities for enforcing team rules. Inform the team that you have no intention of chasing around looking for players who are breaking the rules. Tell them that their team will be only as good or bad as they want to make it.

2. A coach should try to estimate the threshold of every player. That is, he should develop a sensitivity regarding the reaction of different players to different kinds of treatment. One player may react positively to criticism. The same treatment may ruin another boy.

3. In general, a coach should recognize the fact that guidance is entirely different in its effect when given privately. Never publicly berate a boy during a game. The worst thing a coach can do is humiliate a boy in front of others. Even the play-for-pay boys try to abide by this principle. Early in his managerial career, Gene Mauch, now manager of the Montreal Expos, dressed down one of his players in front of the entire ball club. After the game, Mauch called a team meeting and apologized to the player, not for getting down on him but for not showing the player enough respect to do it privately.

4. In general, the less successful a player is, the more severely criticism affects him. Therefore, able players, whose prestige is thoroughly established, should be the first to be criticized or disciplined, not the last.

5. A coach should avoid punishing the entire squad for a listless performance by only a few players. He should always single out the violators and deal with them individually.

6. A coach should never personalize an infraction. He cannot afford to permit a desire for revenge to dictate his coaching methods. He must keep in mind that his command is delegated to him by his players. That authority should be exercised only if it can be used to help a player. He must believe in human dignity as a basic quality of man, regardless of the behavior of that man.

7. Coaches are human and will certainly make errors in judgment. It will be impossible for a coach to make the right decision all the time, but as long as he acts in sincerity, rather than in anger, or with a feeling of personal retribution he will weather the storm of indignation and resentment that always follows disciplinary action.

Principles of Teaching

Coaching is teaching in its highest form. Most coaches realize early in their careers that their successes will be determined not by what they know personally but by what they are able to teach their players. Coaching is a form of dramatic art in that the teacher must bring his material to life by his own visual interpretations. His ability to present the fundamentals in an effective manner will also influence squad morale.

The following principles of teaching have been found to be particularly appropriate in the coaching situation:

1. As a rule, sports learning is worthless for competitive use unless it is a habit-response to perception. An athlete should be drilled consistently on a relatively few important skills. (In my first years of coaching I can recall having my squads spend almost as much time perfecting a pickoff play as they did defending the sacrifice bunt. I later discovered that it pays to use that valuable practice time on those situations that the team will have to cope with the most.) The performance of these movements has to become

second nature to him. If he is presented with too many alternatives this becomes impossible.

2. Drills should be planned so that competition is utilized as much as possible. Regardless of how badly a player wants to excel, performing the same task over and over again will become boring unless additional motivational factors are used. From a practical standpoint this can be accomplished by:

a. Keeping a record of an individual's progress in learning a particular skill.

b. Pitting one player against another, or one group against another in squad drills.

c. Establishing a means of rewarding players for their accomplishments in practice.

3. In presenting a new and difficult skill, teach the general idea first, then go back to the details. My ignorance of this principle early in my coaching career almost led to my completely destroying the confidence of one boy. He was a catcher, but to my way of thinking he was not throwing properly. Within the course of a few minutes I had given him five or six suggestions on how he might improve his throwing. The boy became so confused that he literally forgot how to throw! For a time he couldn't even throw the ball back to the pitcher, let alone to second base.

4. Keep in mind that boys learn in different ways and at a variety of rates. For example, some of the slowest learners may develop into the best athletes. A particular boy may be the last to learn a skill, but he may also learn it more thoroughly than the faster learners.

5. A coach should use visual and verbal cues whenever possible. Using a lot of words to describe a relatively simple skill will add to a player's confusion. For example, telling a player to *"throw* his bat at the ball" will give him an immediate picture of what is meant by bringing the bat around quickly with the wrists.

6. Caution athletes against performing most skills with great speed or force. Generally speaking, control is impaired when there is maximum muscular involvement.

7. Early practices should be planned with the assumption that the whole squad is inexperienced. The coach should teach skills from scratch in order that they serve as new experiences for the beginner and reviews for the veteran.

8. A boy has to be convinced that he is making a mistake before a change in performance is possible. His coach must take this factor into consideration before he attempts to correct a fault. For example, the boy who is hitting over .300 will be hard to convince that he is doing anything wrong at the plate. His coach must exercise some patience and wait until the player comes to him and expresses a need for help.

9. Advice is usually more acceptable to the player if it is given privately and personally.

10. Remind a player of his mistakes every time he does not seem to be aware of what he is doing wrong. If a boy makes a particular mistake five times, but is corrected only once, he isn't being conditioned against that error.

11. Corrections should generally be made immediately, especially if it is during practice. It won't have the same effect a couple of hours or days later.

12. Plan the teaching of skills so that there is a minimum of possible responses to game situations. Choice reactions take longer than simple reactions. For example, a runner on third base will get a better start toward home if he is taught *always* to try to score on a ground ball to the infield in this situation.

13. A coach should know when to work and when to stop. As a rule, the body increases in endurance by working at its maximum for a reasonably short period of time, then resting until the next day. Therefore, short, well-organized practice sessions provide the best conditions for effective teaching and training.

22

Planning and Conducting Practice

The organization of his practice sessions is one of the most difficult and important tasks a baseball coach has to face. With from fifteen to twenty players on a squad, and each of them needing individual attention, he certainly has his work cut out for him if he expects any learning to take place. He must teach the basic skills of nine different defensive positions as well as the various offensive fundamentals of the game. To make the job just that much more difficult, most baseball coaches are forced to tackle this situation alone, without an assistant.

Many coaches overcome these conditions and do provide a meaningful practice experience for their players. Here are some of the techniques that baseball coaches have used to compensate for the difficulty of their rather unique assignment:

1. They organize each practice session so thoroughly that each player is accounted for during every minute of the workout.

2. They establish a practice routine with which the squad can become thoroughly familiar, thereby eliminating time wasted on explaining new procedures.

3. They provide enough equipment to keep drills going at a regular pace. For example:

    a. Enough baseballs are available so that no more than two players have to play catch with one ball. (Believe it or not, I was watching a Little League team practice recently and they had three baseballs and two bats to use among twenty-two players!

How can a boy enjoy the game if he never gets to handle a bat and ball?)

b. There are enough bats to allow at least half the squad to be working on batting drills of one kind or another.

c. Two sets of catchers gear are available so that batting practice and intra-squad games do not have to be held up for catchers to exchange equipment.

d. Enough batting helmets are available so that hitters do not hold up practice while they hunt for the one helmet that fits them.

4. They provide field facilities that allow for maximum participation for all players. For example:

a. A portable batting cage is available so two groups can take batting practice at the same time.

b. A pitcher's practice area is available to enable every pitcher on the squad sufficient throwing. This facility might include:

1) At least two additional mounds, rubbers and home plates.

2) Pitching control strings.

c. A protective screen for the batting practice pitcher.

d. A screen for the protection of the first baseman during batting practice.

e. Several batting tees.

5. They make good use of players, particularly pitchers, as fungo hitters. In fact, a coach will be in a better position to supervise the workout and will be able to provide more instruction if he leaves this responsibility almost entirely up to his players.

6. They encourage players to help each other. For example, a boy who has pretty well mastered the fundamentals of sliding should be put to work helping those athletes who are weak at sliding. One day last season I must have spent a good forty-five minutes with one boy trying to teach him how to slide. When my attention was needed elsewhere I asked one of the other players, a good slider, if he would continue working with my pupil. I returned in less than ten minutes and the boy was executing a perfect bent-leg slide!

7. They do an exceptional job of teaching self-discipline. Knowing that he cannot possibly watch every player all the time, the baseball coach must convince his athletes that it is up to them to make use of every minute of practice time.

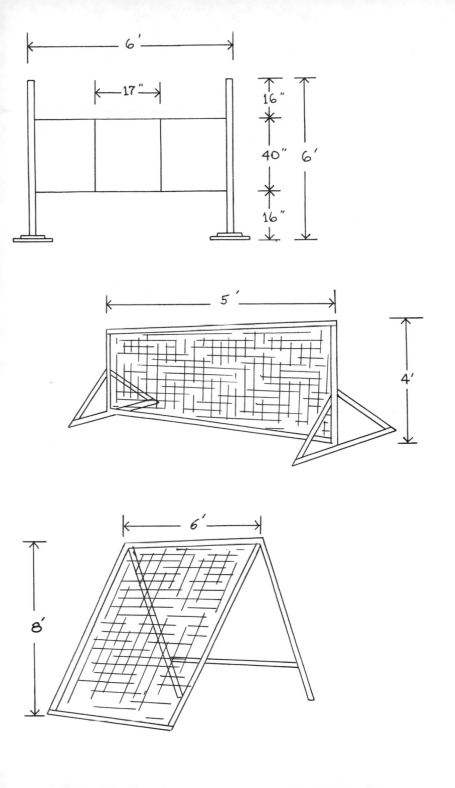

A Practice Routine

Generally speaking, there are two accepted ways of organizing a baseball practice. Some coaches like to operate on a completion theory. They set out to accomplish a certain amount of work during a session and do not quit until the job is done. The other commonly used system is the timed schedule. That is, each drill to be used, as well as the entire practice session, is set on a time limit.

Although there are advantages to either technique, most coaches are forced to operate on a time limit whether they like it or not. For this reason, the approach we will describe in detail here will be the timed schedule.

Our procedure has been to divide the practice schedule into seven basic kinds of drills:

1. Warm-up Drills
2. Skill Drills
3. Dummy Drills
4. All-purpose Drill
5. Live-situation Drills
6. Pitcher-conditioning Drills
7. Squad-conditioning Drills

The coach can select from a number of drills within each of these categories. On some occasions he may want to use several drills from one category and omit the drills from another category entirely. For example, early in the season he may wish to concentrate on skill drills and not bother with live-situation drills. Or, on the day before a ball game, he may want to use most of the available practice time for batting drills.

The drills that follow are examples of some of the basic team drills that have been used effectively by baseball coaches. The wise coach thoroughly indoctrinates his squad on the procedures for performing the drills they will be using over and over again throughout the season. Once the team is familiar with his routine, he can begin to concentrate on teaching skills rather than drills. New drills may be substituted for variety or for work on a specific weakness, but as a rule, an athlete will find it easier to learn intricate skills when he can concentrate entirely on his performance.

Preparation

In order to keep things running smoothly on the practice field, a coach will have to spend some time beforehand plotting out the day's workout. Although coaches vary in the amount of detail they go into in planning their practice, the drills to be used and player assignments in each should definitely be included on the schedule. Ideally, the practice plan is then posted so that players can refer to it before and during the workout. A sample of a rather detailed practice schedule is presented later in the book.

In addition to having a well-organized schedule, the coach may want to establish a few team rules regarding practice procedure. For example:

1. Require the squad to run a lap around the entire field (or whatever) for each baseball that is missing at the end of the workout.

2. Forbid players from congregating in pairs or small groups during practice, particularly shaggers during batting drills.

3. Assign warm-up partners, by position, at the beginning of the season. Allow an outfielder to throw only to another outfielder; infielders to infielders; pitchers to pitchers, and catchers to catchers. This procedure should be followed whenever possible because the distance a player should throw and the type of throw he will use will vary with the position he plays.

4. Discourage players from wearing their warm-up jackets during drills. If a boy works up a sweat with his jacket on, then he will have nothing to wear following the drill.

5. Insist that players report to practice looking like baseball players. Unless the squad is fortunate enough to have practice uniforms, the best bet is to require players to wear:

    a. Loose-fitting pants (sweat pants are excellent)
    b. A baseball undershirt or sweatshirt
    c. A baseball cap (the team cap if possible)
    d. Sweat socks
    e. Spikes

6. Forbid sitting on the bench or on the ground, except in cases of sickness or injury.

DATE *March 25*

PRACTICE SCHEDULE

TIME		EQUIPMENT ASSIGNMENTS

3:00 WARM-UP DRILLS
(20 minutes)

1. Calisthenics	Bat Bag – Young
2. Pick-ups	Ball Bag – Yoshimura
3. Throwing	Medicine Kit – Hamamoto
	Helmets – Wright
	Bases – Murphy

3:20 SKILL DRILL: Bunting (20 minutes)

Group 1 (Diamond)		Group 2 (Batting Cage)	
1. Larks	5. Read	1. Hightower	5. Brooks
2. Lusk	6. Preston	2. Gilmore	6. Black
3. Raymond	7. Chew	3. Geandrot	7. French
4. Skeels	8. Nichols	4. Stevens	8. Brown

3:40 DUMMY SITUATIONS: Fungo Drill (20 minutes)

Situations:	Defense:
1. Pitchers covering 1B	P – Brasher, Hammitt
2. Sacrifice situations	C – Smith
3. Double-play situations	1B – Majors
4. Get one situations	2B – Wong
	3B – Boschetti
	SS – Anderson

4:00 LIVE-SITUATION DRILL: Intra-squad Game (1 hr.)

P – Stevens	LF – Shupe	P – Parker	LF – Ramirez
C – McGrew	CF – Huggins	C – Threlkeld	CF – Allen
1B – Faraclas	RF – Couch	1B – Hill	RF – Harris
2B – Campbell		2B – Hubert	
3B – Belsey		3B – Fujinaga	
SS – Ashcraft		SS – Henderson	

5:00 SQUAD-CONDITIONING DRILLS   PITCHER-CONDITIONING DRILLS
(15 min.)

1. Whistle Drill	1. Sprints – 10
2. Coaching Drill	2. Fly-ball Drill

5:15 SHOWER

270

7. Generally, establish an atmosphere of continuous activity. Tell the squad if everyone is busy, a baseball practice should look like a three-ring circus. The Dodger training camps when Branch Rickey directed them must have been something to watch. Rickey was so thoroughly organized that every player had to account for every minute he was on the field. Of course, Rickey had the equipment, facilities and coaches to make such a program work, and those of us in amateur ball do not. However, we can certainly do our best to see that every boy is kept busy.

WARM-UP DRILLS

These drills are designed to ready the squad for activities that call for a maximum physical effort. Early in the season, several or all of these drills may be appropriate. Later in the year, and on extremely warm days, perhaps only one or two of them will be needed. The team should perform these drills together and with a lot of snap. The tempo for an entire practice can be established during warm-up drills.

When everyone is ready, the captain or a designated leader leads the squad on a slow jog around the outside edge of the outfield to the opposite foul line.

Calisthenics

1. Upon returning from their jog around the field the squad begins to form a circle. The first players to arrive clap their hands and shout to their teammates to stimulate some enthusiasm.

2. A double-arms distance should separate each player from those on either side of him.

3. When the complete circle has been formed the captain leads them through the following exercise routine:

    a. 10 jumping jacks
    b. 10 windmills
    c. 10 side bends
    d. 10 windups (right arm)
    e. 10 windups (left arm)
    f. 10 kick-ups (right leg)
    g. 10 kick-ups (left leg)
    h. 10 hill climbers

4. The squad goes through the same exercises, in the same order, every day.

5. The captain calls out the exercise and counts the individual movements. The rest of the team counts the repetitions.

Pick-ups

1. The squad divides into pairs, one baseball in each group.

2. Partners face each other about 15 feet apart. One boy, the feeder, rolls the ball to his partner's left, and then to his right.

3. The receiver races back and forth in a semicircle; moving over to his right, he picks the ball up, returns it underhand to the feeder and then moves back to his left to repeat the same procedure.

4. The first player picks the ball up 25 times and then they switch places and the other player does 25.

5. This drill should be done quickly; the feeder should really work his partner.

6. Gloves may or may not be used, but correct fielding fundamentals should be practiced.

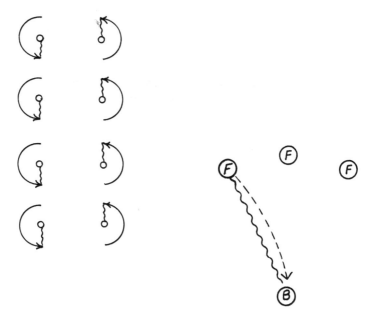

Pepper

1. Two pairs of players combine to form a group of four. One player becomes the batter, the other three are fielders.

2. For best results, the batter should stand up against a backstop or fence, especially with extremely young players. The fielders stand double-arms' distance apart and about 30 feet from the batter.

3. Of course, the procedure is to have the fielders throw the ball to the batter, who strokes it back to them.

a. The batter does *not* use a full swing. He chokes up on the bat, concentrates on watching the ball hit the bat and swings down on the ball.

b. The fielders practice fielding ground balls and getting rid of the ball quickly.

4. An element of competition can be added by playing "work-up":

a. Each time a fielder catches a ground ball the batter gets one point charged against him. Each time a fielder catches a ball in the air, the batter is charged 2 points.

b. If no errors are made before the batter is charged with 15 points, the fielder on the far right becomes the next hitter.

c. If a fielder makes an error, the points against the hitter are voided, and that fielder moves to the end of the line.

d. If a batter should miss a good pitch completely, he must give up his turn at bat at that point.

5. With experienced players, this drill can be performed with just two boys in a group, one batter and one fielder. There should never be more than five players in a game of pepper.

6. This is probably the oldest drill in baseball, but it can also be the best if it is played with a lot of hustle and chatter.

7. To keep the game going, one player should keep an extra ball in his pocket to be used when the one they are playing with gets by the hitter or a fielder.

Throwing

1. Few young players warm up their arms properly. We look upon this as one of the most valuable drills in our daily practice. A coach should insist that his players throw the ball correctly and warm up sufficiently for their position.

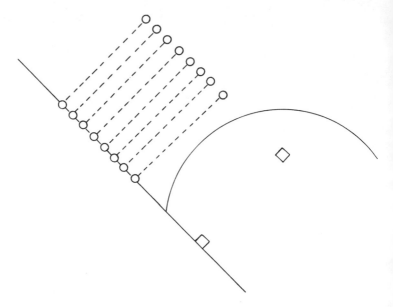

2. As we indicated previously, warm-up partners should play the same position whenever possible.

3. For reasons of safety, all players should throw in the same direction and there should be at least 15 feet between a player and the one standing next to him.

4. The warm-up procedure should vary somewhat by position:

a. Pitchers should start throwing about 40 feet apart and should gradually increase the distance until they are throwing about 75 feet.

b. Catchers should begin the drill about 30 feet apart and throwing from one knee. That is, the knee on the throwing side should be on the ground so the player has to throw the ball primarily with his wrist, using an overhand delivery. After a minute or two of this, they should stand up and throw normally, gradually increasing the distance to about 150 feet.

c. Infielders should start throwing about 40 feet apart and gradually increase the distance until they are throwing about 150 feet apart. At the very end of the drill, they should come up to about 60 feet and work on getting rid of the ball quickly and throwing the ball from where they receive it.

d. Outfielders should start throwing at 40 feet and gradually move back until they are about 175 feet apart. On the extremely long throws, they should work on "crow hopping" into the throw.

5. In each case, players must concentrate on throwing properly: learning to grip the ball without looking at it; delivering the ball overhand; striding in-line with the receiver; and aiming at a target.

6. If it is performed properly and the participants concentrate on what they are doing, this drill should take no more than 10 minutes, once the players' arms are in shape.

SKILL DRILLS

These drills provide players with an opportunity to concentrate on the basic skills of the game. The squad is usually divided into groups by position or otherwise, depending on the drills to be used and the facilities available. One veteran player should be placed in charge of each group.

Bunting Drill

1. Divide the squad into two groups, listing the batting order and designating a pitcher and catcher for each group. Assign one group to the main backstop and send the other group to the batting cage or any other area where some sort of a backstop is provided.

2. The pitcher (any player who can get the ball over) throws half-speed fastballs only.

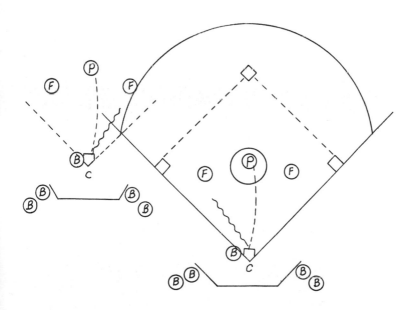

3. The batter is given one of the following assignments:

a. 5 sacrifice bunts.

b. 5 bunts for a hit.

c. 5 squeeze bunts.

d. Bunt 5 times as directed by the on-deck hitter.

4. Those waiting to bunt stand in line and judge the batter's performance. Two of these players shag the bunts from either side of the pitcher.

5. A foul ball counts as a bunt.

6. The catcher and pitcher bunt last.

7. Repeat the drill as many rounds as time permits.

8. Throughout the drill the group leader (a good bunter) or the coach offers suggestions to players who need help.

9. To provide an element of competition:

a. Have players keep track of the number of times they bunt successfully.

b. Mark the spots where a bunt can be most effectively placed and give these areas a numerical value. See which player can accumulate the highest score. These areas can be designated by drawing circles with lime or by simply laying out some old blankets or gunny sacks.

Stroking Drill

1. This batting drill is designed to give players a maximum number of swings against medium-speed pitching. Players should concentrate on hitting the ball where it is pitched and not hitting for power.

2. The squad is divided into batting groups of three or four each, depending on the total number of players involved. The groups are identified by number. The batting order within each group is listed on the practice schedule.

3. Each group is given a certain amount of time to hit. For example, within a 40-minute time period, four groups of four players each could hit for 10 minutes apiece. The hitters in a group could take turns taking 5 cuts each until their 10-minute time period is up.

4. In order to keep the drill running smoothly, a few other procedures should be followed:

a. The group batting is responsible for shagging all foul balls.

b. The first player listed in the group slated to hit next throws to the group at the plate. His responsibility is to *make* the batter hit every pitch he throws.

c. The second player listed in the next group shags for the pitcher.

d. All of the remaining players shag in the outfield until it is time for them to assume another assignment or take their turn at bat.

e. A catcher is usually not needed in this drill.

5. If two batting areas are available, the same drill can be run at each facility.

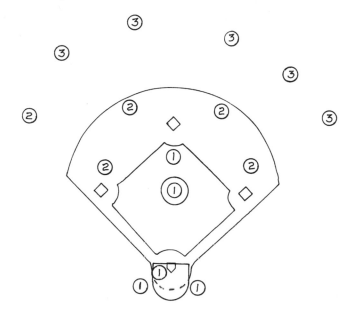

Sliding Drill

1. The purpose of this drill is to give players an opportunity to learn and practice the fundamentals of the bent-leg slide.

2. The squad is divided into three groups, and a good slider is designated as the leader of each.

3. The drill can be performed on any area of the outfield where the grass is relatively heavy and well-matted.

4. Players are instructed to remove their shoes and slide in their stockings.

5. The three groups line up single file, with a loose bag (or glove) in front of each.

6. The progression for teaching inexperienced players how to slide should be as follows:

    a. The basic position for the bent-leg slide is taught first by having the players all sit down on the grass and assume the correct position. The coach and/or group leader checks out each player.

    b. The next step is to have each player walk through the approach to the bag and sit down in the correct position.

    c. Then, they gradually move farther back and speed-up their approach until they are sliding into the bag full speed.

7. After each boy slides, he replaces the bag for the next slider.

8. As soon as most of the players have learned the basic fundamentals, the squad can work on the variations of the bent-leg slide:

    a. The pop-up slide.

    b. The back-door slide.

9. When all three variations have been taught, each group can play "follow the leader." Whichever variation the leader performs, his groups must also execute.

10. This drill can be used even more effectively on wet grass or by having the players slide on blankets indoors on a hardwood floor.

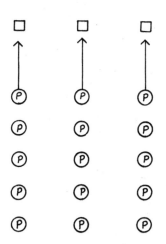

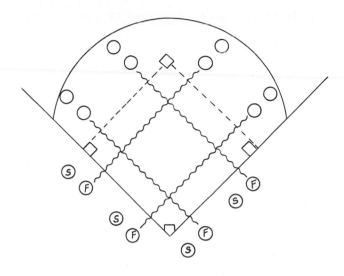

Ground-ball Drill

1. The purpose of this drill is to give infielders or the entire squad an opportunity to practice fielding a maximum number of ground balls in a short time period.

2. The squad is divided into four groups. The regular infielder at each position serves as the leader for his group. One group lines up at each infield position.

3. Players rotate assignments. The last player listed in each group fungoes until each of the players in the group has received 10 ground balls, then another player fungoes.

4. After a player fields a ground ball, he simply lobs the ball back to the fungo hitter and readies himself to field another.

5. An element of competition can be added by having players within each group keep track of their errors. The four best fielders (one from each group) can then be pitted against each other in a final showdown.

6. The coach should circulate around behind the fielders throughout the drill and offer suggestions for improvement.

Infield Skill Drill

1. Purpose: To give infielders an opportunity to work on the basic skills of their positions.

2. One or more infielders are assigned to each position.

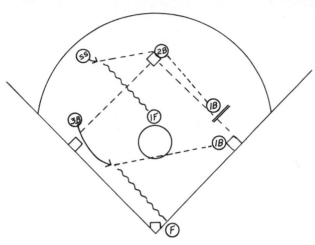

3. The shortstops and second baseman work together on the double play:

a. One player stands just behind the mound and rolls all kinds of ground balls to the shortstop, who fields the ball and throws to the second baseman covering second base. He makes his pivot and throws to another extra player standing in the baseline about halfway to first base.

b. The same procedure is then repeated with the second baseman fielding the ball and the shortstop making the pivot.

c. For safety, a protective screen should be placed on the baseline in front of the first baseman.

4. The first and third basemen work together on fielding bunts and slow-hit balls:

a. An extra player throws or fungoes ground balls to the third baseman who makes the play to first base.

b. Then the same procedure is repeated with the first baseman fielding the ball and throwing to third base.

5. Infielders rotate from each assignment after a specified number of plays.

6. The coach circulates around behind the players and offers suggestions for improvement.

Outfield Skill Drill

1. Purpose: To give outfielders an opportunity to work on the basic skills of outfield play.

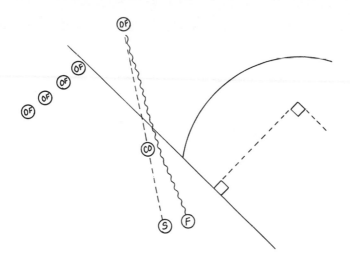

2. All of the outfielders line up along the foul line about 100 feet beyond the edge of the infield. One player acts as a relay man and another shags for the fungo hitter.

3. One by one, each outfielder jogs out, assumes a "ready" position and fields the ball that is hit to him. The fungo hitter gives each outfielder an opportunity to work on fielding each of the following types of batted balls:

    a. Ground balls—hard hit, bounding and slow-rollers.

    b. Line drives—straight at him, to either side and over his head.

    c. Fly balls—short, to either side, over his head and in the sun.

4. Every play is performed under game conditions. The fielder hurries to get position on the ball and makes a throw into the cut-off man.

5. For best results, the coach should try to use a player to fungo the ball so that he can remain out by the outfielders and offer suggestions for improvement.

6. Rotate fungo, shagging and relay assignments periodically.

Fly-ball Drill

1. Purpose: To give a team practice at fielding fly balls, especially those that require communication between two or more players.

2. Divide the squad into two complete defensive teams. With less than two complete teams available, assign extra players to their positions later in the drill.

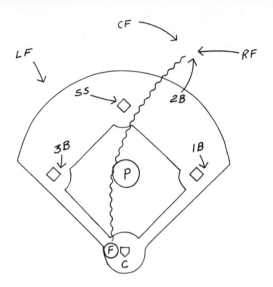

3. With everyone in position, the coach fungoes fly balls, attempting to place most of them between two or more players:

    a. Down the baselines toward home plate.

    b. In front of the outfielders and behind the infielders.

    c. Behind first and third base.

    d. In the area of the pitcher's mound.

4. The coach should insist that every ball is called for and that every base is covered.

5. As a variation, call all of the outfielders in and hit pop flies behind the infielders. This will give the infielders needed work on going back for balls hit over their heads.

Infield-outfield Drill

This drill is commonly used just prior to the beginning of a ball game. It is also used quite often during practice sessions to give infielders and outfielders an opportunity to work on the basic defensive skills. With a limited amount of time available, it can be used as it is described in Chapter 23. If more than 15 minutes can be allotted for this drill, the coach may wish to add any of the following variations to the basic drill:

1. Hit as many fly balls and ground balls to each player as time permits.

2. Using two or more catchers, roll bunts out in front of the

plate in rapid succession and have the catchers take turns fielding the ball and making the throw as directed by the coach.

3. Hit about 15 ground balls in a row to each infielder. Make him move to his left, right and in for the ball so that he will be thoroughly exhausted by the time he is finished.

4. Have all of the infielders play back on the edge of the grass and hit the ball as hard as you can to each player. Offer a milkshake to the boy who stays in there the longest without making an error.

DUMMY DRILLS

These drills are designed to teach players how to react to the various offensive and defensive situations that occur in game competition. Each situation is re-created to give the player the actual experience of performing the play himself. These drills are referred to as "dummy" drills because the participants do not really compete but simply learn their assignments.

Fungo Drill

1. Purpose: To give the offense and defense an opportunity to carry out their responsibilities in the game situations that are most likely to occur in a ball game.

2. The coach, standing in the batter's box, assigns baserunners and calls out the game situation. The pitcher takes his windup and throws the ball easily into the catcher. At this point, the coach either lets the ball go through or fungoes another ball in the desired direction.

3. Using this drill, a coach can take his players through almost every defensive and offensive situation:

a. Passed-ball situations:

1) All of the pitchers assemble at the mound and the catchers take turns behind the plate. Everyone else lines up to run at third base.

2) The pitcher deliberately throws the ball by the catcher and covers home plate. The catcher retrieves the ball and throws to the pitcher for the tag.

3) The baserunners work on getting a jump and trying to score on the passed ball.

b. Pitcher covering 1B situations:

1) First basemen take their position and baserunners run from home plate.

2) The ball is fungoed to the first baseman who feeds it to the pitcher covering first base.

3) Baserunners work on going down the line and running through the bag.

4) The second baseman is then added, and the ball is fungoed between the first and second baseman.

5) The pitcher covers the bag and takes the long throw as described in Chapter 17.

6) The second baseman calls off the first baseman if he can make the play.

c. Pitcher-to-second-base double-play situations:

1) The shortstop(s) is added and half of the extra players go down to first base to run.

2) The coach then fungoes ground balls back to the pitcher, who throws to second base to start the double play.

3) The shortstop and second baseman work on co-ordinating the base-covering assignment.

4) The baserunners work on taking their lead and getting a jump on the batted ball but do not slide at second.

d. Sacrifice-bunt situations:

1) The third baseman is added and baserunners are assigned at first or first and second base.

2) The coach squares around and dumps a bunt down either baseline or at the pitcher.

3) The defensive team works on their bunt coverages, and the baserunners practice offensive responsibilities under the same circumstances.

e. Double-play situations:

1) Runners are assigned at first, first and second, first and third, or at all three bases.

2) Ground balls are hit to every infielder and each works on his particular double-play assignments.

f. "Get one" situations:

1) Any number of baserunner situations are set up and the ball is fungoed on the ground to the infield.

2) Infielders work on making the play to the plate, looking the runner back and throwing to first, or throwing for a force out.

3) Baserunners work on deciding when to go and when not to go on a ground ball.

g. Relay and cut-off situations:

1) Outfielders are then added and balls of all kinds are fungoed to the outfield to create the various relay and cut-off situations that may occur.

2) Baserunners are particularly aggressive so that outfielders and relay men are given a lot of opportunities to make their throws.

3) Throughout these drills the baserunners run full-speed but do not slide.

4) On a given day, the entire drill can be used or only that phase of it on which the team needs the most work.

5) Once the team has learned their assignments fairly well, a more realistic fielding situation can be created if the coach actually hits the ball that the pitcher delivers.

6) To give every player a chance to work both offensively and defensively, a coach should rotate two complete teams or use alternates, depending on the number of players available.

Steal Situation Drill

1. Purpose: To work on the offensive and defensive fundamentals of the steal play.

2. Designate one player as the batter. Tell him to alternate hitting righthanded and lefthanded. Also, have him either swing to miss the ball, fake a bunt, or merely take the pitch.

3. Rotate pitchers and catchers. Make sure their arms are thoroughly warmed up prior to the drill.

4. To work on stealing or defensing the steal of second base:

a. Have the first basemen, second basemen and shortstops join the pitchers and catchers in the field.

b. The remainder of the squad line up at first base and take turns attempting to steal second base.

5. To work on stealing or defensing the steal of third base:

a. Have the third basemen take the field and the first basemen run the bases with the rest of the squad.

b. To begin with, have the baserunners line up behind second and steal third only. Then, divide them in half and have one group steal second while the other is stealing third.

6. To work on stealing or defensing the steal of home:

a. Have the second basemen run the bases from third with the rest of the squad.

7. To work on the offensive and defensive aspects of the double steal:

a. Place a complete infield in the field along with the pitchers and catchers.

b. Divide the remaining players in half, with one group running from first and the rest from third.

1) Tell the runner on first to execute any of the three variations of the double steal and to either hold up and get caught in a rundown or steal second base.

2) Tell the runner on third to try to score or fake stealing home.

8. Make sure that baserunners rotate assignments. Every player should have at least one opportunity to perform each assignment.

9. Since this is basically a "dummy" drill, baserunners do not slide. However, they should run outside the baseline and hustle past the bag to make the timing as realistic as possible.

10. This drill is used most effectively when the team concentrates only on one or two steal situations per session. The coach can work with either the offense or the defense or both, depending on the needs of the squad. For example, he may want to work primarily with the catchers. An excellent method of measuring the quickness with which a catcher gets rid of his throws is to use a stop watch. For a valid test, start the watch when the pitch enters the glove and stop it when it is caught by the infielder covering the bag.

Pickoff and Rundown Drill

1. Purpose: To work on the offensive and defensive fundamentals of the pickoff and rundown plays.

2. Send all of the pitchers and catchers to their respective positions. Make sure their arms are thoroughly warmed up prior to the drill.

3. To work on the pickoff at first base and the rundown between first and second:

a. Have the first basemen, second basemen and shortstops take their positions.

b. The remainder of the squad takes turns running at first base. They take an exaggerated lead and allow themselves to be picked off. Once they are in a rundown they work on their offensive responsibilities under those circumstances.

c. The defense works on their pickoff plays to first and, ultimately, the rundown play.

4. To work on the pickoff at second base and the rundown between second and third:

a. Have the third basemen take the field and the first basemen run the bases with the rest of the squad.

b. The baserunners line up behind second base and take turns allowing themselves to be picked off of second base.

5. To work on the pickoff at third base and the rundown between third and home:

a. Have the second basemen run from third with the rest of the squad.

b. The baserunners allow themselves to be caught off third and then do everything they can to evade the tag in the ensuing rundown.

6. To provide an element of competition to the drill, the squad can be divided into groups and compete against each other:

a. Sets of infielders can compete to see who can retire a runner caught in a rundown with the fewest throws or in the shortest time period (use a stop watch).

b. Baserunners can compete against each other to see who is best at getting out of a rundown:

1) Award a runner three points if he is successful in getting to the next base.

2) Award a runner two points if he is able to return safely to the base he came from (after being caught in a rundown).

3) Award a runner one point if he is able to force the defense into making three throws or more before tagging him out.

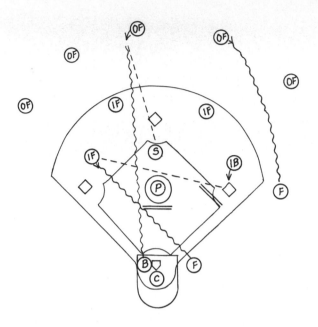

ALL-PURPOSE DRILL

This drill is almost a practice session in itself. With the proper facilities available and a fairly mature squad, a coach can use this drill to work on almost every basic offensive and defensive skill. Because players are working on a variety of skills at the same time, the drill is extremely time consuming. For this reason, it should be used only when the coach can afford to devote at least half of the day's workout to this particular activity.

1. Purpose:

a. To provide pitchers with an opportunity to throw off the mound to live hitters.

b. To provide catchers, infielders and outfielders an opportunity to practice the skills of their positions.

c. To give batters an opportunity to bat and bunt against regular pitchers.

d. To provide some opportunity for the development of base-running skills.

2. Special facilities needed:

a. A protective screen for the pitcher.

b. A protective screen for the first baseman.

3. This drill must be particularly well-planned if every player is to benefit from it. The following information should appear on a posted practice schedule:

a. The order in which pitchers and their catchers are to participate.

b. The batting order and hitting assignment.

c. Special assignments, such as conditioning, and the names of the players to be involved.

4. Every player must be thoroughly familiar with his responsibilities as he proceeds from one phase of the drill to the next.

a. Batters:

1) Check the practice schedule for batting order and hitting assignment.

2) Rotate from the field to shagger behind the pitcher, to on-deck hitter, to batter.

3) Run out the last swing whether it is fair, foul or hit at all.

4) Take your lead off first base and steal second on the first pitch to the following hitter. Do not slide.

5) Take a lead off second and break for third on the next pitch. Then take your place in the field.

b. Pitchers:

1) Check the schedule for when you are to pitch; be warmed up and ready to throw when you are needed.

2) Throw from the stretch when the batter is bunting.

3) Concentrate on throwing strikes and let the hitters know what you are throwing.

4) Work on form, but don't waste a lot of time by taking a long, slow windup.

c. Catchers:

1) Warm up the pitcher you are assigned to and go in with him.

2) Catch as you would in a ball game, except do not give the pitcher signals. Let him signal you which pitch is coming.

3) Keep track of the hitter's cuts.

d. First basemen:

1) Alternate taking throws from the infielders and catching ground balls from the fungo hitter.

2) Bounce the ball on one hop to the fungo hitter if he does not have a shagger.

e. Infielders:

1) Take turns fielding ground balls.

2) An extra infielder fungoes a round of 10 balls to each infielder, then is replaced by one of the others.

3) Throws are made to second or first base.

f. Outfielders:

1) Occupy their own positions as much as possible. With more than three outfielders available, they should spread out and cover the entire field rather than clump together in one area.

2) Work on getting a jump on every batted ball and making the fielding plays correctly.

3) Whenever possible, rotate fungoing fly balls and ground balls to each other.

5. With baseballs flying all over the place there are some very important safety precautions that every player must observe:

a. With a lefthanded hitter at the plate, infielders must not throw to first base as the first baseman should be watching the hitter.

b. Fungo hitters must hit the ball *between* pitches and not at the same time a ball is being pitched to the batter.

c. Infielders should make their throws only after fielding a ball fungoed to them—not after fielding a ball off the hitter's bat.

d. Fielders must always return the ball to the shagger (behind the pitcher) on the ground.

e. The shagger behind the pitcher should stand halfway between the mound and second base. If he stands too close to the pitcher, he may be hit by a line drive if it gets by the pitcher.

6. Depending on the time available and the size of the squad, the hitters may be given any of several assignments. For example:

a. Round One: 2 sacrifice bunts; 6 cuts (not fair balls)

b. Round Two: 1 bunt for a hit; 4 cuts

c. Round Three: 3 cuts

7. The method in which pitchers are used can also vary:

a. Assign each pitcher a certain time limit on the mound.

b. Assign each pitcher a certain number of batters to pitch to.

c. Rotate two pitchers every four batters, using the extra pitcher as a shagger while he is waiting to resume pitching.

LIVE-SITUATION DRILLS

These drills are used to provide players with an opportunity to work on skills under conditions that are as similar to those in actual game competition as possible. The tendency is for players to approach this competition with something less than a 100 per cent effort. They find it difficult to really get serious about competing against their own teammates. Therefore, the coach should use every means available to him to motivate his athletes to perform at their best. Unless every athlete is hustling, these drills are not worth the time put into them and could even be dangerous.

Offensive Play Drill

1. Purpose: To give players practice executing the offensive plays to be used in game competition.

2. Divide the squad into three offensive teams, the combination of any two of which will form a complete defensive team. For example, with fifteen players available in all, three offensive teams of five players each can be formed. With one team at the plate, the other two are combined to form the defense.

3. These teams must be well thought out and listed on the practice schedule. Some players will have to play defensive positions that are not their own. The coach should make an effort to place every athlete in a position at which he can do a reasonably good job.

4. The first offensive team remains at the plate until each of its players has an opportunity to execute the assigned offensive series. The last batter listed in the order runs at first base. Then, each of the other batters take a turn running immediately following his turn at bat.

5. Each batter remains in the batter's box until he has had an opportunity to execute one of the following sets of offensive plays:

   a. Starting with a runner on first base: sacrifice him to second; move him to third with a ground ball to the rightfield side of the infield; bring him home with a squeeze bunt.

   b. Starting with runners on first and second: sacrifice the runners to second and third; score the runner on third with a sacrifice squeeze; score the last runner with a suicide squeeze bunt.

c. Starting with a runner on first base: execute the hit-and-run play to advance him to third; score him with a suicide-squeeze bunt; then, bunt for a base hit and run it out.

6. Here are some additional tips that will make the drill run smoothly:

a. Have pitchers throw as hard as they can without losing accuracy.

b. Give each batter two strikes to execute each skill within his assigned series. If he fails to execute the play in two tries, the runner automatically advances to the next base.

c. Caution the defense against adjusting their positions for the play before they would normally be able to in actual competition.

d. Have baserunners run full-speed and slide when the situation presents itself.

e. Use batting orders that are approximately the same as those used in regular competition. For example, the first offensive team might be made up of the first five hitters in the team's regular batting order.

7. Provide an additional incentive for players by keeping a record of the number of runs each offensive team scores.

Intra-squad Game

1. Purpose: To provide players with an opportunity to compete against each other under actual game-like conditions.

2. Set a time limit after which no new inning may begin.

3. Separate the squad into teams:

a. With eighteen or more players available, merely divide the squad in half.

b. With less than two full teams available, divide the squad into three offensive teams, the combination of any two of which will make up a complete defensive team.

4. Appoint a captain for each team and make him responsible for:

a. Keeping track of the number of runs his team scores.

b. Seeing that the last two hitters coach the bases.

c. Directing his team's offensive strategy.

5. To save time, give the team at bat 6 outs before changing sides.

6. Use a pinch-runner if the batter receives a base on balls. The hitter remains at the plate and the pitcher starts over on him.

7. Pitchers may be used in any one of a number of ways:

a. Schedule two pitchers for the drill and have them rotate every 6 outs.

b. List a pitching order and have each pitcher throw for a certain time period.

8. With limited time available, start each batter with a 2-ball and 1-strike count.

9. Provide an additional incentive for the teams by offering a reward for the winner. For example, give the winning team an extra round of batting practice or excuse them from conditioning drills.

10. For best results, the coach should umpire the game if another adult is unavailable.

Offensive Scrimmage

1. Purpose: To work on all phases of offensive-team development under game-type conditions.

2. Arrange to have another team work their defense against your offense, or select the best possible defensive team from your reserves.

3. Divide your team into two or three groups of four or five players each, depending on size of the squad. The first two groups should consist of those athletes who normally make up the team's starting line-up.

4. Rotate these batting groups against the defense. Switch groups at the end of 6 outs, after each hitter in the group has batted or after a certain period of time. Have the groups waiting to bat assigned to another drill.

5. The playing rules are exactly as they would be in a normal ball game except that the same team remains on defense throughout.

6. Regular team signals should be used and base coaches should practice their responsibilities.

7. A responsible player should be assigned to umpire behind the pitcher as the coach should be concentrating on directing his team at bat.

8. An additional incentive can be provided by offering a reward to the batting group that scores the most runs.

9. One effective variation to this drill is to place a baserunner or runners on base from the beginning of the inning. The offense can then work on their techniques for advancing the runner and bringing him in to score.

Defensive Scrimmage

1. Purpose: To provide the defensive team an opportunity to work on their responsibilities under game-type conditions.

2. Place the top defensive team in the field. If you use a regular pitcher, have him lay the ball in there and make the batters hit the ball.

3. Organize the remaining players into batting groups and have them do everything in their power to make it tough for the defense. Encourage them to bunt for a base hit, try every conceivable kind of offensive play and run the bases with reckless abandon. In fact, have each player keep track of his total bases and reward the boy who accumulates the highest score with a Coke after practice.

4. Clean the bases after every 6 outs but leave the same defense in the field. Tell the defense:

a. That they have to run a lap for every run they allow, or

b. That they don't get to bat themselves until they have retired every offensive player at least once (or twice, etc.).

PITCHER-CONDITIONING DRILLS

These drills are extremely important in providing pitchers with enough running to keep their legs in shape. One of these drills should be performed daily by each pitcher. There is only one exception to this rule. A boy should do very little running on the day preceding a starting assignment.

The best time during practice for a pitcher to do his running is just before he goes in to take his shower. It would not be a good idea for a pitcher to work up a sweat and then have to stand around in the cool air.

Normally, a coach will not be able to direct these drills himself. If this is the case, he should assign another player with this responsibility. One excellent way of handling this is to give each catcher the permanent responsibility for seeing that a certain pitcher or pitchers are properly conditioned.

Snake Drill

1. Give the pitcher in the best shape a stop watch and have him lead the rest of the staff on an irregular course around the ball park for a specified amount of time.
2. The players run in a single-file line and must stay together.
3. The amount of time assigned would depend on the stage of the season and the maturity of the squad. It would also depend on whether other conditioning drills are also planned for that day.

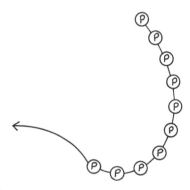

Sprint Drill

1. Running sprints can be extremely boring. For this reason, this method of conditioning should be avoided unless a pitcher has to do his running on his own.
2. Set up a course of about 50 yards in length.
3. The player sprints in one direction and walks back to the starting point. Insist that he actually sprint the entire 50 yards.
4. Ten sprints are usually enough for a boy of high school age.

Fly-ball Drill

1. Line the pitchers up along the foul line in deep rightfield.
2. The coach stands near the mound with a bucket of baseballs

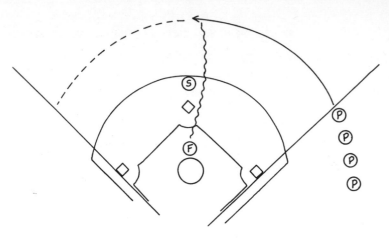

and fungoes the ball to each pitcher as he races toward centerfield. He tries to hit the ball out in front of the player so he has to really stretch his legs to catch up with it. If the player does not catch the ball, he must retrieve, throw it in to a shagger and continue on over to the leftfield foul line.

3. After each pitcher has made the trip across the outfield, they repeat the same procedure back toward the rightfield line.

4. A relay man should be provided out beyond second base so the pitchers do not have to make long throws.

5. High school pitchers should be able to make at least 10 trips at midseason.

Quarterback Drill

1. Have each pitcher get a ball and line up behind first base on the edge of the outfield grass.

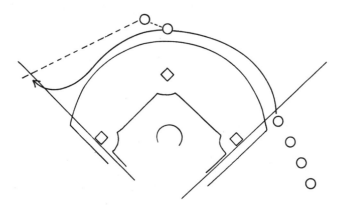

2. The coach or another player stands on the outfield grass behind second base. One at a time, the pitchers jog toward the coach and underhand their ball to him.

3. As the player passes the coach he begins to sprint; when he approaches the leftfield foul line the coach yells "right" or "left" and the player breaks in that direction to receive a throw from the coach. Again, the coach leads him so he really has to stretch out his legs.

4. As soon as each pitcher has completed a trip, the same procedure is repeated back the other way.

5. A high school age pitcher should be able to do 10 trips without undue strain.

SQUAD-CONDITIONING DRILLS

The following drills are designed for use in conditioning the entire squad. Most of them provide for some skill development as well. A team will use these drills early in the season more than they will after they have actually begun game competition. However, at least one of these drills or one like one of these should be used at every practice session.

Relays

1. This drill is an old one and may appear to be somewhat juvenile to the experienced athlete. However, we have found it to be a good conditioner for baseball players, particularly during the early training season. It is also a good morale booster as it provides some light relief from more rigorous and serious drills.

2. Divide the squad into teams of about four or five. Although it is generally best to separate the faster boys so the teams are equal, it might be fun to assign them to relay teams by position. For example: The pitchers, infielders and outfielders could have separate teams and the catchers and first basemen could join together to form a team.

3. Line the teams up side by side, with a glove about 30 yards in front of the first man in each line.

4. The teams then run relay races against each other. The participants must run around the glove and return to their lines.

5. Any of the following variations from a regular forward sprint could be included:

a. Running backward.

b. Hop on one foot.

c. Wheelbarrow race—one player holds the legs of a partner who walks on his hands.

d. Horseback ride.

e. Seal walk—participant crosses his lower legs and walks on his hands.

f. Crab walk—running on all fours.

g. Inverted crab walk—on all fours with the back facing the ground.

6. The competition can be intensified by setting some stakes beforehand. For example, the winningest team might be excused from helping to carry in equipment.

Whistle Drill

1. Divide the squad into four equal groups and assign each group to a base (including home plate).

2. The coach stands on the mound with a whistle. One man from each group takes off from his base and chases the man in front of him. When each player has circled the bases once, the coach blows the whistle and the runners stop and return to the base at which they started.

3. The same procedure is then repeated with the next four players.

4. The coach should insist that the players circle the bases properly. If a player misses a base, have him run again with the next group.

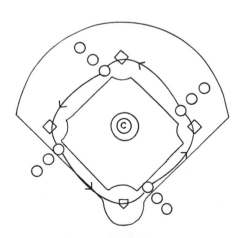

5. A variation to this drill would be to divide the squad into eight groups and have runners start from a point halfway between each base as well.

6. The coach should blow his whistle to stop the group running only when every player is really hustling.

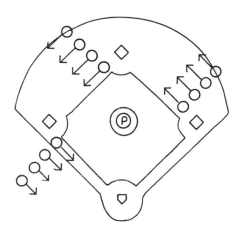

Lead Drill

1. Divide the squad into three equal groups and have each group line up at a base. The first man in line takes his lead in the baseline and the remainder of his group do the same behind him.

2. The coach stands on the mound and represents a pitcher taking his stretch with a runner on base. If he throws home, the baserunners sprint to the next base and stop. If the coach fakes a pickoff move to any base, all baserunners return to their respective bases.

3. Baserunners must be disciplined to work on taking an appropriate lead, getting the jump on the pitcher and getting back to the bag properly.

4. The same procedure is repeated until every player has had several opportunities to run from each base.

Timing Drill

1. Select a boy who can throw the ball over the plate with some consistency. Direct a few more boys to shag balls and have the remainder of the squad line up at home plate to hit.

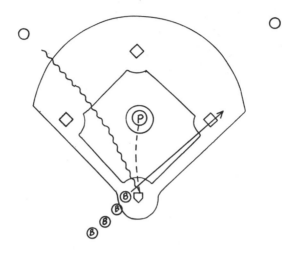

2. One at a time, the batters go up to the plate, take a full swing at the ball and race down the line past first base. The coach uses a stop watch to time each boy from the instant his bat touches the ball to when his foot touches first base.

3. The same procedure can be repeated with the batter running to second, third and then all the way around the bases.

4. The best performances of each player should be recorded at the beginning of the season and after they have been drilled on the proper fundamentals.

5. It might be of interest to the coach to compare a player's time in actual competition with his performance in this drill. He might come up with some concrete evidence that a particular boy is not making a 100 per cent effort.

Coaching Drill

1. This is an excellent drill to end each day's practice session.

2. The squad lines up at home plate and one by one, each player races down the line toward first base.

3. The first runner runs through the bag and becomes the first-base coach. The second player starts just as his predecessor finishes. He either runs on through the bag, rounds the base and goes to

second, or rounds the bag and returns to first, depending on the directions of the base coach. Each of the other players does the same, and each takes a turn at coaching a runner.

4. The last player in line continues around the bases to third and becomes the coach at that base. The first player now takes a lead off first and breaks for second. He rounds the bag and continues on to third or returns to second base, depending on the directions given by the third-base coach.

5. After each runner has gone through this phase of the drill, and has coached a runner rounding second, they all line up at second. Each player then takes his lead off second base and breaks for third. He rounds the bag and either tries to score or returns to third base, depending on the directions of the base coach.

6. Again, each player coaches a runner rounding third after having performed that phase of the drill himself.

7. It is vitally important that the base coaches utilize proper coaching signals (see Chapter 8).

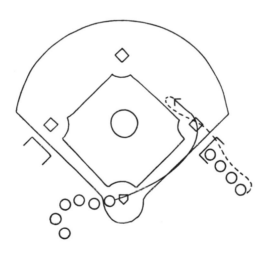

23

Game Preparation and Strategy

A good coach is more than a leader of young men and a teacher of baseball skills. He is also a technician in the art of managing one team against another in competition.

This responsibility begins early in the season when he first starts to analyze the abilities of his players in an effort to determine the kind of team he will be able to field. If the squad is blessed with a liberal amount of talent in all of the essential areas, then it stands to reason that the coach's own capabilities as a teacher and manager will be somewhat less critical in terms of the team's potential for success.

On most occasions, however, a coach will discover that he has good pitching or good hitting or adequate fielding, but not all of these. His job then becomes one of making the most of the talents that his players do have and selecting a line-up that can execute the type of game strategy that has proven to be most effective at that level of play.

Selecting the Team

Although the decisions associated with selecting a line-up will be difficult no matter how it is approached, the nature of the game, particularly at the lower levels, should make some choices rather evident.

First of all, there simply never has been a winning baseball team that did not have good pitching. If a coach discovers he has a weakness in this area, then he had better begin shifting his talent around until he finds a boy or two who can get the opposing batters out with some consistency. A colleague of mine was faced with this predicament once and he solved the problem by asking his all-league shortstop to learn how to pitch. The boy became an all-league pitcher and led his team to the championship.

He must also find a solid athlete who can catch that pitcher. A good catcher can be the difference between a mediocre pitcher being a good pitcher or a good pitcher being a great one.

Most coaches also agree that the selection of a second baseman, shortstop and centerfielder should have top priority.

The offensive ability of these players is generally conceded to be of secondary importance. That is, a coach will fill these positions with an athlete who excels on defense before he will use a boy who hits well but is somewhat weaker defensively. The theory behind this is that the weaker defender would probably cost the team more runs by his mistakes in the field at these particular positions than he could possibly produce with his more potent bat.

Regardless of the talent at their disposal and their level of competition, every coach strives to develop this "strength up the middle." However, the extent to which he can afford to apply this kind of thinking to his selection of the remainder of the line-up will depend upon two important factors: the strength of his pitching staff—whether it is strong enough to compensate for what the team will lack in its batting attack as a result of playing the better defensive players— and the general maturity and consistency of all players at that level of competition.

If a major league manager uses his top defenders to give him strength up the middle, then he will almost always emphasize offensive ability at the other positions. This is dictated by the kind of strategy that has proven to be most effective at that level of play. Most major league clubs like to go for the big inning. They seldom bunt and they steal even less because these plays simply do not have the chances of being successful as they do at lower levels. Percentages favor taking a minimum of chances and waiting for one of their big sluggers to knock the ball out of the park. (Of course, the Los Angeles Dodger and St. Louis Cardinal teams of recent years have been good running and bunting clubs, and their successes may inspire other professional organizations to build for speed too.)

The coach at the lower levels cannot afford to pattern his line-up after that used by most major league teams. The percentages do not favor the home run, and scoring runs in bunches. The greatest chances for success, at the high school level on down, come from playing for one run at a time from the first inning on. This is true for a number of reasons:

1. Very few non-professional teams have enough good hitters in the line-up to produce hits with any degree of consistency.

2. The defensive capabilities of the players at this level is such that the bunting and running are extremely effective. And these skills are much more readily taught than hitting, especially hitting for power.

3. High school and youth league teams usually play only seven innings. Even if the line-up were blessed with a number of good hitters, they simply do not have as many opportunities to put together a big inning.

4. If a team is playing for one run from the start, there is a good chance they will take an early lead in the game. The team that "draws first blood" will be given a psychological lift. This factor is probably important at all levels of play, but it may be particularly true with younger athletes.

5. The one-run-at-a-time approach to offensive strategy will also tend to improve the caliber of the defense. The big, slow-footed athlete who may hit with power but represent a liability on defense, would probably not be in the line-up. The faster boy who can bunt, run and play defense would be the more valuable player.

Arranging the Batting Order

The strategy that a team can use with the greatest percentages for success should also influence the arrangement of the batting order. Most professional managers design their order in much the same way. The player to occupy each spot in the order must have some fairly definite qualifications for that particular assignment.

1. The leadoff hitter is a high-average hitter, an excellent bunter and a good baserunner. He usually has very little power because the weakest hitters on the team precede him in the order. There are exceptions to this rule. Willie Mays, who has hit over 600 home runs in his career, almost always bats in the first or second slot

when he competes in the annual All-Star Game. Of course, Mays is also an exceptional baserunner, and the manager has hitters like Henry Aaron and Roberto Clemente available to drive in the runs.

2. The number-two hitter usually has many of the same qualifications as the leadoff man. Ideally, he is a lefthanded batter and rarely strikes out. The fact that he swings from the left side of the plate means that he presents more of a hindrance to the catcher if a runner on first tries to steal, he is more likely to hit a ball to the right side to advance a baserunner, and with the first baseman holding a runner on first, he has a big hole through which to hit the ball.

3. The number-three hitter is almost always the best all-around offensive player on the team. He hits for an average, has good power and can run the bases.

4. The cleanup hitter is usually the second-best all-around hitter on the team. He usually has good power and is known for his ability to produce with runners on base. He is generally the slower of the two if there is little else to chose from between the number three and four hitters.

5. The number-five batter hits with power but may or may not hit for an average. He has many of the same qualities as the number-four hitter but to a lesser degree.

6. The number-six batter is normally the sixth best offensive player, regardless of his particular talents. He may have skills similar to those of the first two batters, or he may hit with power.

7. Depending on the team's overall batting strength, the number-seven hitter may or may not have any unique talents. More often than not, he is an outstanding defensive player, who is in the line-up for his fielding ability and not for what he can produce at the plate.

8. The number-eight hitter usually falls in the same category. However, since the pitcher follows him in the order, he is often a player who is capable of hitting an occasional home run.

9. The pitcher is almost always the number-nine hitter in this kind of a batting order. He has made the squad on the basis of his pitching ability alone, and he does not play often enough to develop any of the offensive abilities that he does have.

Of course this kind of a batting order would make sense at any level of play if the coach or manager has the personnel to fill each of these slots. As we have said before, rarely will teams below the major league level find enough consistent hitters to implement the type of offensive strategy for which this kind of order is designed.

One year we were fortunate enough to have four switch-hitters in our line-up, and they all hit over .300. Making out the line-up card for that team was simple, but we still didn't have the kind of personnel that would warrant our using a pro-type line-up.

The non-professional coach would be wiser if he were to arrange his line-up almost entirely on the basis of hitting consistency, bunting ability and speed on the bases. The big, slow power-hitter should be confined to the bottom of the order if he is used at all.

This kind of arrangement would be more in keeping with the one-run-at-a-time offensive philosophy. With the best hitters at the top of the order, the team is likely to score in the first inning and jump to an early lead. The better hitters would also bat a maximum number of times in the game.

And of course, since the pitcher on most amateur teams is one of the better all-around athletes, he should not be automatically relegated to the number-nine position in the order. However, even if he is one of the team's top three or four hitters, he probably should not bat that high in the order. The pitcher should be required to do as little running as possible and placing him at the top of the order might force the coach to be more conservative in strategy.

Game Strategy

The first concern in executing any offensive attack is to get runners on base. Even the team that is blessed with a number of good hitters will occasionally find itself confronted with a situation where a pitcher literally has them eating out of his hand. The best thing a team can do under these circumstances is to attempt to break up the pitcher's momentum. This is best accomplished by:

1. Making liberal use of the bunt for a base hit. Even if the attempt is unsuccessful, the pitcher is likely to begin thinking more about his fielding and less about pitching.

2. Having the poorer hitters take more pitches, forcing the pitcher to throw more and thus perhaps tire.

3. Having hitters shift around in the batter's box, stand closer to the plate and generally distract the pitcher.

4. Having all hitters cut down on their swings and work on getting on base rather than hitting for power. This would be especially true if the pitcher is accumulating a lot of strike-outs.

Once the foot is in the door and a runner is on base, the team can go to work trying to bring him around to score. The following suggestions would be appropriate for teams using a one-run-at-a-time philosophy. The reader should refer to Chapter 7 for a detailed description of the offensive maneuvers mentioned.

1. With a runner on first base and no outs:

a. Use the sacrifice bunt frequently. It is the easiest method of getting a ground ball into play and thus increasing the possibilities of an error. The runner is advanced into scoring position and the double-play possibilities are reduced considerably.

b. If the bunting game has been established earlier, consider using the fake bunt and hit, especially if more than one run is needed (see Chapter 7).

c. Steal if the percentages for success are good and you are approaching the bottom of the order. This will put a runner on second with no outs. He can then be sacrificed to third and scored on a squeeze play.

d. Hit away only if you are more than two runs behind, it is late in the game, the pitcher shows definite signs of weakening and/or one of your top hitters is at the plate.

2. With a runner on first and one out:

a. Use the sacrifice bunt only if an extremely slow runner is on first and/or a very weak hitter is at bat.

b. Steal if the percentages for success are good, especially if the last good hitter is at bat.

c. Use the hit-and-run if the batter has demonstrated a consistency in getting a piece of the ball. The hit-and-run should also be considered if the batter has shown a reluctance to swing. This type of hitter is often more effective when he is ordered to swing no matter where the pitch is delivered. I vividly remember giving a boy the hit-and-run signal for exactly this reason, and he knocked out his first extra-base hit of the season to win a ball game for us.

d. The run-and-hit might be considered also, but only if the runner on first has enough speed to have a good chance of making it to second if the pitch is not a strike.

3. With a runner on first and two outs:

a. Steal if the chances for success are good, but not if the number-nine hitter is at the plate. If the runner is thrown out, the same batter must lead off the next inning. A weak hitter might try to bunt for a hit in this situation as the third baseman is normally playing back with two outs.

b. The better hitters, of course, should be hitting away under these circumstances.

4. With a runner on second base and no outs:

a. Sacrifice the runner to third unless one of your top hitters is at the plate. The percentages for scoring a runner from third are much greater than they are from second, especially at the high school level and below.

b. If the batter is allowed to hit away, he should be trying to hit the ball to rightfield. If the ball is hit on the ground to the right side, the runner can advance to third even if the ball does not go through to the outfield.

5. With a runner on second and one out:

a. Seriously consider stealing if the percentages for success are good and you are approaching the bottom of the batting order. If the runner is successful, he can then be scored in a variety of ways other than a base hit.

b. Hit away with a high-percentage hitter at the plate, a slow runner on second and/or when one run is not significant at that point in the game.

6. With a runner on second and two outs:

a. Almost always hit away unless an extremely weak hitter is at bat. A number-nine hitter should be encouraged to take a strike or two, or bunt for a hit if the third baseman is back.

b. Steal with a weak hitter at the plate, but only if the run is critical. The theory here would be to hope for an overthrow so the runner could score, rather than just to advance him to third.

7. With a runner on third base and no outs:

a. All but the weakest of hitters should be allowed to hit away in this situation. The runner should attempt to score only if he is certain he can make it.

b. A safety squeeze might be appropriate if a fairly weak hitter is up and poorer hitters follow.

c. A bunt for a base hit would be sound strategy if better hitters follow.

8. With a runner on third and one out:

a. Hit away with the infield back and a batter at the plate who seldom strikes out.

b. Use the suicide squeeze if the batter can bunt and the infield is playing in for a play at the plate. If the ball is bunted on the ground, the runner will almost always have time to score, regardless of the position of the infield. The runner on third does not have to be extremely fast.

c. If the batter is not a good hitter or bunter and the runner on third does have good speed, consider calling for the safety squeeze. If the batter fails to put the ball on the ground, then the runner can remain at third.

9. With a runner on third and two outs:

a. Hit away under almost all circumstances unless the batter is almost certain to strike out and the runner on third is extremely fast. If this is the case, consider stealing home but only if the pitcher's windup is such that the percentages for success are reasonably good.

10. With runners on first and second and no outs:

a. The sacrifice bunt should be almost automatic in this situation. The double-play possibility is almost eliminated, but even if successful, two runners will be advanced to scoring position.

b. Consider using the fake bunt and hit if the bunting game has already been established, the runner on third is extremely slow and a fairly good hitter is at the plate.

c. Steal only if the runner going to third is almost certain to make it and the last of the good hitters is at the plate.

11. With runners on first and second and one out:

a. The steal should be seriously considered here, especially if the lead runner has good speed and the tail end of the order is up. If successful, a number of possibilities, aside from a base hit, could score the run.

b. The hit-and-run might be considered if the runners on base are not very fast and the batter usually gets a piece of the ball.

12. With runners on first and second and two outs:

a. Hit away under almost all circumstances.

b. With an extremely weak hitter at the plate, the steal might be appropriate if the abilities of the catcher are such that there is a good chance he will overthrow third and allow the runner to come around to score.

13. With runners on first and third and no outs:

a. Consider having the runner on first steal second if the chances for success are at all good. If successful, two runners will be in scoring position and the possibility of the double play is eliminated. The runner on third should break for the plate, then quickly return to the bag to lure the defense into cutting off the throw to second.

b. If the batter at the plate is a weak hitter and two runs are needed, consider trying the safety squeeze, especially if better hitters follow and the runner on third is fast.

14. With runners on first and third and one out:

a. Use a variation of the double steal if the runner on third has good speed, the batter is a poor hitter and only one run is needed.

b. If two runs are needed, use the run-and-hit if the runner on first has fairly good speed, and the hit-and-run if he does not. If the ball is hit anywhere on the ground, two runners should end up in scoring position, and if the ball goes through the infield, one runner will score and another should end up on third.

c. Simply stealing second base might be considered, especially if the last good hitter is at the plate.

d. The safety squeeze would be appropriate if the runner on third has good speed and the batter is only a fair bunter. The suicide squeeze could be used if the batter is a good bunter, but poor hitter, and both baserunners are slow.

15. With runners on first and third and two outs:

a. A variation of the double steal should be almost automatic in this situation, especially if only one run is needed.

b. If two runs are needed, an extremely fast runner on first might be allowed to steal, particularly if the batter at the plate is the last of the good hitters.

c. In rare instances, when two runs are needed and the percentages for success are favorable, the steal home just might be appropriate. Both runners break at the same time, and an inexperienced pitcher could balk or the catcher may throw to second without first checking third.

16. With runners on second and third and no outs:

a. Hit away under almost all circumstances. If an extremely weak hitter is almost certain to strike out, consider calling for the bunt for a base hit.

17. With runners on second and third and one out:

a. The suicide squeeze is a great play in this situation. (I will never forget the day we won the championship game in an Easter week tournament by using the suicide squeeze on two successive pitches in the first inning. Our opposition became so demoralized that the game turned into a rout.) If the ball is bunted on the ground, the lead runner will score almost automatically and the trailing runner may even score on the throw to first to get the batter.

b. The fake bunt and hit might be appropriate here too, especially if the defense is looking for the squeeze and the batter is a fairly good hitter.

c. Hit away with a top hitter at the plate and/or more than two runs are needed.

18. With runners on second and third and two outs:

a. Hit away under almost all circumstances.

b. Attempt to steal home only if the chances for success are good and the batter is very likely to strike out if he is allowed to swing.

19. With the bases loaded and no outs:

a. Hit away under all conditions.

20. With the bases loaded and one out:

a. Hit away with all but the weakest of batters. The squeeze plays are not normally as effective under these conditions as the defense has a force play at the plate.

21. With the bases loaded and two outs:

a. Hit away in most instances but consider calling for the steal home if the batter is likely to strike out and an extremely fast runner is on third.

b. With a three-and-one or three-and-two count on a batter who is almost certain to strike out, the steal might be an excellent play. With the runner breaking for home the pitcher may be hard pressed to get the ball over the plate. This play could be attempted even if the runner on third were not particularly fast.

As each of these situations develop, the coach must not only decide which play has the best percentages for success, but also when to call for that play. For example, most big league managers would call for the hit-and-run when the pitcher is well behind in the count. The theory here is that the batter is more likely to get a good pitch to hit because the pitcher cannot afford to throw a pitchout, even if he expects the play.

However, as a general rule, the most opportune time to attempt the majority of these plays with younger players is on the first pitch to the batter. Pitchers at the lower levels are in the habit of getting the first pitch down the middle and the batter is likely to get a good ball to bunt or hit, whichever the case may be. If the play is a steal, then the batter will still have two strikes to deliver a base hit if the play is successful. In addition to these factors, fewer signals are missed on the first pitch because players are more alert for signals at this time.

We have been describing circumstances that are certainly realistic for most high school and youth league coaches. Of course, there are coaches at these levels who do have the kind of talent that would allow them to go for the big inning and generally avoid the one-run-at-a-time philosophy. Perhaps the coach who finds himself in this situation would be making the most of his material if he did not confuse his hitters with a lot of set plays but simply turned them loose at the plate.

But for those of us who are forced to peck away at our opponents, the philosophy we have presented here should be extremely appropriate. Even if the opposing team has a commanding lead, a team can continue to use the one-run-at-a-time strategy to some extent. The trailing team that is scoring a run here and there is not as apt to abandon hope as the team that sits back and waits for the big inning. Simply breaking the ice and scoring the first run can instill confidence in a club and may cause its opponent to crack. In fact, many big innings are started by playing for just one or two runs. Of course, as the game progresses, the team that is trailing by a considerable margin must gradually place more emphasis on the big inning, regardless of the abilities of its hitters.

The Defense

A word or two should certainly be included here about defensive strategy. If a team has very little in the way of offensive strength, then its best bet is to develop an outstanding defense. Most experts are of the opinion that defensive ability, like bunting, can be taught, whereas batting ability can only be improved.

From a strategical point of view, the coach who has a great deal of confidence in his defense and very little in his offense should always play for the shutout. His philosophy should be that his club cannot be defeated if his opponents can't score. This approach works extremely well with younger players, but it does involve taking a few chances:

1. The first and third basemen play fairly close to the hitter to cut off all bunt possibilities.

2. The second baseman and shortstop play relatively deep to keep ground balls from going through into the outfield.

3. The outfield plays relatively shallow to prevent short fly balls from dropping in front of them.

4. The team literally masters their defensive assignments to the extent that each player knows exactly what he should be doing in every possible situation.

5. With a runner on third base, the infield almost always plays in to cut off a run at the plate.

Non-Playing Assignments

As we mentioned before in discussing team morale, the baseball coach faces a difficult task if he hopes to keep all of his players involved in the ball game. This *is* a problem but it can be licked if each player is made to feel that he actually is participating to some degree. Every player on the squad should be given a definite responsibility for each game. The assignments described below should be distributed amongst those players on the squad who are not in the starting line-up. Some thought should go into assigning these tasks and the coach should insist that each of them is performed conscientiously.

Coaching the Bases: These assignments are usually reserved for two veteran players who have a thorough knowledge of the game.

The most qualified of the two should be the third-base coach. A detailed description of base coaching responsibilities is presented in Chapter 8.

Stealing Signals: Although every player should be alert for opportunities to pick off an opponent's signals, the best bet is to assign several players specifically to this task. The leader of the group should be assigned to watch the opposing coach. Another boy is assigned to watch the third-base coach and another the first-base coach. All three of these players sit together and keep a running commentary going on the actions of the people they are assigned to watch. At the end of each inning the leader reports their findings to the coach.

Keeping Pitching Charts: Some kind of a record should always be maintained on the pitcher's performance, and this is best accomplished by another pitcher. Although there are several different kinds of charts that may be used, most of them provide for a recording of the different kinds of pitches thrown, where they were thrown in the strike zone, and the sequence in which they were thrown. This kind of information can be useful to the pitcher in the game, and maintaining the charts can be learning experience for the boy given this responsibility.

Notifying the Catcher on Steal and Squeeze Plays: One player, usually a reserve catcher or first baseman, is given the responsibility of shouting "there he goes" when a runner attempts to steal a base or score on a suicide-squeeze play. Although there are players on the field who have this assignment, they are often so far away from the catcher that he is unable to hear them.

Warming Up the Extra Outfielder: A reserve outfielder is given the assignment of playing catch with one of the three outfielders just before the beginning of their defensive half of each inning. This will allow the other two to throw to each other rather than having all three outfielders play catch in a three-cornered fashion.

The Bull-pen Catcher: A reserve catcher should be given bull-pen duty. He should have a good baseball and his glove in hand and ready to use whenever the coach gives the call for a relief pitcher to warm up. This responsibility should be assigned; not all ballplayers are good receivers.

The Relief Pitcher: It is generally a good idea for the coach to let the pitcher who will be used in relief know that he may be used in this capacity. Some coaches go so far as to designate one pitcher for long relief (to be used if relief is needed early in the game) and another for short relief (in the late innings). The pitcher or pitchers who are given this assignment should sit next to the player keeping the pitching charts and become thoroughly acquainted with the opposing batting order.

Dugout Duty: One player can be assigned the responsibility of keeping the bench area in reasonably good shape. If he is an enterprising young man, he might find a batboy who will do this for him. Normally, this job is given to the rookie on the squad. It definitely should not be assigned as a disciplinary measure.

Miscellaneous Chores

Baseball coaches probably have their most frustrating moments before a ball game even begins. For a home game, the field has to be prepared, the umpires have to be notified and arrangements must be made for the visiting team. If the game is to be played away from home, travel arrangements must be taken care of. And for every game, home or away, equipment has to be transported to the ball park and a multitude of little "housekeeping" chores must be performed before the contest can get underway. Unfortunately, most of these responsibilities are assumed by the coach himself.

A coach can eliminate many pregame headaches if he develops a system for taking care of all these non-coaching responsibilities. One of the best techniques I know of is to develop a pregame check list. With a list of the equipment that will be needed as well as a list of all those duties that must be performed, a coach can see that things are taken care of beforehand and will be better able to concentrate on the game itself once the team takes the field.

Because each coach faces a situation unique in itself, we will not go into any detail in describing the specific items that might be included on this check list. The main thing is to have some sort of system for keeping track of those little tasks and responsibilities that can become annoying if they are neglected.

Pregame Warm-up

The manner in which a team goes through its warm-up routine just prior to each ball game may have a considerable influence on the players' readiness to compete. Pregame drills should be such that they help to prepare the athlete physically and mentally for his particular role in the contest. They must be extremely well organized so that every player has an assigned responsibility. A standard warm-up procedure should be established early and then used throughout the season. If a set routine is not followed, pregame jitters are apt to be intensified in the more emotional athletes. Although the coach should insist that his players perform these drills enthusiastically, he should refrain from trying to do any teaching at this time.

The drills used will vary considerably depending upon the amount of time available. Most high school teams, for example, are not allowed to take batting practice before a ball game. Other restrictions may be imposed because of limited facilities. However, some coaches are in a position to run their squads through a complete warm-up routine. Therefore, our intent here will be to outline a procedure that might be used if conditions were ideal in terms of time and facilities. Those coaches who are restricted in these respects can modify the procedure according to their particular situation.

Essential to the planning of a warm-up routine is the time schedule leading up to the start of the contest. The league in which the two squads are competing is usually responsible for establishing such a schedule. If this is not the case, the home club should assume the responsibility and inform the visiting team about it before the day of the game.

The following schedule would be appropriate if the game were scheduled to begin at 1:00 P.M.

11:30–12:00   Home Team Batting Practice
12:00–12:30   Visiting Team Batting Practice
12:30–12:40   Home Team Infield-Outfield Drill
12:40–12:50   Visiting Team Infield-Outfield Drill
12:50– 1:00   Presentation of Line-ups and Review of Ground Rules

Let's take a look at one way in which the home team could make use of this time schedule:

11:15: Batting practice pitcher begins to warm up.

11:25: The remainder of the squad takes the field and jogs one lap around the outfield.

11:30: Batting practice begins.

1. The team is divided into three batting groups. The make-up of these groups would depend on the size of the squad. An 18-man squad might be grouped as follows:

Group ⚹1 consists of the first 6 men in the batting order.

Group ⚹2 consists of the last 3 men in the order and the top 3 reserve players.

Group ⚹3 consists of the remaining players with the exception of the pitchers.

2. The half-hour time period is then utilized in the following manner:

Round One: Group ⚹1 bunts 2 and takes 6 cuts.
        Group ⚹2 bunts 1 and takes 4 cuts.
        Group ⚹3 takes 3 cuts.

Round Two: Group ⚹1 takes 3 cuts.
        Group ⚹2 takes 1 cut each until time runs out.

3. The key to getting the most from this drill is the batting practice pitcher. He should literally "make" the batter hit every pitch. He should throw fastballs only unless he can throw curves with the same consistency. His job is to help the hitters get their timing down—not to fool them. He should always let the batter know when he intends to throw a curve or change speeds.

4. Additional assignments are made as follows:

a. Two reserve catchers should alternate behind the plate.

b. Two pitchers should be assigned to shag behind the mound and keep the batting practice pitcher supplied with baseballs.

c. The remainder of the squad shags in the outfield. These players should form a semicircle from one foul line to the other and should not congregate in groups.

5. Here are a few additional suggestions that will enable a team to make maximum use of the time available:

a. Hitters must hustle in and out of the batter's box.

b. The batting practice pitcher should use an abbreviated windup and should not waste time between pitches.

c. Every player knows his assignment and sees that he is in the right place at the right time.

12:00:   Calisthenics, throwing and pepper league.

If a team were not allowed to take batting practice, it would probably begin its pregame drills at this point.

1. Depending on the weather and the coach's point of view, the team may or may not go through their regular exercise routine. We have found that most younger athletes will not take the time to warm up properly unless the team does it as a group. Therefore, we like to have the team circle up and run through the exercise routine described in Chapter 22.

2. Following exercises, the team warms up their arms by using the same routine described in the previous chapter.

3. As soon as a player feels his arm is thoroughly warm, he and his partner begin playing pepper league (see Chapter 22). When each of them has had an opportunity to hit a round, they return to the bench for a brief rest.

12:30:   Infield-Outfield Drill.

The home team traditionally takes the field for its infield-outfield drill first. There are as many ways to perform this drill as there are teams. Our approach is not uncommon and is probably as good as any. The important thing is that the team is familiar with the routine and every player knows where he is to go and what he is supposed to do.

1. The team hustles onto the field together.

2. Specific responsibilities:

a. The fungo hitter:

1) Hits to the outfielders from the area of the pitcher's mound.

2) Hits ground balls to the third baseman and second baseman from the rightfield side of the plate and to the shortstop and first baseman from the leftfield side. This will give the ball an angle of direction more like that of a batted ball.

3) Eliminate delays by having an extra ball or two in your pocket.

4) Hit balls that are fairly easy to handle so players can go into the game with some degree of confidence.

b. The players:

1) Perform each movement deliberately and naturally; don't make a race out of this drill.

2) Throw all extra balls into the plate on the ground.

3) Infielders fake a tag on all throws from the catcher.

4) All relay assignments are performed as they would be in game competition.

5) To save time, play all line drives to infielders as ground balls.

3. Procedure:

a. Outfield throws:

1) LF throws once to 3B, twice to 2B, and twice home.

2) CF throws once to 2B, twice to 3B, and twice home.

3) RF throws once to 2B, twice to 3B, and twice home.

b. As each outfielder completes his throws he begins fielding balls hit to him by a previously assigned fungo hitter.

c. The catcher receives the last throw from the rightfielder and starts it around the infield in the prescribed manner.

d. The coach is then ready to move into the home-plate area to begin the infield portion of the drill. He calls out the directions at the beginning of each round, then fungoes the ball to one infielder after the other. The player fields the ball and makes the throw as indicated:

Round One: "Bring it in, no throws"

    3B – C
    SS – C
    2B – C
    1B – C

Round Two: "Get one, no throws"

    3B – 1B – C
    SS – 1B – C
    2B – 1B – C
    1B – 2B – 1B – C
    Bunt down 3B line, C – 1B – 3B – C

Round Three: "Get one, throws"
   3B – 1B – C – 3B – C
   SS – 1B – C – SS – 3B – C
   2B – 1B – C – 2B – 3B – C
   1B – SS – 1B – C
   Bunt down 1B line, C – 1B – 3B – C

Round Four: "Get two, no throws"
   3B – 2B – 1B – C
   SS – 2B – 1B – C
   2B – SS – 1B – C
   1B (breaking from the bag) – SS – 1B – C
   Bunt in front of plate, C – SS – 1B – C

Round Five: "Get two, throws"
   3B – 2B – 1B – C – 3B – C
   SS – 2B – 1B – C – SS – 3B – C
   2B – SS – 1B – C – 2B – 3B – C
   1B (breaking from the bag) – SS – 1B – C
   Bunt in front of plate, C – 2B – 1B – C

Round Six: "Get one, hurry it" (Ball hit slowly)
   3B – 1B – C (fake to 2B) – 3B – C
   SS – 1B – C – SS (cut-off position) – C
   2B – 1B – C – 2B (cut-off position) – C
   1B – 3B – C
   Bunt down 3B line, C – 3B – 1B – C

Round Seven: "Bring it in"
   3B – C
   SS – C
   2B – C
   1B – C
   Pop fly to catcher

4. If each team is given the field a full 15 minutes, every player on the squad should be involved in this drill:

a. Extra outfielders can make their throws right along with the regulars.

b. Extra infielders can be taken care of in either of two ways:
1) If there are only a couple of extra players, they can be rotated in with the starters.
2) If a complete second infield is available, the infield portion of the drill can be divided in half. The starting players would go through a short version of the drill, and the "second infield" would do the same.

12:45: The starting pitcher begins warming up.

The starting pitcher should begin warming up approximately 15 minutes before he is scheduled to take the mound. The time needed will vary with the individual and the weather conditions.

The coach should provide him with a catcher, not just any extra ballplayer who happens to be available.

Most pitchers warm up gradually until they are able to throw their fastball full-speed. He then develops his curve and any other pitches he uses in the same manner.

Once he feels he is thoroughly warm, he should throw 15 to 20 pitches just as he will have to in competition: throwing from the stretch as well as the full windup; mixing up the different kinds of pitches; changing speeds; throwing to spots. For this final phase of the warm-up period, it is always a good idea to have a batter standing up at the plate to make the conditions as realistic as possible.

Ideally, the starting pitcher should complete his warm-up just a minute or two before the game begins.

12:50: Presentation of line-ups and discussion of ground rules.

At this point the coaches or the captains from both teams meet at home plate. Each team should provide two copies of its line-up: one copy for the umpire-in-chief and the other for the opposing coach.

The ground rules are generally explained by the home team representative.

1:00: PLAY BALL!

The Game Plan

Obviously, all of these activities leading up to the game, as well as those extra chores that must be taken care of during the contest, must be delegated in a well-organized manner. The best way we know of to do this is to develop a game-plan form. Prior to each contest, the coach fills out this form and posts it so that everyone concerned can see for himself just what his responsibilities will be on that particular day.

GAME PLAN

"Jackets" vs. _____ at_____ time_____

Equipment Assignments:

Ball Bag_____
Helmets_____
Bats_____
Medicine Kit_____

Pre-Game Assignments:

Pre-Game Drill: Fungo_____
                 Fungo to OF_____
                       Shag _____
Warm-up Pitcher_____
        Batter_____

Game Assignments:

Long Relief_____Short Relief_____
Bull Pen Catchers_____,_____
Base Coaches: First_____Third_____
Notify Catcher on Steal and Squeeze_____
Warm-up Extra Outfielder_____
Scout Team: 1_____2_____3_____
Dugout Duty_____
Pitching Charts_____
Scorebook_____

Post Game Assignments:

Notify Newspapers_____
Fines_____
Equipment Check_____

ROSTER

1_____ 9_____
2_____ 10_____
3_____ 11_____
4_____ 12_____
5_____ 13_____
6_____ 14_____
7_____ 15_____
8_____ 16_____

Starting Line-up:

1_____
2_____
3_____
4_____
5_____
6_____
7_____
8_____
9_____

The Final Inning

Well, I guess that about wraps it up. We have tried to describe the game as we think it might be played, coached and enjoyed. Of course, no single publication could possibly be all-inclusive on this subject.

As we have said before, baseball is a fantastically intricate game from the technical standpoint alone. These pages offer but one of a number of different approaches to the teaching of fundamentals and the implementation of baseball strategy.

Our personal bias is also evident by the manner in which we discuss baseball as a builder of character. We happen to be one of those old-fashioned individuals who feel that winning is not everything. We believe that baseball and other sports provide one of the most ideal teaching situations available. Not just for teaching skills but also for molding young boys into mature and honest men. We certainly hope that those who read this material will find our arguments for such a philosophy convincing and useful.

Baseball has meant a great deal to this writer. I played it almost religiously as a boy, and the fact that I failed to realize my dreams of stardom in the major leagues has not reduced my love for the game in the slightest. And now, as a coach, I am discovering that my enthusiasm and knowledge of baseball has given me an excellent means of communication with many young boys. I think it is safe to say that the satisfactions I received from the game as a player do not compare with those I am enjoying as a coach.

INDEX

All-purpose baseball practice drill, 288–90

Alou, Matty, 11

Arm swing of the pitcher, 89–90

Ashburn, Richie, and use of head-first slide, 49

Back-door slide, 48–49

Balance of baseball bat, 13, 14

Balk, and the pitcher, 95

Ballplayers, famous (in alphabetical order): Alou, Matty, 11; Ashburn, Richie, 49; Boudreau, Lou, 228; Boyer, Ken, 19; Clemente, Roberto, 11; Cobb, Ty, 1, 16, 36, 38; Dark, Alvin, 223; Feller, Bob, 228; Gomez, Lefty, 90, 180; Gordon, Joe, 26; Green, Pumpsie, 108; Hodges, Gil, 130; Hornsby, Rogers, 236; Hubbell, Carl, 101; Lopez, Hector, 51; McCovey, Willie, 136; Mantle, Mickey, 6; Marichal, Juan, 88, 101; Maris, Roger, 51; Martin, Pepper, 50; Mays, Willie, 2, 4–5, 26, 54, 80; Miller, Stu, 97; Pierce, Billy, 97; Richardson, Bobby, 151; Robinson, Jackie, 3; Spahn, Warren, 99; Thomson, Bobby, 3; Wagner, Honus, 1; Williams, Ted, 10, 11, 16; Wills, Maury, 36, 48; Wynn, Early, 108

Base coaches, general rule for, 69; as a non-playing assignment, 314. *See also* Coaching; Coaching the bases; Coaching philosophy

Baserunner on base, holding, by first baseman, 136–37

Baserunners, and the sacrifice bunt, 57–58

Baserunning, fundamentals of, 36–43; running form, 36–37; baserunning from home plate, 37–39; from first base, 39–41; rounding second base, 41; baserunning from second base, 41; approaching third base, 42; from third base, 42–43; approaching home plate, 43. *See also* Hand signals of coaches to baserunner; Runners on bases, rules for, in offensive game situations

Bases, coaching the: general rule for, 69; at first base, 70–72; at third base, 72–75; at home plate, 76. *See also* Defense, communi-

man, 266; batting tees, 266; preparation for practice, 269

Practice routine and schedule, 268; seven basic kinds of drills, 268, 270; team rules, regarding practice procedure, 269

Pregame warmup, 316

Preseason training for ballplayers, 246–51

Protective screens for batting practice pitcher and first baseman, as equipment for practice sessions, 266, 288

Psychological factors essential to batting success, 12

"Pulling" an outside pitch, 22

Pulling the head, as common batting fault, 25

Push bunt, 32–33

Push-off, stride, and throw of the pitcher, 90–91

Qualifications, basic and physical, needed for playing baseball, 4–5. *See also* qualifications for playing individual positions, under name of individual position

Quarterback drill, 296–97

"Ready position" of all fielders, 77–78

Receiving position of catcher, 114–15

Regular double steal, 61

Relay assignments and cut-off plays: of first baseman, 139–40; of second baseman, 156; of third baseman, 165–66; of shortstop, 177–78; other relay and cut-off situations, 210–22

Relay drills, 297–98

Relief pitcher, 314–15

Richardson, Bobby, 151

Rickey, Branch, 271

Robinson, Jackie, 3

Rocker pivot, by second baseman, 154, 155

"Rubbed off" signal by coach, 68

Rubbers and home plates, needed for practice sessions, 266

Run and hit, 64

Rundown situations, 207–9; pick-off and rundown drill, 286–87

Runner on base, holding a, by first baseman, 136–37

Runners on bases, rules for, in offensive game situations: on first base, 51–52; on second base, 52–53; on third base, 53–54; general principles for all baserunners, 54–55; baserunners and the sacrifice bunt, 57–78. *See also* Base stealing

Running form, and fundamentals of baserunning, 36–37. *See also* Baserunning, fundamentals of; Hand signals of coaches to baserunners, 38–43

Sacrifice bunts, 29–31, 57–58; defensive handling of, 190, 193, 194. *See also* Bunting, fundamentals of

Safety squeeze, 57–58

Screens, protective, for batting practice pitchers and first baseman, as equipment for practice sessions, 266, 288

Screwball: how to swing at, 24; how to pitch, 100–1

Scrimmage: offensive, 293–94; defensive, 294–95

Second base, playing, 143–58; qualifications for playing second base, 143–44; field positions of, 144; basic fielding plays, 144–45, 147–49; covering second base, 149–54; on tag plays, 149–51;